10 0499139 4

D1381033

Surviving Domestic Violence

Surviving Domestic Violence

Gender, Poverty and Agency

Paula Wilcox
University of Brighton

NOTTINGHAM
UNIVERSITY LIBRARY

© Paula Wilcox 2006

All rights reserved. No reproduction, copy or transmission of this publication may be made without written permission.

No paragraph of this publication may be reproduced, copied or transmitted save with written permission or in accordance with the provisions of the Copyright, Designs and Patents Act 1988, or under the terms of any licence permitting limited copying issued by the Copyright Licensing Agency, 90 Tottenham Court Road, London W1T 4LP.

Any person who does any unauthorized act in relation to this publication may be liable to criminal prosecution and civil claims for damages.

The author has asserted her right to be identified as the author of this work in accordance with the Copyright, Designs and Patents Act 1988.

First published 2006 by
PALGRAVE MACMILLAN
Houndmills, Basingstoke, Hampshire RG21 6XS and
175 Fifth Avenue, New York, N. Y. 10010
Companies and representatives throughout the world

PALGRAVE MACMILLAN is the global academic imprint of the Palgrave Macmillan division of St. Martin's Press, LLC and of Palgrave Macmillan Ltd. Macmillan® is a registered trademark in the United States, United Kingdom and other countries. Palgrave is a registered trademark in the European Union and other countries.

ISBN-13: 978–1–4039–4113–8   hardback
ISBN-10: 1–4039–4113–0   hardback

This book is printed on paper suitable for recycling and made from fully managed and sustained forest sources.

A catalogue record for this book is available from the British Library.

Library of Congress Cataloging-in-Publication Data
Wilcox, Paula, 1951-
    Surviving domestic violence : gender, poverty, and agency / Paula Wilcox.
       p. cm.
    Includes bibliographical references and index.
    ISBN 1–4039–4113–0 (cloth : alk. paper)
    1. Abused women. 2. Victims of family violence. 3. Women–Social conditions. I. Title.

HV1444.W55 2006
616.85'822–dc22   2005055564

loo499139 4

10   9   8   7   6   5   4   3   2   1
15   14 13 12 11 10 09 08 07 06

Printed and bound in Great Britain by
Antony Rowe Ltd, Chippenham and Eastbourne

For Will

Contents

List of Tables

Acknowledgements

I would like to thank first and foremost the amazing women who made this book possible; they had such resourcefulness and courage in surviving domestic violence and were then prepared to share their lives with me so generously. A big thank you also goes to all the women in the local domestic violence forum who supported me throughout the fieldwork and beyond.

Friends and family have had a lot to put up with over the last eighteen months. Jo Harrison, Will Johnston, Elaine Flynn, Karen Salinger, I owe you all so much and promise to get back to 'normality' soon!

I am very lucky indeed to have had the best possible support from colleagues and friends in the academic world at the Universities of Brighton, Portsmouth and elsewhere; without Sue Balloch there would have been no book proposal, Helen Jones has been absolutely wonderful as my 'friendly reader', as have Lynda Measor, Yvonne Bradshaw, Cathy Humphreys, Helen Baker and Liz Kelly for their perceptive feedback on various chapters. Other people who have been very supportive in various other ways are: Renate Prowse and Chas Wilson Karen Leander, Chris Piggott. Kate Olliver-Kneafsey, Eileen Berrington, Peter Squires, Marilyn Taylor, Evan Stark, Norman Johnson, Tony Jefferson and Christine Jennet. As everyone always says all remaining errors and omissions are my own.

To the people I met in Copenhagen where I spent five months writing this book I owe a debt of gratitude for making the stay such a wonderful one (no pun intended!).

To the editors at Palgrave Macmillan; Briar Towers, Jill Lake and Jen Nelson, thank you for this opportunity and for making it so easy to work with you. Thanks also to the publisher Elsevier for permission to publish material previously published as 'Me mother's bank and me nanan's, you know, support: Women who left domestic violence in England and issues of informal support', *Women's Studies International Forum*, 2000, 23(1), 1–13.

This research study was funded by the Economic and Social Research Council.

Introduction

Yes I should think the last seven years have been the worst of the lot ... I wanted to do things with my life and he just wouldn't let me (Jill).

I'd say I'm a survivor mmm I'm much, much stronger, because now I have to make me own decisions, I can't turn to anybody else for help in a situation that concerns just me, myself... I just feel a better person all round. If I want to do anything I'll go out and do it and there's nobody stopping me from doing it (Louise).

My central focus in this book is on women's agency in the face of the constraints of gender, domestic violence[1] and poverty. All of the women participants in this study, like Jill[2] and Louise, took many actions and overcame multiple obstacles in moving through and away from abusive and violent relationships. I have called my book '*Surviving domestic violence*' to reflect my focus on agency and in tribute to all women who have survived domestic violence, and also as a reference back to Liz Kelly's book '*Surviving sexual violence*' (1988) which was influential in my development as a researcher and of course in the field more generally.

In this book I try to reflect the changing and complex ways in which women's identities are formed in today's world (Braidotti, 2005). By prioritising women's own words, yet not seeing these as unproblematic, and by acknowledging my responsibility in analysing and interpreting their words, I hope to contribute towards understanding change and continuity in terms of gender (Lundgren, 1998). By asking women about responses (spontaneous and actively sought) from the people they came into contact with, I hope to contribute towards

1

understanding the importance of social networks and communities in enhancing women's agency and in acting against domestic violence (Kelly, 1988).

As a feminist researcher and activist, I am committed to research which challenges ideas and practices which perpetuate inequalities and exclusions of all kinds. In this study, however, my data allow me to say more about the intersection of gender with poverty and less about the intersection of gender with 'race' as the women in my sample were all white, working class, heterosexual women. Exploring the intersection of gender with poverty and the impact on agency in domestic violence, I address both institutionalised social relations and discourse. Language is extremely powerful but a focus on text alone does not reflect the heterogeneity of 'reality'. By taking white, working class women's perceptions of their experience of subordination in abusive heterosexual relationships as my starting point (Ramazanoglu with Holland, 2002, p. 99) I claim the possibility of knowledge (even if partial) of 'reality'. Studying violence brought me right up against the materiality of embodied existence, whilst studying women in poverty brought me face-to-face with the tangible materiality of poverty, and these experiences influenced my hybrid feminist approach; to ignore the material realities of women's lives and reduce violence and poverty to discourse alone would be doing a disservice to the lives of the women who participated in this research so generously.

My interest in domestic violence was shaped by my own childhood experiences of violence in childhood, of paternal aggression, and by adult experiences of interviewing and working with women survivors of domestic violence.[3] For many people, like myself, first knowledge of violence is discovered in childhood, rather than constructed, in the sense that first experiences of physical violence impact directly on the body. I well remember the visceral nature of shock and embarrassment felt in my own body when a seven-year-old friend of mine (a girl) threatened to hit me with a stick if I jumped over a certain space and then carried out her threat. I had mistakenly assumed she was joking.

I also draw on tools and insights from social constructionist approaches, conceptualising agency as constructed by women in communicative interaction with others, such interactions however being mediated by relations of power and by cultural discourse. Through interaction, norms for women in relation to heterosexuality, the family, marriage and motherhood are communicated, and the responses women receive to disclosing abuse contribute to women's understandings of domestic violence. My own example of experiencing violence as a child demonstrates how knowledge (which informs agency) is developed through the body, as well as in construction with others.

This book is an argument about the importance of analysing women's experiences of domestic violence as distinctly gendered (as well as raced, classed, etc), in opposition to gender-neutral or gender equivalence approaches. All forms of violence have certain similarities with other forms of violence but the experience of male violence against women 'in the home' is different because of the particular gender order of the society we live in. The overall argument I make builds on earlier feminist work on women's agency and domestic violence (Kelly, 1988; Hoff, 1990) but I examine more closely the mechanisms of patriarchal[4] control and examine the responses of others, as well as focusing on the forms of resistance used by women. Before proceeding, I want to look first at the importance of naming and definition since language is an integral part of the gender order and is often the way power relationships are expressed.

Naming and defining domestic violence

Until the nineteenth century, state discourse on male violence in the home, as 'violence', or as 'crime', did not exist and domestic violence was viewed as a private and personal matter. Private in that it happened behind closed doors, in *his* 'castle', with little outside intervention from state or community. Personal in that responsibility for the violence, and for dealing with the violence, was placed onto women. The 'unhappy wife' has long featured in songs and literature and 'maladapted wives', known as malmariée in France and malmaritata[5] in Italy, were received into women's asylums in considerable numbers across early modern Europe, as Cohen (1992, p. 161) details.

In the nineteenth and late twentieth centuries strong feminist challenges to the dominant construction of male violence in the home as private and personal emerged, critiquing the non-interventionist stance of the state. In the 1970s and 1980s feminists researched into, and campaigned against, all forms of violence against women, at the same time developing networks of refuges/shelters and other support services. This work brought a new discourse on male violence against women into the public arena providing 'a vehicle for change' (Dobash and Dobash, 1992), clearly a significant shift in the gender order. The public naming of domestic violence also meant that women were now more likely to receive improved/improving services from a range of social agencies.[6] However, the move from feminist discourse on domestic violence to public discourse brought new dilemmas and contradictions as feminist understandings came up against age-old, traditional discourse on domestic violence, 'a discourse of denial, minimisation and woman-blame' (Radford, 2003, p. 34).

Violence has always been a slippery concept, definitions can be broad and inclusive or narrow and exclusive. Johan Galtung (1975), for instance, uses the concept 'structural violence' in referring to the widest possible range of social injustices and inequalities endured by groups of people in the world. Others define violence more narrowly drawing on legal discourse. Gail Mason (2002) for example refers to violence as 'the exercise of physical force by one person/s upon the body of another. By physical force, I mean, pushing, shoving, hitting, punching, or otherwise harming or hurting the person who is targeted; which, in turn, often produces emotional and psychological harm' (2002, p. 5). Each definition captures different aspects and forms of violence, highlighting the way in which defining is a crucial political act. Responses to violence, through the law, policy and practice, are shaped by choice of definition; definition determines what and how the subject is researched, what becomes visible and known about it and how it is understood (Itzin, 2000a) and this has concrete effects on people's lives.

A recent significant debate on the relatively new public discourse on domestic violence is the emphasis on *physical* violence and its tendency to obscure sexual, emotional and material violence/s. This has been an outcome of the predominant ways in which domestic violence came into public view. Firstly, the physical injuries women sustain in domestic violence are extremely serious and can be life-threatening. Secondly, *physical* injuries are more likely to bring victims into contact with refuges/shelters, criminal justice and other social agencies. Thirdly, in our visual culture demonstrating the *physical* injuries sustained by women is easier than demonstrating other forms of injury.[7]

Legal definitions of domestic violence, identifying behaviours which could be defined as crimes, played a key role in the prioritisation of *physical* violence and seeing domestic violence crimes as discrete 'incidents' whereas feminists tend to conceive of domestic violence as a process of coercive control over time. Despite conceptual problems, the law and legalistic definitions have been (and remain) politically and socially crucial in the long struggle for legitimacy (Gramsci's 'battle of ideas', 1971), which finally brought domestic violence into the public sphere.

The problems raised by emphasising physical violence/s are being recognised as concern over the relative silencing of sexual, emotional and psychological violence against women (and children) grows. Feminist researchers have shown that women experience *emotional* abuse as a 'deeper and more central form of abuse' (Kirkwood, 1993, p. 44) and moreover women are far more likely to conceptualise *verbal* abuse as an expression of violence (Burman, Brown and Batchelor, 2003). Stark (2004) proposes that a concept of 'coercive control' may be more appropriate than one of 'violence'.

I argue, however, that we need to hold onto the term 'violence' in relation to all aspects of male abuse against women, partly in view of the seriousness of physical injuries sustained in many cases, but also because, as Radford argues, overly-broad definitions can 'result in the minimisation of domestic violence through its reconstruction as an equal opportunities issue in which men are as likely as women to be victimised and women represented as perpetrators' (2003, p. 34). My preference for the definition of violence against women (and domestic violence) is that outlined in the UN Beijing Declaration and Platform of Action (1995). This is preferable in that it is gendered as well as being sensitive to cultural differences and so I quote it in full as reflecting my own position:

D. Violence Against Women

113. The term 'violence against women' means any act of gender-based violence that results in, or is likely to result in, physical, sexual or psychological harm or suffering to women, including threats of such acts, coercion or arbitrary deprivation of liberty, whether occurring in public or private life. Accordingly, violence against women encompasses but is not limited to the following:

    a. Physical, sexual and psychological violence occurring in the family, including battering, sexual abuse of female children in the household, dowry-related violence, marital rape, female genital mutilation and other traditional practices harmful to women, non-spousal violence and violence related to exploitation;

    b. Physical, sexual and psychological violence occurring within the general community, including rape, sexual abuse, sexual harassment and intimidation at work, in educational institutions and elsewhere, trafficking in women and forced prostitution;

    c. Physical, sexual and psychological violence perpetrated or condoned by the State, wherever it occurs (UN Beijing Declaration and Platform of Action, 1995).

The gendered aspect of this definition is fundamental as feminist domestic violence researchers have consistently argued, and evidenced, women are preponderantly victimised by male perpetrators. Yet increasingly, claims are being made in the west that women and men are equally victimised (see for example Steinmetz, 1977/8; Fiebert, 1997; Archer, 2000). This is, therefore, an important time to revisit a feminist, gendered analysis of domestic violence.

Gender and domestic violence

Gendered relations are complex and changing, as already noted, however, there are clearly patterns of gender which tend to endure over time. Here I find the concept of each society having a 'gender order' useful. This concept was identified by Jill Matthews (1984) and developed by Connell (1987, 2002). Matthews argues that every known society distinguishes between women and men (although in varying ways) but the concept of the gender order (unlike 'patriarchy') enables distinctions to be made between the general form of gender relations and their specific content; thus 'it is not logically necessary that gender orders should be hierarchical, inequitable or oppressive' (1984, p. 13). Connell, too, sees the gender order as the wider gender patterns in society and argues that within the gender order there are different institutional 'gender regimes'. Both Matthews' and Connell's works are useful in thinking about how continuities remain, in spite of change; 'the gender regimes of institutions usually correspond to the overall gender order, but may depart from it. This is important for change. Some institutions change quickly, others lag; or to put it another way, change often starts in one sector of society and takes time to seep through into other sectors' (Connell, 2002, p. 54). At the level of the heterosexual couple, Lundgren (1998) has theorised domestic violence as a process of normalisation; as part of the way in which violence is seen, justified and experienced as 'normal'; the control and violence exercised over time narrowing women's possibilities for agency. In analysing domestic violence I argue the importance of studying at all three levels; gender order, gender regime and interaction; as well as encompassing responses from others in women's social networks and the wider community.

The notion of gender regimes enables us to look at how change and continuity happens in different institutions; two institutions relevant in this book are paid employment (Chapter 5) and the heterosexual family (Chapter 3). In the area of paid employment for example, significant shifts in the gender order have taken place in western societies. Women are increasingly employed in the public sector, are increasingly represented in government and are increasingly visible in the visual media (if not yet in positions of editorial power in large numbers). Walby (2002) has characterised this transition as a movement from a domestic to a public 'gender regime'. However, women continue to face structural disadvantages in the labour market; in particular those women in a lower social class and/or with few or no qualifications, as those in this study. Within the heterosexual family, gendered patterns of domestic work and caring remain relatively static with children primarily cared for by mothers, and fathers primarily seen as economic providers. Within this relatively conservative institution, domestic violence is a context in which men seek to enforce and maintain traditional gender difference/dichotomies and male privileges.[8]

We are able to refer to traditional gender relations because we have a *history* of gender relations going back thousands of years where men's privilege and notions of ownership over women have been the norm. This historical perspective is essential to understanding domestic violence, just as the history of 'race' is to understanding racism (Pence, 2005b). Domestic violence is rooted in a history of structural male dominance (through heterosexual relationships) and is embedded in the dynamics of patriarchal families. As a result even non-violent control tactics take on *meanings* they would not normally have in the absence of their connection with violence. Male domination has been enshrined in our legal systems which have only latterly started to respond to shifting cultural and gendered norms. A major contribution of feminist research on domestic violence has been to draw on historical perspectives on gender relations and to identify domestic violence as part of this ongoing (although changing) history (Dobash and Dobash, 1979, 1992[9]; Borkowski, Murch and Walker, 1983; Maynard, 1985; Hanmer and Saunders, 1984; Stark and Flitcraft, 1985; Pleck, 1987; Kelly, 1988, 1994; Yllo and Bograd, 1988; Mama, 1989, 2000; Stanko, 1988, 1990; Mullender and Morley, 1994; Richie, 1996; Hanmer and Itzin, 2000). To therefore equate violence against men ('in the home') by women as equivalent to male violence against women ('in the home') is to ignore the historical evidence and misunderstand this social phenomenon.

There is a wealth of statistical evidence in the present day, which supports a historical and gendered theory of domestic violence with the direction of violence in the home being mainly from men to women. Statistics in Britain reveal that one in four women will experience violence from a known man at some point in her life and two women are killed each week by a current or former male partner (Home Office, 1998, 2003).[10] In the US, although the number/reports of violent crimes by intimate partners against females declined from 1993 to 2001, it remained the case that intimate partner violence made up 20 per cent of all nonfatal violent crimes experienced by women in 2001 and 1,247 women were killed by an intimate partner in 2000 (US Department of Justice, 2002). In Australia the 1996 Australian Bureau of Statistics 'Women's Safety Survey' reveals that 23 per cent of women who had ever been married or been in a de facto relationship had experienced violence in that relationship; 1.1 million women experienced violence by a previous partner during and after the relationship; women were nearly four times more likely to experience violence by a man than by a woman (cited in Carrington and Phillips, 2003).

Conceptualising domestic violence as gendered, as primarily male violence against women in the home and a different experience, clearly brings into question existing ahistorical gender-neutral stances. As domestic violence is increasingly being mainstreamed feminist understandings, based on a history of gender relations may be distorted through gender-neutral definition and discourses.

Gender-neutrality and domestic violence

Gender-neutral approaches risk conflating differently gendered experiences and I am concerned that valuable knowledge about women's *gendered* experiences of male violence, painstakingly garnered over the past 35 years, may be subsumed within a broader discourse which attempts to cover all forms of violence in the home. Having said this, I am not arguing that violence against men, or elder abuse, or any other form of violence or abuse 'in the home' is not important, rather that each requires its own understanding (located historically and culturally) and responses. Nor am I arguing that all women's experiences are identical since different groups of women will experience specific differences, as well as similarities, as a consequence of domestic violence; for example differences would include classed stereotypes of violence, and racialised representations of violence and racism experienced by minoritised women (see Batsleer et al., 2002).

People have differing perceptions of gender-neutrality but two meanings have predominated in the west. Firstly, historically there has been a presumed 'gender-neutral' approach to research, policy and legislation, which might better be described as 'gender blindness'. This is a framework which simply ignores women and men's differently gendered identities both historically and in current practice both at home and in public. It relies on an ahistorical assumption of 'unitary, rational individuals' whose experiences can be universalised (Henriques et al., 1984). This assumption has been heavily critiqued both for its androcentricity and for perpetuating the status quo in gender relations. Secondly, there is a 'progressive' model of formal gender-neutrality, informed by liberalism, which currently frames political, policy and legislative documents, exemplified in the adoption of gender-neutral language; for instance use of the term 'parenting' rather than gendered terms such as 'mothering/fathering'. This model supposedly reflects the changing nature of gender relations in the family and society, but this model is problematic since it too hides continuing gender inequalities and the gendered nature of the social world. I look at several examples of the impact of gender-neutral policy which take no account of gendered and cultural differences and how this in fact tends to reproduce systematic discrimination. A key example with reference to domestic violence is that of the issues currently being debated around joint custody for parents when there is domestic violence (see Chapter 3).

My perspective on domestic violence, drawing on the feminist research above, and my own feminist activism, is that it is a gendered experience which has no parallel amongst men. The crucial difference is that male violence against adult female partners/spouses in the home is based in historically gendered relations and fuses in very particular ways with the overall gender order and regimes in contemporary western society; in particular the second-class status and social constraints experienced by women (Kimmel, 2002; Saunders, 2002; Stark, 2004; Pence, 2005a).

The research

The empirical research was based on participant observation, in-depth interviews and group discussions with 20, white, working class women victim/survivors of violence. The 'community' I studied was both spatial and interest-based, focused on a particular neighbourhood on a local authority council estate, and on female victim/survivors of domestic violence with similar backgrounds and experiences. Given this particular group of women the intersection of poverty/disadvantage with gender was especially important.

The research involved an ethnographic study in a small neighbourhood on a council housing estate in the North of England. Many people on the estate lived on welfare benefits: 30 per cent in receipt of income support and 19 per cent unemployed. Of all families with children 40 per cent had no wage earner, 26 per cent of these were single parent families (mainly mothers), of which 82 per cent were not in employment (City Council, 1995, pp. 120–1). It was women's agency which highlighted domestic violence as the major problem for women on this estate. Local women (activists, workers and others) organised a women's day at which this issue emerged as of utmost concern. At the time of the study this estate was one onto which women fleeing violence were being re-housed. In 1993 a local practitioner domestic violence forum was set up on the estate and I became a member of this group. Most of the women who participated were approached via forum members, and given a letter from myself to ensure voluntary participation in the study. Two others were put in touch with me through contact with other agencies such as refuges/hostels and advice centres. The research was built on working as far as possible with women as peers and co-participants in the research, involving in-depth interviews, group discussions and observations. All participants were assured of confidentiality and anonymity with reference to their identity and in addition to a consent form, consent was requested at other intervals. In terms of the safety of the women and myself I made sure that they had all separated from their abusive partners if visiting their homes and the location of survivor support group meetings was kept secure as far as was possible.

Observations in a support group of 20 survivors were carried out, as were a series of in-depth interviews with ten white, working class women (Betty, Jill*, Louise*, Lucy*, Janice*, Sally, Mandy, Catherine, Christine and Rachel [*not in survivors group]) whose ages ranged from 25 to 43-years-old. All had experienced one abusive and violent relationship but one woman had experienced three such relationships (grandfather and two husbands). The majority of the women studied had moved varying distances, from six to 70 miles, away from their own homes and communities. The ten women interviewed had 31 children amongst them (one had one child, two had two children, four had three children, two had four children, and one had six children) and there were also other children of the women in the survivors group with whom I also interacted. Most of the children had spent at least some time living with their mothers' abusive partners.

In the in-depth interviews I focused on women's experiences of control, abuse and violence and their perceptions of their support contexts. It is in my analysis that the gendered nature of women's experiences became apparent as explicit discussions of gender occurred infrequently in the interviews. Whilst carrying out my field work I needed to work out a means of summarising and classifying the mass of data I was collecting. In this I was influenced by Glaser and Strauss' (1967) work on grounded theory and used their constant comparative method. In grounded theory data are systematically coded into as many themes as possible, and as the categories emerge they are refined by the researcher as s/he begins to consider how they relate to one another and what the theoretical implications are. As Bulmer argues (1979, p. 668) the process of conceptualisation is, however, not reducible to simple formulae and carrying out the analysis was an iterative process, going backwards and forwards between my growing knowledge of the literature, my own previous experiences, the interview transcripts and observational field notes.

In my study there are data supporting the proposal that women find it difficult to disclose domestic violence. They often found it hard to name their experiences as violence and sometimes minimised their experiences. Hesitancies in women's speech patterns often denoted problems in speaking out about the violence they had experienced, and laughter (examples of which will be seen throughout the quoted extracts from interviews) indicated a range of complex emotions. Feeling shame and being ashamed were recurrent themes in the interviews (see Chapter 2).

Structure of the book

Structuring this work, in the inevitable linear fashion of books, has been difficult since I was exploring a constellation of influences, experiences and responses all of which came into play over time and which also interacted with one another. Women differed in which factors had the most impact on them overall, and at different times some factors predominated whilst others tended to fade into the background. All were significant at some point in time. I have had to make choices which may (wrongly) indicate that some factors are more important than others so I ask readers to see each chapter as one piece of a jigsaw which fitted together form a complex whole.

In this book I look at domestic violence, but also women's agency and resistance to it, focusing on one key social dimension in each of seven chapters: 'power', 'emotion', 'children', 'home', 'economic', 'informal support' and 'community'. In each dimension I document and analyse the impact of gender, poverty and domestic violence on women's actions in trying to build violence-free lives for themselves and their children.

Chapter 1 looks at issues of power and force in abusive heterosexual relationships. In Chapter 2 the key role that emotional dynamics play in domestic violence is explored, in particular the role of shame, whilst Chapter 3 focuses on the nature of abuse towards mothers but also the abuse children encountered. Chapter 4 discusses meanings of home for women experiencing domestic violence and Chapter 5 looks at how economic factors impact on the financial and material contexts of women and children. Chapter 6 examines responses to women from their family and friends and Chapter 7 looks at support in the community more broadly and draws conclusions about the enhancement of women's support.

I conclude this introduction with a recent quotation from the Deputy Secretary-General of the UN Committee for CEDAW (Convention on the Elimination of All Forms of Discrimination Against Women) which I believe highlights the continuing need for *gendered* analyses:

> *Marking the twenty-fifth anniversary of the adoption of the Convention to Eliminate All Forms of Discrimination Against Women (CEDAW), the UN Committee for CEDAW announced that no country in the world has achieved full equality between men and women in law and in practice. The Deputy Secretary-General, Louis Frechette, asserted that women are still 'significantly under-represented in public life', and still suffer from violence and sexual harassment in their daily lives.* (UN News Service reported in *Feminist Daily News Wire*, 18 October 2004).

1
Coercion and 'Consensus'

> ... and when it come to birthdays and things like that he used to
> fall out wi' me so he didn't have to buy me anything, or owt like
> that, until he felt as though you know, he knew he was going to lose
> me again, so he bought me an orchid. I don't know why he thought,
> I hated orchids! I hate orchids! (laughs) I hate orchids! He once
> bought me an eternity ring and erm it was second [hand], it were
> only twelve pounds, but it were something special, you know,
> I thought he was actually being nice, you know. And then as soon
> as he'd bought it he went, 'and don't ask for anything else because
> you're not getting it', you know, I thought, oh God you've spoilt it
> again! (Sally)

Introduction

The practices of men in their efforts to control their wives/partners,
and women's agency in the face of such practices, are the focal points
of this chapter. As Sally reveals above, the enactment of male power
and control in violent heterosexual relationships does not rely on
violent acts alone. Women often experience this behaviour as bewil-
dering, which makes it difficult for them to know how to react (and
I take up this point later in the chapter). As seen in the introduction to
this book not only do women find it difficult to speak about domestic
violence they tend to deny or minimise the violence they experience
from men, indeed are often encouraged so to do (see Kelly and
Radford, 1996). Nevertheless, when women *are* encouraged to speak
about their experiences it is clear that the majority are constantly
active in their attempts to make sense of their relationships, and to do
something about it.

In the context of male coercive and violent acts it is questionable whether the concept of 'consensus' is an appropriate one and I place the concept of 'consensus' in inverted commas to indicate its problematic nature. Research reveals that women stay in relationships with violent men for between seven to 12 years before leaving (Women's Aid, 2001 cited in Humphreys and Thiara, 2002) and this would imply some level or form of 'consensus'. However, whereas traditionally 'consensus' and coercion have been conceptualised as dichotomous ideas, in reflecting on what women told me, it was clear that the two concepts cannot easily be teased apart in contexts where power relations are unbalanced. Women's accounts of their experiences of male violence and control in this chapter provide important evidence of how a form of 'coercive-consensus' is achieved.

This 'coercive-consensus' is at times 'maintained' and at times challenged by the women themselves, as well as by the people in women's social networks. Where existing definitions of domestic violence have tended to focus solely on the heterosexual couple this has hidden the way in which involvement in, and impacts of, violence ripple outwards affecting children, other members of the family, members of friendship groups and members of the wider community, such as neighbours. Other people are important resources that women could, and can, draw upon to challenge violence. How these others respond, therefore, is an integral and important aspect in (potentially) challenging violence and in enhancing women's agency. So it is essential to assess how and whether male coercive acts impact on the ability of women to seek and obtain support from others.

In this chapter, to try and better understand what is going on in terms of what I term a 'coercive-consensus' in violent heterosexual relations, I will look first at previous theorising on power and domestic violence which has been influential in feminist thinking. I will then examine how men act to achieve a form of 'coercive-consensus', how this can extend to women's wider support networks and how women respond.

Theorising power and domestic violence

Feminist researchers conceptualise male violence against women as having developed as part of a long history of male institutions, male dominance and men's notions of ownership over women. A major contribution of feminist research, therefore, has been to identify men as primarily the perpetrators of domestic violence. From the 1970s feminist research examined the *extent* of physical, sexual, psychological and economic violence against women in the private sphere and the *range* of violences suffered by women, as well as the *meanings* such violence have for women (see for example Brownmiller, 1975; Smart, 1976; Dobash and Dobash, 1979; Stanko, 1985; Hanmer and Maynard, 1987; Kelly, 1988). Importantly too emphasising the connections that exist amongst different forms of male violence 'in the public arena on the streets, in the public-private world of work and the private space of a woman's home' (Kelly and Radford, 1996, p. 22), termed a '*continuum of violence*' by Kelly (1988).

Black feminists challenged the universalised notion of 'woman' arguing that there are differences *between* women (Carby, 1982; hooks, 1982; Mohanty et al., 1991) which also constitute power relations and looked at the intersection of 'race' with other social divisions in experiences of violence (see e.g. Thornton Dill, 1988; Mama, 1989, 2000; Richie, 1996; Warner and Pantling, 2002; Gupta, 2003). This work greatly enhances our understanding of the multiplicity of experiences around domestic violence; it remains important, nevertheless, to retain Hanmer's idea that however diverse cultures may be 'the boundaries specifying correct behaviour for women are not those that bind men to society and cultures ...' (2000, p. 11). Or to follow Lundgren 'if we focus too much on the variable aspects of gender norms the roof may fall in' (1998, p. 197).

Early feminist thought has been problematised as predominantly conceptualising power as a negative force, some 'thing' which men 'have' and wield over women, thereby determining women's lives. This view of power was influenced by an early feminist focus on women who were the most downtrodden and oppressed in society; 'We identify with all women. We define our best interest as that of the poorest, most brutally exploited woman' (Item 6 in the Redstockings Manifesto, 1969). This model of power and gender relations was *invaluable* in capturing knowledge of women's experiences of structural oppression and looking at *who* has power, but was perhaps less valuable in helping us to understand 'how power, as a property of social relationships, is generated' (Crossley, 2005, p. 213). It failed to capture fully the multiplicity of power, its dynamic, processual and contradictory nature. As Bordo (1993, p. 190) points out this model makes it difficult to adequately theorise individual men who feel tyrannised by existing power relations (for instance). Others have argued that taken in its strongest version it can seem to deny women the possibility of exercising power; 'when power is understood as a possession, the corollary is usually to juxtapose the powerful with the powerless' (Hollway, 1996, p. 73).

Any argument which claims women are powerless must be treated with caution since feminism is, and always has been, premised on the possibility of resistance to, and transformation of, men's dominance over women; and hence is built on women's agency and power, although hedged by constraints (Kelly, 1988).

Since the 1970s and 1980s feminist work continued to develop more nuanced understandings of power, and here some drew from, but developed and gendered, the work of Foucault (see insightful examples in Ramazanoglu, 1993). Foucault (1980, 1983) challenges the traditional view of power as some 'thing' which individuals possess and the idea that power is necessarily negative (comprising violence, force and coercion). Foucault's development of his model of power involves recognising the existence of multiple power relations where power is never possessed, nor does it proceed from a particular source, but rather is considered to circulate in a diffuse way throughout society. Where power exists, he argues, there is always also resistance. This analysis of power as 'neutral', and hence potentially available to all, led to him emphasising the *instability* of power relations.

Foucault's (1983) claim that power is 'never in anybody's hands' is problematic for feminists, however, since it does not help us to understand the specific patterns of male power: '... through some relatively stable sex/gender or patriarchal system, men possess power which they hold over women (and subordinate men and children). In feminist theory women, in spite of the social divisions between them, are seen as very generally dominated by men' (Ramazanoglu and Holland, 1993, p. 239). Foucault's conceptualisation of power then is rather too diffused through society making it difficult to capture the systematic nature of male power (similarly that of class, 'race' and sexuality) and where and how such power is reproduced; power is '... so dispersed through the body of society that it has little relation to the traditional centres of political and economic decision making in capitalist social orders' (Tombs and Whyte, 2002, p. 223) or to traditional male dominance over decision making in patriarchal[1] societies. Foucault's approach is helpful however in demonstrating that power need not be negative, that it is unstable, relational and complex, and that we are all implicated in power relations in our daily lives.

Aspects of Giddens' analyses of power are also useful as a way of seeing power in nuanced ways. Fundamental to his conceptualisation of power is that in order for human beings to know how to 'go on' in life there has to be an interlacing of meaning, normative elements and power which occurs in all human interactions. As he explains it the basic relation between action (agency) and power is to be able to act otherwise, that is 'being able to intervene in the world, or refrain from such intervention, with the effect of influencing a specific process or state of affairs' (1984, p. 14). He points out that there are many interesting cases in the social sciences where the individual is confined by a range of specifiable circumstances. This would certainly apply to women experiencing male violence, but having little choice does not mean that women are merely forced into reaction; '... all forms of dependence offer some resources whereby those who are subordinate can influence the activities of their superiors. This is what I call the *dialectic of control* in social systems' (ibid., p. 16). However, I argue in this book that those resources are limited and women (subordinates), in order to resist men's actions to control them, often have to take deceptive and/or indirect actions. Where Giddens argues that the outward appearance of compliance is often the result of a *rational* assessment of a particular situation and possible alternative forms of action, that does not automatically entail agreement (ibid., p. 15). I agree but argue that we need to extend this argument by adding the impact of embodied experiences on agency (this chapter), as well as the emotional dynamics (see Chapter 2) in heterosexual relationships. The data in this study lend support to his theory that '... the normative elements of social systems are contingent claims which have to be sustained and "made to count" through the effective mobilization of sanctions in the contexts of actual encounters' (1984, p. 30). So for male partners to exercise control over their wives/female partners they need to effectively mobilise sanctions and 'rewards' over time.

For women to effectively resist such control, they too need to mobilise such resources as they have access to. In this respect Lundgren's (1998) notion of the man's hand, which strikes but also comforts the woman (an 'intentional switching between violence and warmth' (ibid., p. 171)), is important in understanding women's sense of bewilderment and uncertainty in how to act for the best. This switching between seemingly loving and hateful behaviour, she argues, contributes towards women's internalisation of the violence. At the same time externalisation of the violence is also important in that men become symbolic gods who control 'their' women's lives. Lundgren (ibid.) theorises the process of violence over time as a process of normalisation; as part of the way in which violence is seen, justified and experienced as 'normal' or 'acceptable' behaviour in women's lives, and argues that the space for women's agency is reduced to a minimum. Lundgren's conceptualisation is important,[2] however women in this study *were* able to act otherwise (even though it took them a long time and many acts) and it is equally important to see how such agency was enabled and how it might be enhanced in future.

Moving the perspective on domestic violence out from gendered interactions between specific (gendered) individuals, I also find the notion of a 'gender order' (the wider gender patterns in society) and institutional gender regimes helpful in trying to understand continuities and change in gendered power relations (Matthews, 1984; Connell, 1987, 2002). In any society there are numerous social institutions: the state, the school, the family and so on, each of these institutions having its own gender regime (patterns and texts produced by that institution), usually but not always corresponding to the overall gender order. Indeed any gender regime is itself likely to give complex and contradictory messages (ibid., p. 80) and is subject to change. Importantly too, the norms of such gender regimes are not passively accepted by people. In childhood, girls and boys are constantly active in taking up, adapting and/or rejecting such norms (back to Foucault's notion of resistance). However, it is equally true to say that gender learning is not shapeless, it is shaped in particular directions; 'Children learn about, and shape in their own lives, patterns of practice – the configurations of gender practice in personal life that we call "femininity" and "masculinity"' (ibid., p. 81). Here then we have both the agency of individual women and men as well as the constraints of gender regimes in a particular gender order: 'Gender patterns develop in personal life as a series of encounters with the constraints and possibilities of the existing gender order' (ibid., p. 82).

I now turn to look at how the above gendered issues, of agency and constraint, played out in the gender regime of the family, in the everyday lives of the heterosexual women participating in this study. What we will see emerging from this data is that power is at play at all levels, as Connell says: 'everyday life is an arena of gender politics, not an escape from it' (1995, p. 3) but shaped in particular directions.

Expectation and reality in heterosexual relationships

All the women participants reported how their relationships were positive at first (as all relationships are or presumably they would never get started). This finding mirrors the 'wonderful' early days identified by African American women in Richie's study (1996, p. 70). In looking at how women describe the early days of their relationships, gendered ideologies, expectations and identities are evident. Sally, for instance, reveals facets of her gendered identity and expectations of a heterosexual relationship when she reflects on her boyfriend's 'positive' behaviour towards her in the early days, talking about how he treated her 'like a lady' and how she was charmed by him. Other researchers have noted that in some cases male abusers can be charming (see for example Horley, 2002) and this is also the impression he gives others in her social network. This creates difficulties for her at a later stage when trying to convince them that he really is violent towards her.

> **Paula:** *And how did he treat you at first?*
> **Sally:** *Like I say, like a lady, opening doors for you and, you know, like a real charmer, yeah, he could charm birds off trees, you know…*

Being treated 'like a lady' is evocative of notions of chivalry and male protection.[3] Through his job as a bouncer and, as she saw it, his physical strength and proven ability to fight, he projected a gender identity of 'hegemonic' masculinity[4] (Connell, 1987, 1995). Sally had experienced violence (bullying) as a child and found herself attracted to him for these reasons (although in retrospect she saw the irony in this situation):

> **Paula:** *And what had happened before in his previous marriage did you know about that?*
> **Sally:** *I knew a little bit, but what I could see in him weren't the person other people were telling me about, you see, so I tried to trust my own instincts rather than other people's, which I shouldn't have done I suppose … just another thing that I think attracted me to him were the fact that he could protect me because he could fight, which is a stupid thing really, but I'd been picked on at school, and things like that, for most of me life and it were actually somebody that could stick up for me and be, you know, like protective.*
> **Paula:** *So it was the protection, somebody you thought could keep you safe?*
> **Sally:** *Yeah, yeah, ah ha, (laughs) weird isn't it.*

Sally was aware that there had been problems in his previous marriage as one or two people in her social network had tried to warn her about his past behaviour and potential dangerousness. However, partly because she was in the early stages of the relationship, and partly because what she was being told did not square with how he was treating her at this time, she decided to rely on her own judgement. This is an example of where a woman's agency (informed by dominant cultural stereotypes) is evident but worked against her own best interests. Whilst her friends were giving her valuable information about this man's previous behaviour, she was not prepared to listen. This is one area where girls and young women need to be made aware of the serious nature of domestic violence, the importance of taking other women's experiences seriously and hence to make better informed decisions.

The severity and range of abuse/violence experienced by the women in my study was similar to that identified in previous research and so I do not intend to repeat what has already been documented elsewhere (see for example Dobash and Dobash, 1979; Kelly, 1988; Hoff, 1990; Kirkwood, 1993; Richie, 1996; Weiss, 2000). Richie (1996) found that violence in her study typically began after the second year of being together whereas the women in this study described controlling behaviour and incidents of violence starting at a much earlier stage, usually within the first year. It must be stressed, however, that early in the relationship controlling incidents were seen by the women as being normal and 'what you do' in a heterosexual relationship.

There was a level of dominant practices from their boyfriends/partners which women were, at least early on, prepared to see as 'normal' behaviour. Sally again described several of what she called 'minor' incidents of jealousy in the early stages of the relationship, saying: *I just thought he cared about me, I just thought it were like what you do.* It was not uncommon for women to rationalise dominant male behaviour in this way. Women's accounts also support other research evidence that at the same time women often minimise their experiences of abuse and violence and indeed find it hard to name their experiences as violence (Kelly and Radford, 1996). As a result they were prepared to defer to male control to a certain degree. Rationalisation and minimisation both contribute to the constellation of factors influencing women's continuance in abusive relationships. Betty's quote below reveals this tendency to minimise violence and also illustrates the way in which men tell women that they are responsible for the abuse they are suffering. Men often justified their violence as due to something their partners had done, a 'reversal of responsibility' (Kelly, 1988, p. 179), or a supposed character trait in this case that Betty is 'mad':

Paula: *When did he start being violent to you then, how did it all start?*
Betty: *Oh dear, at wedding day he decided to get paralytic drunk but he didn't hit me he was just really nasty.*

Paula: *So he hadn't been at all violent before that Betty?*
Betty: *Oh, he'd cracked me a few times but he said it were because I was mad.*

Social constructionist[5] approaches argue that masculinities and femininities are achieved as performative (Butler, 1990) and in order for masculinity/ies to be effectively dominant they have to be continuously 'made to count' (Giddens, 1984). Evidence in the present study revealed that compulsion in relation to women's and children's behaviour in the home was essential to this practice of dominant masculinity. In the present study women described their male partners as having traditional attitudes towards gender differentiation and gender roles in the family (see Quaid and Itzin, 2000). As Jill said: *He wanted a stop-at-home wife and a very old fashioned type of wife ... he liked his meals on the table when he got in from work.*

Men who believe that their control is legitimate and who wish to sustain traditional cultural values[6] on gender in the family (research evidence reveals) are more likely to become perpetrators of domestic violence (Dobash et al., 1996). The male partners of the women participants actively endorsed and acted out traditional, dominant masculinity and were prepared to try and enforce traditional femininity on their wives/partners.

In this study the exercise of controlling acts by men extended into *every* aspect of household life/practice, including areas, which conventionally might be considered the traditional remit of the female partner, such as what the family could and could not eat. In answer to a question about the ways in which her husband exercised control, Jill said: *Have you got three hours (laughs)? Right I couldn't smoke, I couldn't have chicken, certain fish I couldn't have. If I went out I'd have to be in at such and such a time else he'd come looking for me, erm, oh, what wouldn't he allow me to do, looking back, I can't think to be honest but there were so many things that he wouldn't allow me to do.*

A key finding in this study (see also Lundgren, 1998) is that male power and control is achieved through the use of seemingly positive actions as well as abusive or violent actions and, commonly, the use of positive and negative actions at one and the same time; as Sally explains in her account at the opening of this chapter about the orchids and the eternity ring. This narrative highlights how seemingly innocuous behaviour may instead be an alternative form of control. Fearing that she is going to leave him (because of his intolerable behaviour) he buys her an orchid. Ostensibly, the orchid is a present, however, it is not a true gift as it is something that she hates which comes with strings attached; a way of making her stay with him on his terms. The eternity ring is also not a true gift. It too is a tool of control, a gift given along with a threat not to make any demands on him. Lundgren's notion of the soft and hard hand is also apt in this context; as we can see the 'orchid' and the 'ring' are 'rewards' (positive sanctions) or in her terms the 'comforting hand', which women may experience (or want to experience) as being a change in their partner, a change back to his original 'real' self (1998, p. 185) harking back to the early 'wonderful' days, the threat representing the hard hand.

The levels of uncertainty women experienced as to when, where or on what grounds controlling or violent acts would be exercised was a further significant finding of this research. Women described their partners as having rapidly changing behaviours; Betty, for example, describes this:

> *I mean he could be sat here like normal and then just like that, for no reason at all he'd change, and he'd say, 'do this! do this! get that!' and I used to. Not very often admitted, I used to answer back, I daren't answer back, but on the few occasions I have, oh, he's knocked ten tons of shit out of me, honestly, I wasn't supposed to answer back and he used to say that to me as if I were a little kid, 'don't answer me back' and I used to think God what is he playing at!*

Sally describes a similar situation of uncertainty and how a form of 'coercive-consensus' was achieved in the relationship through his repetitive practices of dominance and her fear of his reprisals, all the while not knowing when they would occur:

> *You could be having a conversation and next minute he'd turned on you and you didn't even know what he'd said, or what you'd said, or it were just, having to be careful of every word you said and, you know, like give him money so, you know, he could go out in his car and not be angry that day, sort of thing. It was awful, sending me upstairs because he'd had enough of one of little uns making noise, and we didn't have no carpets upstairs and if one of the little uns dropped some noise he would shout upstairs 'if you don't ...' you know swear words sort of thing, and you had to be quiet, just everything, he had to control everything.*

Whilst domestic violence is repetitive over time and patterned, in the sense that the objective is clearly about men asserting their control, the women could discern no definite pattern as to when and where this would occur. As Sally says above, she was never sure when it was going to happen next, or over what grounds, and it was the level of anticipation and uncertainty (will he or won't he react aggressively) that women found so debilitating. Betty puts it differently, at first saying that she always knew when the violence was going to happen (which seems to counter my point) as she describes her body shaking in anticipation of his arrival. However, it is clear from what she says later on that she is in fact expecting to be beaten *every time* he comes home, but sometimes as she says he would surprise her by being 'all lovey-dovey' when he came in (Lundgren's alternating hand again):

Betty: *It were right funny, because I always knew when I were going to get beaten and some nights ...*
Paula: *You could tell then?*
Betty: *I could tell, straight away, I used to have right funny feelings.*
Paula: *What sort of things?*
Betty: *I don't know I'd be sat there, I'd be normal as owt like I'm sat here now. I mean you can't imagine me normal I know (laughs), but I were sometimes and I'd be watching telly and it would get to about ten o'clock and all my body used to shake and I'd go, oh God and I, oh God, I felt cold chill up my face, and I'd be sat like this, sat shaking, and you could bet your bottom dollar if I were like that, he never took a key, and I used to go and open door and first thing I got were a punch in the face, and I knew every time when he were going to hit me, I knew and I were ready for it then. And sometimes he come in all lovey dovey and everything and he was as right as rain, but sometimes he just used to beat me all over the house.* (my emphasis)

Where women are living from day-to-day in an abusive relationship, sometimes feeling 'normal' (as Betty describes) but often dreading an outbreak of violence, it is not surprising that women may give an outward appearance of compliance. This is partly the result of a rational assessment of the situation, and a weighing up of possible alternative forms of action, rather than entailing agreement to such treatment (Giddens, 1984, p. 15). But it is also partly about women's emotional responses to the control and abuse (as in the example of the orchid and the ring and see Chapter 2) and partly about embodied responses of anxiety and fear (as Betty's shaking body). Sally, for example, clearly feeling ambivalent about repressing her own feelings and needs, says below that she 'put up with it', making a conscious decision to bracket these feelings (as far as she could) and look forward to the good times (which happen even in violent relationships):

> *He made you feel that you weren't worthy of anything else anyway so you just put up with it, you just lived for the nice bits, you know like if he'd say 'let's go away for the day today' and you'd live for them days and just hope that others didn't come about (small laugh) by just trying to keep your mouth shut and I couldn't do it all the time though I had to rebel a little bit (laughs)* (Sally).

As these women reveal, the use of abusive and violent means of controlling behaviour undermined any early promise the relationship had shown, and over time as the husband/male partner's behaviour continued to be violent, women's resentment and anger build up. At this point, male acts of power are more overtly coercive and women started to question their former acceptance of the legitimacy of male dominance (Pilcher and Whelehan, 2004).

As time went on and the abuse continued the women in this study became less and less happy to accede to men's acts of control without resistance, and in many cases took more direct actions in resisting these acts. It was when women decided to seriously and overtly resist being controlled that the men increased their levels of abuse/violence in order to reinstate and maintain their notion of 'social order' (as Betty demonstrates in the quotation on p. 22). Jill, who had suffered years of emotional abuse found that as she tried to lead a more independent life, doing voluntary work and so on, her husband increased his level of abuse to physical violence:

> *I went to the solicitors because, when he actually started getting violent, I went to the solicitors to get an injunction on him and he said that if I did that to him he'd cause as much trouble as he could, and I just didn't want that I'd had enough. So he says, 'the only way you're going to get me out is by doing it my way'.*

The example of the orchid and the ring, as well as those which illustrate women's uncertainty about when violence is going to occur, contest Walker's (1984) concept of the cycle of violence, where she conceptualises domestic violence as going through three phases: a tension building phase, followed by the acute battering incident, followed by kind, contrite and loving behaviour (sometimes referred to as the 'honeymoon' stage). As we have seen women often do not know when abusive or violent acts are going to occur, and the men's behaviour was experienced as random, and coercive. The mobilisation of rewards and sanctions were intentionally used by male partners whenever they wished to assert control. However, when women continued to resist their male partner's wishes they often experienced more 'severe' (in the sense of more physically violent rather than implying a hierarchy of severity) violence (see also Kelly, 1988).

At the same time, however, the relative instability of men's power is also revealed in that if such power was truly stable and secure, there would be no threat to their power and no need for them to wield abuse and violence to regain control.

I now turn to look at women's social networks and how coercion was also wielded by the male partner in relation to the extent to which women were able to maintain contact with family and friends. Although this forms an integral part of the 'coercive-consensus' context achieved I have separated out this section for analytical reasons as in this book I have a particular focus on the support of other people in women's social networks.

Coercion and women's social networks

It is important that women's wider social networks are not overlooked as they often have been (see however Hoff, 1990; Kirkwood, 1993). It is still the case that women are more likely than men to spend a greater proportion of their lives embedded in close, intimate relationships with others (family, children, friends) and such relationships and co-present interactions may tend to reinforce traditional, hegemonic meanings of experience. Ribbens (1994) and Edwards (1993) refer to women and men's 'different ways of being in the world' (cited in Ribbens McCarthy and Edwards, 2001, p. 770)[7] and such differences in women and men's lives imply the need to pay attention to specific, concrete details of women's daily lives in interaction with others.

The most significant finding as regards to coercion and its impact on women's support networks was the extent of control exercised by male partners in preventing women from seeing their friends, and even family. All of the women interviewed had difficulty in maintaining contacts with their family and friends due to the controls exercised by their male partner. Women's opportunities for supportive interactions were severely curtailed over time and women were often coerced into accepting his friends as her friends. Over time women's potential support network diminished leading to increasing isolation and men's increasing surveillance of their wives or partners.

I asked the women how this had been accomplished and Christine reveals the efforts that men were prepared to put in to ensure women became more isolated from their friends over time: *Mmm, he just used to row and row until I gave up.* In a number of cases husbands/partners drove women's friends away with inappropriate and insulting behaviour when the friends were visiting their home; for example by embarrassing her, by ignoring her friends, by insisting on being there all the time and/or by constantly butting into the conversation, as Louise points out: ... *they only used to come when he wasn't there because they didn't like him. Because like he used to walk in and never used to talk to them you know.*

In other cases the male partners would be as 'nice as pie' when her friends were there but as soon as they had gone they would start a row, 'slag the friends off', and/or threaten her if she dared to ask them to the house again. Women described these insults as a form of violence; as we saw in the introduction to this book women tend to experience levels of verbal abuse as an expression of violence (Burman, Brown and Batchelor, 2003). When I asked Sally if she had been forced to stop seeing her friends she told me how this happened: *Yeah, yeah. I ended up with none at all [friends]. No, if anybody came to the house, everybody were a slag you know. He didn't like 'em they were a slag, you know what I mean. He'd speak to them great while they were there, then soon as they walked out of the door that's what they'd be and 'don't fetch them here again' sort of thing.*

If the friend was a single woman, then that woman was seen as even more problematic, calling a woman a 'slag' is offensively gendered discourse with connotations of 'loose sexuality' (Lees, 1993, p. 297) and reveals the men's view that they are in control of 'their' women's sexuality. Male concern with taking charge of a heterosexual relationship is a common finding of research on domestic violence (Dobash and Dobash, 1979) and women's accounts in this study uphold this. As Jill clearly recollects: *I knew [friend] before but because she was on her own, if I went out with her I think she'd be a threat because she were on her own, you know, automatic ... So I couldn't actually go out with [friend] because she was single and she's too much of a threat.* Dobash and Dobash identified four interrelated 'sources of conflict' which they argue are predictive of men's violence: Men's possessiveness and jealousy; men's expectations regarding women's domestic work; men's sense of the right to punish 'their' women for wrong doing; the importance to men of maintaining or exercising their position of authority (1979, p. 268). In this case we see men's possessiveness projected onto the woman's single women friends who are perceived by the male partner as more likely to be sexually active and lead 'their' woman into associating with other men, hence their use of the term 'slag' as a means of ending the friendship.

Most of the women in this study were expected to drop their friends (and to a lesser extent family) and make friends with their partners' family and his friends' wives. Even when women did this, close surveillance was nevertheless maintained:

Jill: *I started going out with some of his friends, but I lost all my friends. You know his friends' wives [we would] all go out as a foursome.*

Paula: *Was he OK with this?*

Jill: *Yes, but he'd keep a close eye on me if I was, if I spoke more to his friend than I should have done, then I was eyeing him up type of thing.*

What is clear from the evidence presented is how much effort men had to put into imposing their will on women, and that women were prepared to resist men's attempts to control them as far as they could (and this varied from woman to woman) however, most lost contact with at least some friends. On the one hand this supports the idea that men's power is relatively unstable and fragile (Foucault) or else why did they have to put so much effort into controlling the women. On the other hand they were relatively successful in reducing women's potential support networks. Usually, however, women persisted in maintaining contact with at least one female friend (even if secretively) and close family members (see Chapter 6).

Nevertheless, the disadvantage these women faced in having diminished support networks on leaving cannot be overemphasised, since maintaining socially supportive interactions with peers and family is central to human health and well-being. Indeed Scheff argues that the maintenance of social bonds is the 'most crucial motive' for humans and threats to social bonds generate intense feelings, and survival is threatened when social bonds are not maintained (1990, p. 4).

I now turn to examine how the women themselves dealt with controlling and abusive interactions to continue to assess how far women were able to 'act otherwise' (Giddens, 1984). Again I have separated this section out for analytical reasons, clearly women's responses to men's efforts to control them are interwoven into the broader fabric of their lives.

Women's resistance

There are various ways in which women respond to controlling and abusive practices from their male partners. One way of analysing their responses is to see them in terms of resistance and coping (Kelly, 1988), another way is in terms of reaction, resolution and resistance (Griffiths, 2000). I would not want to generalise women's responses to domestic violence, as women react in a range of different ways, except to say that women's agency was present in all cases. Many women tried to tackle it on their own through individual agency believing themselves fully capable of doing so (see Chapter 2).

On encountering early experiences of violence an expression of initial shock and disbelief, after the 'idyllic' early stages of the relationship, was virtually universal, as Mandy said: *It's like coming out of a warm bath, being picked up and dropped into a freezing cold bath, the shock just sends you off guard.* This shock could lead to taking many other forms of action, such as questioning, talking it through, trying to understand and especially initially to women trying to adapt their own behaviour. A major struggle was with the feeling that somehow they were to be blamed for his behaviour (see Chapter 2). Most women felt guilty and tried to adjust their behaviour to suit what the men wanted, as Louise:

> *Oh, yeah, yeah, like, all the interests he had, like he used to do stock car racing, and I always went with him, you know to wherever he wanted to go. And if he went to a football match, and if he were playing football I used to go with him, I always went with him and you know tried to support him and that, but no, it didn't seem to help, no.*

Other women said they tried to make sure they did nothing to make him anxious, to meet his demands and anticipate his needs. Trying to avoid violence by keeping their mouths shut and not saying what they thought (we saw this with Sally earlier) was another strategy women used to try and prevent violence:

> *It's not only that when they like you know on Saturday when he were like starting up his argument there were loads of things in me mind I wanted to like shout at him and I'm thinking, 'no, you know, keep your mouth shut because you know what he can do to you', I mean he could quite capably kill me, walk o'er me and go and get in car and drive off, quite easily, do you know what I mean* (Mandy).

However, as Kelly also found such 'avoidance strategies did not prevent violence recurring, although it is possible that in some cases, they may have limited its frequency' (1988, p. 180). Other strategies used by women were perhaps even more self-destructive, some women turned to drugs and alcohol as a means of coping with the controlling behaviour and to keep the relationship, as Betty says:

> *I'd been on libriums for ages because my nerves were right bad and they had to send for doctor to come out to me, at [place name], because me nerves just cracked, they just totally cracked up.*

Women saw the use of drugs and/or alcohol as one way of suppressing or preventing the feelings associated with the abusive relationship. But they also tried to distance themselves from their emotions by mentally switching off from what was going on:

> *Because in a lot of ways, because you get, well you don't know, but women that's been battered you can shut off, you don't have to know nowt you don't want to know, that's how I used to be. I mean he used to beat me and then he'd say, 'who's done that to you?' he knew very well who'd done it to me. I mean I used to have my face out here and my lips hanging out (laughs) and everything, and he'd say 'who'd done it?' (Betty).*

Lundgren has written about the way in which abused women retreat from their bodies in this way and the women she studied (who were members of a tight-knit religious group) integrated to their husbands' worldview and became different people:

> When a woman is abused, it is impossible for her to be *completely* present in her painful, violated body. She has to 'break loose' from her body. Like a prostitute or a sexually abused child, she may separate her body from her 'self', repress her body, make it into an *object*. She cannot feel the feelings with her 'self'; that would be too painful, so she estranges herself from her body and flees to a *symbolic* world as a survival strategy; 'she' is no longer her body (1998, p. 192).

However, Betty (quoted above) reveals that this strategy of blocking is usually only partially 'successful' since it is obvious that Betty remained aware of his duplicity and abuse throughout. Women also directly resisted male power and control by direct confrontation, responding to aggression with aggression, as Sally recounts:

> *All I can remember is about this time is that he said he were never going to do any, he'd lost all that weight and you know and all this and er, it*

sounds stupid, but me friend phoned up and asked me if I wanted to go blackberry picking and because he didn't want me to go he threatened to hit me and that just did it, he'd threatened to hit me a couple of weeks ago, yeah, and we'd actually had a fight, and I'd had two black eyes, and I'd actually hit him back for first time in my life.

Women also succeeded in finding other ways and means to resist and subvert their partner's will by devious means, as Betty explains:

If I went to me mum's I was supposed to get there for a certain time and get back for a certain time. If he told me I couldn't go I wasn't supposed to go and I used to have to tell the next door neighbour 'If he says have I been out say no, because I've told him I were stopping in today'. I used to whizz round right quick, do me work, race to me mum's then race back home before he got home from work, and I always had to have his dinner waiting for him.

However, even when resisting as Betty does, we can see that there are gendered beliefs underpinning her ability to 'act otherwise' (Giddens, 1984). So whilst Betty covertly goes to see her mum, she nevertheless makes sure that she does the housework and that his dinner is on the table. In examining the capacity of women to resist male coercion it is necessary to redefine what we mean by resistance and the different ways in which resistance may be carried out. Conventionally resistance is often conceptualised through a masculinist lens as being aggressive and active, however, whilst women's resistance could be, and was often, confrontational it could also be expressed in other ways.

What is of significance is that part of women's resistance in this study was to turn to informal supporters (see Chapter 6) and some also consulted social agencies for help in resisting such risks; the police, social services, voluntary organisations, etc. My study revealed a range of different responses from formal agencies some encouragingly positive but also inappropriate and insensitive (see Chapter 7).

Conclusion

Mostly with him he had to be in control, he had to be in control over everything, absolutely everything, noise, furniture, anything, windows being cleaned to his satisfaction, everything you know, he had to be in control over absolutely everything in end (Sally).

In talking with women about their experiences I have tried to uncover some of the practices through which male power was maintained and (largely) reproduced in these heterosexual relationships. Male partners held polarised views of gender roles (drawing on beliefs about male dominance) and attempted to impose these on the women. To impose a version of dominant masculinity involved real effort and work by them; including insistent will power, women perceived their male partners as prepared to push verbal arguments to the limit without negotiating compromise solutions (or alternatively refusing to make any response to women's attempted negotiations)[8] and the mobilisation of seemingly positive rewards (such as gifts) and negative sanctions (abuse and violence). These practices focused on women's roles in the home, but also impinged on their wider liberty, limiting women's social contacts and activities.

The practices of control were ongoing over time with women living with an underlying fear of when and where abusive (or violent) acts would occur. Indeed physical violence was often unnecessary to preserve this process of 'coercive-consensus'. This is important in understanding the cumulative effect over time of, what may seem from the outside, 'minor' infringements of women's emotional and physical integrity. It is also vital to recognise that for a considerable length of time women may not define their partner's actions as violent violence or abuse; 'The complexity of recognising and naming men's actions as abuse is one important but neglected, reason why many women do not seek outside support and stay with abusive men' (Kelly and Radford, 1996, p. 28).

Women were not passive, however, they responded actively to men's behaviour using a variety of different strategies to try and understand and negotiate (see Chapter 2), to contain and/or stop these practices. To see women's efforts to avoid men's controlling actions by adapting their behaviour, by mentally blocking out the violence, by turning to substance abuse and so on, as passive is misleading. These are all agentic acts of self-preservation (even though they may appear to be self-destructive) since where women resisted more overtly and persistently their partners increased their levels of violence. For women, knowledge of how to act in these contexts involved a rational assessment of what was happening but also embodied knowledge of fear (such as Betty's physical shaking) and an attempt to resolve emotional responses in the relationship.

In all cases the space women had in which to take action was constrained by men's controlling practices, but also to a degree by their own gendered beliefs, and also by other means in the various social dimensions of their lives: by their responsibility for childcare (Chapter 3), for the home (Chapter 4), in their paid work (Chapter 5), in relation to family and friends (Chapter 6) and the wider community (Chapter 7). Moreover, a further constraint was the way in which male partners' practices switched between warmth and violence (Lundgren, 1998, p. 171) and this formed part of the gendered emotional dynamics I look at in Chapter 2.

2
Love and Shame

Part of you keeps trying and trying to make it alright, you know. I'd sit for, when he was there, and the states he'd come in, and afterwards I'd always sit for hours and talk to him and try and work, understand him and what was going through his head, and try and work it out, but he'd never, he'd just return to what he was like (Christine).

Introduction

Polarised and hierarchical concepts of *reason* – associated with masculinity, and *emotion* – associated with femininity, form the typical context for western thinking (Seidler, 1987; Bryson, 1992) and promote the stereotypes: 'emotional women' and 'rational men'. The increase of sex segregation (men seen as active in the public sphere and women in the private sphere), which occurred as part of the industrialisation of western societies from the middle of the nineteenth century onwards, helped to embed these gendered stereotypes as cultural norms. In modernity, men are increasingly seen as individuals, as able to act independently, whereas women are 'cast as incapable of becoming fully agentic .... In the course of this transmutation women are locked into and overwhelmed by their corporeality, while men rise above it and are defined, determined and distinguished by their sociality' (Marshall and Witz, 2002, p. 6). The exception to this general 'rule', however, is that women *are* seen as having greater agency in the area of emotions and emotional management, particularly in the private realm of the family. As Brody argues, men are expected to keep emotional expression to a minimum, with the exception of anger, pride and contempt, and women are expected to show love and care and to promote social bonding through the emotions of warmth, empathy, respect and shame (1999, pp. 4–5).

In this chapter I look in depth, therefore, at gendered emotional dynamics in families where male acts of control and violence were occurring, focusing on the couple relationship (see Chapter 3 for a focus on emotional abuse and children). I argue that women's agentic status as regards emotions in heterosexual/family relationships is an important facet of an holistic understanding of how abusive men often manage to remain in their relationships for relatively long periods of time. This is *not* to argue in the least that women are responsible for their own victimhood, but that the complexities of gendered emotional dynamics form one more facet in the constellation of factors which make the continuation of an intimate partnership, even in the face of abuse and violence, more rather than less likely.

There are three main strands to my argument here. The first is that women continue to be constructed as responsible for emotions and caring in the heterosexual family and this has concrete effects on women's lives. Women tend to take this responsibility seriously, and most women are confident in their abilities in this respect as compared with men. The second is the importance of addressing the emotions of shame and blame[1] experienced by women for a number of different reasons. Challenging these emotions is vital since they compound the difficulties women already experience in speaking out about their experiences and hence delay their efforts to seek support in effecting change. The third is that, although it may help to understand the meaning of love in the couple relationships, women are clearly *not* only absorbed in this relationship; they also have other interests such as their children, their homes, their work (paid and unpaid), and other relationships with family and friends. All of these bring their own rewards and form alternative facets of women's lives.

In order to develop these strands of thought, I look at what women said to me when reflecting on their emotional states during their abusive relationship and how they felt after leaving. To do this I first define what I mean by 'emotions', then I examine the wider social construction of heterosexual love, moving on to focus on the emotional dynamics in domestic violence, in particular men's emotional abuse of women, and finally analyse how shame and blame become key emotions experienced by women which impacted on the extent of their outward-looking agency.

Emotions and gender

I define emotions drawing on Denzin (1984), who argues that emotions are experiences which are felt through the body (in Chapter 1 we saw how Betty experienced the emotion of fear through her body) and on Barbalet who says emotion is 'an experience of involvement ... that immediate contact with the world the self has through involvement' (2002, p. 1). However, the expression or display of emotions in adults can be distinct from such felt emotions; adults learn to mask or regulate their emotions, suppressing anger for example. Brody (1999, p. 19) argues that on existing evidence, although in certain contexts men and women may express feelings differently, it remains uncertain as to whether they experience feelings differently. Moreover, emotions are often mixed or conflicting and rarely referred to in everyday conversation, even when people are specifically asked to describe their feelings (Shields, 2002). In conversations/interviews which address sensitive and/or stigmatised areas of social life, expressing emotions is even more difficult for most people.

In the present study women participants often found it hard to express how they felt, and emotions in the interviews were frequently revealed in extra-linguistic ways through pauses, sighs, long outbreaths and particularly through laughter; all aspects of what Briggs refers to as the 'indexical meanings' of language (1986, p. 42). I found women's laughter particularly useful in assessing their emotional states as examples occurred throughout the interviews and different types of laughs indicated differing emotions, such as nervousness, self-mockery, rebellion and anger.

Barbalet has argued that *all* human actions require 'appropriate facilitating emotions' (2002, p. 1) contrary to much lay and academic theorising where emotionality is often conceptualised as *extreme* states. In western culture if we describe someone as an 'emotional' person we imply that they express heightened, inappropriate emotional states (Shields, 2002) and the label 'emotional' is often applied to women. Indeed, the notion that women are more emotional than men is deeply embedded in western cultures. This belief tends to be construed as a negative quality when compared with the assumed restraint and reasonableness of 'cool' masculinity. However, as Barbalet (2002) points out, assumed 'masculine' reason also needs emotional states, those of 'calmness, security, confidence'.

Since the late 1970s there has been increasing interest in addressing emotion from social perspectives (Denzin, 1984; Bendelow and

Williams, 1998; Barbalet, 2002) some importantly take a gendered and/or feminist perspective (see for example Hochschild, 1983; Jaggar, 1989; Seidler, 1998; Brody, 1999; Shields, 2002; Fischer, 2000).

As seen in the introduction to this chapter, gendered assumptions have dominated western thinking since the Enlightenment and permeated through and across disciplinary boundaries thereafter. In the social sciences Parsons' work on the heterosexual family was particularly influential. In a structural analysis of the family as a sub-system of society, Parsons, Bales and Shils (1953) characterised the husband-father as the primary 'task-leader' (superordinate) of the system, and differentiated from the wife-mother; arguing that the husband-father's labour market commitments precluded his taking responsibilities inside the family, whereas the wife-mother's role was the skilful management of the emotional problems of the family members (1953, pp. 267–8). Their analysis failed to challenge gendered dichotomies upholding women's role as in the private sphere/emotions and men's role in the public sphere/rationality.

For some time now, such thinking has been critiqued as stereotyping, rather than reflecting social realities. Despite this critique, and the rapidly changing roles of women in western societies, stereotypical beliefs about appropriate 'masculine' and 'feminine' roles and duties persist in many quarters. Williams and Bendelow rightly point out that 'we should not neglect the extent to which they [gender stereotypes] still exert a powerful and pervasive impact on our lives, particularly through the media and marketing' (1996, p. 149). This was certainly the case in this study and it is likely that the impact of polarised gendered assumptions on emotions (as expressed rather than necessarily experienced) operates most starkly in heterosexual relationships where men are attempting to enforce traditionally gendered relations.

Duncombe and Marsden's (1993, 1996, 1998) work has been important in exploring how couples stay together in view of late twentieth century feminist research uncovering how women may be exploited in heterosexual relationships. They also look at the new emphasis on individual self-fulfilment in relationships, Giddens' 'pure relationship' (1991), and find that it is mainly women who keep such relationships going by doing 'emotion work' (Hochschild, 1983). This was the case also in the present study. Moreover, the continuing impact of gendered assumptions means that specific ways of behaving are interpreted differently depending on the gender of the person so acting. As Jackson argues, the 'experience' of love within a heterosexual relationship is differentially gendered and one way this was evidenced in my study was the way in which practical tasks achieved by men were interpreted as expressions of caring and love by women (and men were aware of this).

Love has been seen 'as making women vulnerable, not just to exploitation, but to being hurt by men' (Jackson, 1993, p. 205). Because stereotypes of gender give a central role to women's identities as loving and caring, women may be especially sensitive to the loss of love and be more dependent on others' good opinions (Ferguson and Eyre, 2000). This appears especially relevant to the dynamics of relationships where men are exercising control and violence and how this impacts on women. Jackson (1993) goes on to say that although De Beauvoir and Firestone 'differed in their analysis of the meaning of love for men and women, they agreed that women invest far more in love and that they give far more affection to men than they receive in return. This was not seen as part of women's nature ... but as a product of the material conditions of women's lives. Love was linked to women's search for a positive identity, a sense of themselves as valued, in a society which undervalues and marginalises them'. I have quoted this passage in full as it is important to my argument in this chapter.

Emotions and domestic violence

The emotional dimensions of domestic violence have been less explored than other aspects (see however Kirkwood, 1993). Kirkwood (1993), drawing on NiCarthy (1986), identified emotional abuse through two aspects of women's responses to it: the effect of physical abuse on women's emotional state and abuse enacted at an emotional level, such as verbal insults and emotional deprivation. She found six components (separable for analytical purposes) which describe emotional abuse: 'degradation', 'fear', 'objectification', 'deprivation', 'overburden of responsibility', and 'distortion of subjective reality'; '... in women's lived experience, the components are interwoven in such a way that they comprise a whole which has properties beyond merely the sum of those individual components' (1993, pp. 46–58). There are parallels in this study with Kirkwood's findings, and I draw on her work, however what I am trying to do here is to extend the analysis to look at the process of women's emotions over time, in response specifically to the emotional abuse suffered, but also in relation to the rest of their lives. While important, women's intimate relationship was not all consuming and, moreover, emotions were mixed and dynamic, feelings changed over time, there were good times as well as bad times, even in these abusive relationships. Significantly, women were also highly involved in/with their children (see Chapter 3), who provided many rewards and gratifications (as well as frustrations!), some women had paid or unpaid work commitments (see Chapter 5) and the majority were also in contact with a small number of family members and/or female friends (see Chapter 6). This is an important observation as it too partly accounts for why it is that abusive men managed to remain in these relationships as long as they did.

In order to look at emotions and domestic violence in more depth I look at the following three themes in women's emotional lives: 'love in heterosexual relationships', 'managing emotions in the family', 'nurturing, softness and anger/upset'; conceptualised as aspects of hegemonic femininity. There has been less debate in recent literature over the existence and significance of hegemonic femininity as compared with hegemonic masculinity, however, it is clear from the women's accounts that their verbally expressed and non-linguistically expressed emotions have characteristics which can be termed hegemonic.

Love in a heterosexual relationship

De Beauvoir said 'the word love has by no means the same meaning for both sexes' (p. 652 cited in Jackson, 1993, p. 205). To understand the context women find themselves in, with regard to domestic violence, it is necessary to think about 'love' and the place it holds in our social and cultural worlds and hence our individual, reflexive lives. As Jackson (1993) argues we are surrounded by representations of heterosexual love in our culture '... related to its institutionalisation in marriage and family life' (p. 202). Dominant cultural assumptions are that women form sexual relationships with men (Rich's notion of 'compulsory heterosexuality' 1980) and it is thereafter culturally preferable to get married and have children. The women in this study mainly followed this pattern (although two were not married) and, as seen in Chapter 1, experienced 'wonderful' early days (Richie, 1996) in their relationships, which were described in glowing terms drawing on gendered ideologies, expectations and identities:

> **Paula:** *So how did he treat you at first?*
> **Mandy:** *Brilliant, brilliant. I mean like I say he were from [city] so he moved to [city of study] he went and got a job, couldn't have wished for a better person, absolutely fantastic.*

Being in a heterosexual couple relationship, married or cohabiting, produces strong validating feelings of being in the right place and doing the right thing. Importantly, too, our culture holds powerful messages about the transforming power of love and happy endings, especially of women's love and its ability to change/civilise men. This message was reinforced by a (mythical) story circulating amongst Mandy's friends on the 'perfect relationship':

> *I suppose it's like I were talking to somebody other day and she says er she says you meet people and for like years the blokes have pasted them and everything, and then all of a sudden, overnight, these blokes change and like they've got the perfect relationship* (Mandy).

It is not possible to say how common a story this is but it clearly exists amongst some groups of women and is likely to be supportive in justifying some women's lack of action in terms of seeking support and remaining in the relationship in the hope of a change in their partner's behaviour effected by the transformative power of love. In this study half of the women drew on such a discourse of 'love' whereas the remaining five did not. Two narratives most closely elided with romantic narratives of love overwhelming all other emotions (despite violence); *Oh, he'd cracked me a few times ... but then I thought the sun shone out of him, I was just so much in love with him, I were honestly, I can't think why but ...* (Betty laughs, distancing herself from her former self); *I worshipped the ground he walked on, I thought there were nowt like him* (Rachel). Janice, too, said *I loved him, I really did love him.* On leaving for good, women's feelings were far more ambivalent, only Louise said she still loved her partner, *When I first left him I still loved him, believe it or not, and if he'd have said, 'do you want me to come back?' I would have gone!*

The other five women made no mention of 'love'; Christine explained that for her getting married was as much about escaping her own family, and gaining a surrogate family, as any feelings she had for her partner. Jill talked about only 'feeling close to him' for the first few months. Lucy and Mandy both explained the lasting nature of the relationship to me as their partner having some kind of mysterious hold over them, but which they did not refer to as being love; '*... there's something he's got on me and I can't point it out yet'* (Lucy).

> **Mandy:** *I don't know, he's got, I think, instead of getting to me like physically he got to me psychologically first. I don't know why that I don't like stand me ground wi' him, because there's nobody else walking that I couldn't stand me ground wi', nobody, so I don't know why it is him.*

Paula: *Was it because you loved him that this was different?*
Mandy: *I don't know, I honest to god do not know, I really don't,
I mean like no other bloke could ever, ever hit me.*

Where it might have been expected that narratives of 'love' would
have predominated as explanations for staying in the abusive relationship this was rarely the case, however the idea expressed by Mandy and
Lucy of some form of 'psychological hold' is an interesting one which I
explore below in 'nurturing, softness and anger/upset'.

Managing emotions in the family

Despite women's changing social roles over the last 50 years, feminist
activism and research challenges, the women in this study were all
expected by their male partners to manage the emotions in their families
(and much else besides). And it may be that this role in the family
remains largely with women, perhaps especially where there is poverty
and economic deprivation; '...despite a general growth in social
reflexivity in late modernity, not all men are "in touch" with their emotions. In this respect, there are still marked, albeit less clear-cut, gender
differences in emotionality' (Williams and Bendelow, 1996, p. 149).

This finding of emotional management chimes with Kirkwood's
notion of women's overburden of responsibility; 'Overburdening was
experienced by women as the expenditure of tremendous energy in the
day to day emotional and practical maintenance of their relationships
and family, without return of effort or energy from their partners'
(Kirkwood, 1993, p. 54). Janice was fairly typical and talked about how
her partner would hardly ever be in the house, and told her that
responsibility for the home, the children, the food, the dogs, everything in fact, was hers. She describes how she would not have been
able to cope at all if it had not been for the support of her mother and
sister (see Chapter 6):

*Well anyway, after I'd had our [son] things really got from bad to worse.
He started, it were more or less a case of I'd got to stop in the house, they
were my kids, they were my dogs and er things like that ... Then when
I got them [twins] home he started going out, just get in car and say, 'I'm
going out', and go. Wouldn't say where he was going or owt like that,
he'd work all hours god sent, never be at home. Our [sister] used to come
up every Tuesday and take the full run of house, me mum used to come
up when he were on nights so that I could get sleep. Er, I don't know what
I would have done wi'out em ... he were never there, never in.*

Not only were women responsible for managing their own feelings (see below) but also for managing their partner's 'problems'. That is to try and understand their male partner, to help and support him, but also to promote a sense of intimacy that they value themselves (Duncombe and Marsden, 1998). As Christine (below and in the opening quote to this chapter), they would try to talk to men about emotional issues but often got little response either in exploring emotions or in changing behaviour; according to the women their male partners would sometimes say they couldn't remember what had happened, sometimes they would apologise but would not discuss it, sometimes they would seemingly try to make amends by giving gifts or doing something practical (however, we saw in Chapter 1 this was often far more about reasserting control than any 'real' change in the men) but could not or would not talk about their behaviour: *He can't, he can't talk. No, he can't ... No, he won't, he won't let out his feelings about anything* (Mandy).

The majority of the women in this study reported that their male partners took little or no adult responsibility for the emotional health of the relationship. As Kirkwood also found women experienced this behaviour as strange and inexplicable, 'their descriptions were often related in bewilderment and uncertainty' (1993, p. 55). It seemed clear from the interviews that it was not that these men were completely emotionally illiterate, for instance they *were* aware of how practical tasks and doing things for the women would be interpreted by the women as signs of caring and/or love but intentionally used this awareness as a means of control, of regaining women's approval after violent episodes (as also seen in Chapter 1), as in Mandy's example: *I mean Monday morning ... he come up wi' a tray, cups, teapot, the lot, and made me a cup of tea at side of bed! Never done it in his life, not when I'd just given birth to him [their son], did he ever do it, do you know* (breathes out heavily).

The women worked hard to try and talk to their husbands/partners, indeed women held persistent and strong beliefs in their own ability to get through to their male partners and instigate improvements (which ironically contributed to prolonging the time women spent in the relationship before seeking help) but ultimately they found they were unable to understand their male partner or make any differences to his behaviour; *Can't understand him. I thought I'd be able to understand him but I can't* (Lucy).

Nurturing, softness and anger/upset

Hite concluded that there is a kind of 'emotional contract' in which women are expected to nurture men without reciprocation from men

(1988 cited in Duncombe and Marsden, 1998). I argue that this 'emotional contract' is connected with women's own identities as nurturing (which problematises non-nurturing responses such as anger) and hegemonic femininity. Indeed, in this study, the women drew on dominant discourses around women's identity as nurturing, caring and mothering in a number of ways. One negative aspect of this was to conceptualise their partners as children, their behaviour as childish or '*babyish*'.

> **Jill:** *Because he's got that way with him, you know if you say no, he'll go on, he's just like a kid, as I say, he'll go on and on until you give in and you think, I don't want to do this, why am I doing this!*

Women wonder why they find themselves pandering to this sort of behaviour from an adult, and the answer stems partly from this unspoken, unwritten gendered 'emotional contract' which remains influential, but also due to the way in which male behaviour, perceived as being dependent and needy, hooks into women's own self-identification as being uniquely able to help and support their loved ones. This makes it more difficult to deny the needy person's wishes since this would mean denying one's own self-identity. Mandy's quote below shows how a male partner can gain emotional capital by expressing such needs. At the same time since mothering often gives women a positive identity, mothering can become part of how women relate to their adult male partner:

> *I mean he always says to me, 'you're the only one I feel like secure wi'. 'I've never been so secure with anybody, **only you**', but it's like I say, he's my fourth kid. Now probably to him I'm the security his mother never gave him ... Teatime his meal's on table, supper time, 'oh I'm starved Mandy', I'll say, 'well go and have a look in freezer see what you want and I'll do it you', same as kids ... I run his bath for him ... same as I do kids, I wash and iron his clothes for him* (Mandy, my emphasis).

Love has been identified as dangerous for women (Firestone, 1972; De Beauvoir, 1997 [1949]), but it seems rather to be a more complex gendered emotional symbiosis,[2] linked into women's material and emotional responsibilities for the children and family more generally, which is dangerous for women, the notion of love alone is too simplistic. Indeed, women sometimes recognised that other women's identities as carers were deliberately manipulated by male partners to women's detriment:

Sally: *... there were one woman and that bloke just knew exactly how to get her every time ... all he had to do was have a pretend panic attack and she were back again, yeah ... if she wouldn't come back, all he had to do was to have this like a panic attack, like a fit she called it, and she knew what he were doing but just in case it were a real one* (breathes out very heavily).

However, women were less able to 'see' this as clearly when involved in their own relationship due to their ability to empathise with their male partner's point of view; women described this as being soft, or a soft touch (the notion of softness can be seen as characteristic of hegemonic femininity); *'I was too soft. I was too soft, I just let him get on with it, I've always been right easy going anyway'* (Jill); *'he's coming to our house crying all the time', he's doing this that and other you know and I'm soft you know, I felt sorry for him'* (Sally); *'... and he started crying outside and er like a soft touch I am I let him in'* (Lucy).

Linked to a notion of 'softness' is the inability/difficulty women described in feeling anger about what was happening to them. Initial flashes of anger were described as evaporating away and being replaced by feelings of guilt (see below) and/or sympathy for the male partner; *Once like, once at [place] he like, he slapped me, I went 'don't hit me' and he slapped me again, and I like just dove on him, do you know, and like then suddenly I realised what I were doing, stopped, but then it had gone, that anger inside me had gone, and he battered me all o'er* (laughs, Mandy); Mandy and Sally both expressed an inability to hate anyone: *And I can't hate either, I can't hate anybody, I've never hated anybody, I could say I don't like that or I don't like you or something but I can't hate, I ain't got no hate in me and that's one of me problems I think* (Sally). Gendered stereotypes about anger are evident in Sally's account in that although women experience and express anger they are more likely to be uncomfortable with this emotion (Kring, 2000) and in these cases negate or override feelings of anger; 'masking' or 'emotional regulation' described by Gross and John (1998 cited in Brody, 1999). Women in Griffiths' study (2000) also found it hard to admit to anger even though it was apparent in their stories; 'For women, anger is seen as the loss of self-control whilst for men it is the means of imposing control over others' (2000, p. 138).

Remembering that women are seen, and see themselves, largely as 'in charge of' emotions within the family and so far we have seen examples of women acting to try and manage their own and their partner's emotional issues. I include here a long quote from an interview with Lucy as it seems to bring together many of the issues on women's agency around gendered emotion management and the ways in which a form of gendered emotional symbiosis can occur. It demonstrates the ambivalent feelings involved, how women act to try and restore an emotional balance in the family, attempt to have their partner seek help, and attempt to salvage the relationship even when they consider their partner at fault:

> **Lucy:** *I've tried talking to him about it but he just won't listen. I've told him like, he's got a split personality … I've told him to go and see somebody, to go and see doctor or see somebody … yeah, I mean I've told him to go to like a marriage guidance place and he says, 'no because we're not married' and I says [ex-partner's name], 'you don't have to be married to go and see one of these people' I says like, 'it's just people that listen to both of you' … but he just won't … he knows he's got a problem but he won't admit it. So like we'll be arguing like about a petty thing and he'll just completely blank me out, I mean he will not come and talk to me at all … I mean like when it's my fault I admit it, I mean sometimes it is my fault, but more times than not it is [ex-partner's] but he won't admit it. Like **even when it's his fault I will try to make up** and he just won't want to know, he'll just sit there and blank me out completely, as if I'm talking to him, but I'm just talking to a wall really.*
>
> **Paula:** *Does that then put all the responsibility onto you to have to sort it out?*
>
> **Lucy:** *Yeah, I mean whenever we have an argument, I mean even if, like it's his fault it's me that feels the guilty one, and I shouldn't be, I shouldn't feel the guilty one but every time he argues with me, **if I don't give him his way, it's me that feels guilty** (my emphases).*

Ultimately, without understanding how it happens, women feel they are to blame. Even when women think they are in the right and their partner's abuse is wrong, there is a lack of certainty as to whether their feeling is authentic, as Lucy reveals:

> **Paula:** *Why do you think you feel guilty?*

Lucy: *I don't know, I don't know, but I do. It feels as though it's my fault, I've done it, **I've made the argument**, and then like **devil comes out in me and says it's not your fault**, it's his fault don't be silly. I mean no end of times he's slept down here on settee because he's been, he's just been nowt but a child* (my emphases).

Lucy reveals the core of such ambivalence when she says 'I've made the argument' as here she is acknowledging that she is the one who *raises* issues of contention in the relationship; emotional or practical. Thus she feels responsible, and is responsible in the sense that she is the one who acts and take the initiative *in this context*. By failing to respond to attempts to discuss any problems or initiate change, male partners, such as Lucy's, undermine women's sense of themselves as able to successfully manage emotions in the relationship, thus also undermining their gendered identities. Hence the ambivalent feelings of being guilty/not guilty that Lucy expresses above, which may also be experienced by women in heterosexual relationships more widely. Whilst there are parallels to be drawn between 'normal' heterosexual relationships and abusive ones, it is nevertheless essential to assess the differences, and so I now turn to look more specifically at men's emotionally abusive practices.

Emotional abuse

One of the problems identified in the introduction to this chapter was the difficulty of defining emotions, and so it is also with defining emotional abuse; it cannot be 'categorized and quantified as can physical slaps or kicks' (Kirkwood, 1993, p. 45). The problem is that everyone has mood swings, ups and downs in their emotional feelings, which can result in negative actions/responses from time to time. These actions are not seen as emotionally abusive, unless they form patterned responses over time. In this study emotional abuse was patterned over time but also, more often than not, intertwined with sexual, physical and economic abuse. Moreover, the cultural construction of emotions, entwined with personal biographies, compounded by an emotionally differentiated gender order, makes this area an especially complex one.

One outcome of such complexities is that ostensibly abusive actions may not always be characterised as abusive by women (we have already seen women find it difficult to name men's actions as abusive or violent and tend to minimise or deny it in Chapter 1). In the present study this was particularly the case in the early stages of a relationship (as seen in Chapter 1) as such actions were perceived as 'what you do' in a hetero-sexual relationship. Possessiveness and jealousy may be interpreted by women as signs of the strength of a man's love for them. In her inter-view, Lucy for instance, as she saw it, was not referring to a negative trait when she referred to her ex-partner's jealousy:

> *When I used to go to town wi' him, you know, to get shopping and things like that, everybody used to look ... and er like he used to turn round and say to them, 'what you fucking nosying at?' you know going off like that ... because he's really, really jealous, he doesn't show it, he doesn't tell me that he is, but you can see it.*

However, over time, most women came to realise and see the repetitive nature, often intensifying, of possessive and other controlling actions, as increasingly damaging and as undermining their feelings of self-confidence and self-worth. Much emotional abuse was connected with him getting his own way (as seen in Chapter 1) but another core emo-tionally destructive focus was on women's appearance. This included all aspects of appearance, face, body-shape, hair, clothes, linked to pos-sessiveness in different ways; often expressed as whether men wanted or did not want 'their' wives/partners to be looked at by other men. Betty's husband bought her beautiful clothes, which she initially inter-preted as his gesture of love for her and pride in her appearance. However, it transpired he would only allow her to wear these clothes when she was with him: '*When I were with me husband ... he used to buy me beautiful clothes if I went out with him, if I went to town or anywhere [without him] he'd lock me clothes up*' (Betty). His interest in Betty's appearance had little to do with her as a person, but rather was viewed by him as something that enhanced or detracted from *his* reputation; he clearly saw her as his sexual property (Mooney, 2000). Denying her the use of the clothes he had bought for her (unless with him) empha-sised the breadth of his control; not only could he afford to buy her clothes (through his employment status he gained access to economic resources), but he could define how she should look and when she should look 'good' (naming and defining 'beauty' have been, and are, located in predominantly male institutions), and when she should not (the use of negative sanctions). In this way Betty was highly con-strained in the actions she was able to take in relation to her own body and appearance, and hence her identity; he became the symbolic god who controlled her life (Lundgren, 1998).

It is important to recognise here how the heterosexual gender order intertwines with capitalist structures,[3] emphasising the need for women to be 'attractive' to men also sells products and makes profits. To the extent that this message is internalised by women, the need for male approval can become a key part of women's self-identity.[4] In this study women tended to look to their male partners for approval on how they looked, and adapted their appearance accordingly, but gaining approval was usually an impossible ideal, as Jill explains:

> *Oh, he just used to tell me I were useless all the time mmm, he didn't like the way I dressed, I couldn't wear anything in me hair. Me hair were natural and it had to stay as it were. Erm, if I put anything in me hair, he wouldn't drag it out or anything like that, he'd just say, 'oh that looks awful', **so I used to take it out anyway** ... I mean things like make-up, if I were going out with [female friend] and wearing make-up I'd automatically be on the pull ... but like I say he's never ever paid me a compliment ... He liked me to wear mini skirts, I must admit, er, that's what I couldn't understand because he always said I was fat and frumpy, and all this rubbish, and like I say, when I were thin I weren't good enough because I were too thin and he wanted me to start eating again* (Jill, my emphasis).

After getting him to leave, Jill still felt passionately about the verbal assaults on her self-identity she had suffered over many years and *'the first thing I did when I left him was had me ears pierced, because he wouldn't let me!'* In this way Jill continues to demonstrate her resistance to his control, even though her rebellion has been delayed.

Emotional abuse revolved around women's roles, as wives and mothers. Mandy for example was told by her male partner that she was not fit to be the mother of his child (see Chapter 3). Domestic arrangements, such as cooking and cleaning, were also targets of male abuse. Janice (whose husband was rarely at home) gives an example of this:

> *When he were in, he were bad tempered, ill tempered. Er I'd have dinner done after an afternoon shift for six o'clock, he'd come home, one day his custard were slightly cold he slung the whole dish, and said, 'I'm not bleeding eating that' and slung it straight across work top, things like that.*

Emotional abuse was also about women being forced to do things they did not want to do. This could range from what might be considered relatively 'minor' incidents, for example, Sally was forced to watch horror films: *I used to hate watching them, I really, they really did, even if I think about one now I could have a nightmare,* to sadism, sexual abuse, threats of suicide and/or threats to kill. Mandy's ex-partner cut her eye with his finger nail on one occasion and he not only refused to take her to hospital but he insisted she sit all night stroking his dog, knowing her fear of dogs. Betty's ex-partner brought other women back to their home: *Anyway got kids to bed, he went out, half past two he comes back with a woman, now I mean this were a regular thing, he always fetched women home, he always fetched them home and I were always babysitter! ... she says are you his wife? I said, 'no I'm not', because **I were ashamed to let anybody know I were his wife**, I said, 'no I'm not', I said, 'I'm his sister-in-law', I said, 'he often comes and stops here'* (my emphasis)

Women were told that they were useless and/or stupid and were also emotionally abused through the use of gender-specific slurs. Words like 'tramp, trollop, bitch and slag' were taunts used to refer to women's sexuality in a derogatory and abusive way. The term 'slag', as Sue Lees points out, can be used against any woman, not just women who step out of line from acceptable standards of femininity in hetero-patriarchy (1993, p. 297, see also Chapter 1). Mandy's account demonstrates the way in which sexualised insults are intertwined with sexual and physical violence:

> *Stupid, thick, slag, tart, tramp, whore, er I once fell asleep when I were watching a film he dragged me out of bed and made me stand outside stark naked as punishment, er oh I could tell you loads, god, I could tell you loads! I mean he once had an argument wi' me and he made me stand with me leg up on sink, kicking me down below* (Mandy).

Threats of, or attempted suicide by male partners were reported by half of the women. Rachel's ex-husband, for example, took an overdose of paracetemol and this persuaded her to go back to him for fear that he would kill himself: *And then I left him when I were carrying [baby] and I left him for quite a while, I went and lived with me grandma and next minute I knew he'd took an overdose because I'd left him, and that's what ended up me going back to him ... [his mother] rung me mum up ... and I had to go back didn't I, because I were really worried about him taking this overdose.* Threats of violence and death to themselves and/or their children were not uncommon; Jill's ex-husband attempted to drive onto a motorway on the wrong side of the road as well as asking her to kill him, as did Lucy's ex-partner:

> *... he like pinned me up against the wall and started banging me head against the wall and [shouting] right bitches, and slags, and all abuse ...*

and then erm like when I told him it was over completely he says, 'well I'll tell you what's going to be over', he went in kitchen got a knife, the biggest knife there were and he put it onto his chest, no I mean in his stomach, and he like, got hold of my hand and tried to make me force it into him ... and he says, 'look, if I'm going to stab meself' he says, 'I'm going to fucking take you to a prison as well, as long as your fingerprints are all o'er this they'll think you've killed me'. And I mean he were really, really scaring me (Lucy).

In three other cases women reported rape and being forced to carry out sexual acts. Christine explains how difficult resistance was when children were in the house:

I think I can remember once, the sexual violence, you'd call it rape at the time. Erm, I don't really know what to say about that, it was just that feeling that, he was drunk, and you don't want to, when you've got the kids there as well, well [son] in the next room you know, so what do you do? You can't just, you can't walk off, you can't walk out the door, you can't escape from the situation, so I think you accept it in a sense (Christine).

The word 'acceptance', as Christine uses it here, does not have the usual meaning of this word. She is not saying that she willingly accepted being raped at all, but that in the context she found herself in, with her children in the next room, there was no room for manoeuvre or for doing anything else other than putting up with it; this is an enforced form of 'acceptance', as we saw with coercive-coerc-consensus in Chapter 1.

Intertwining of fear and necessity: the ostensible 'acceptance' of his behaviour

As Christine says about sexual abuse above, fear and concern for the children influence women to consciously manage their own emotional responses to abuse and violence, so as not to invoke further abuse/violence and as a way of minimising damage; as Kirkwood says this is '... both an action of survival and a part of the dynamics in which she loses control over her life' (1993, Note 1, p. 150). Fear was an emotion which women described as impacting on how they expressed their own emotions (see Chapter 1). On reflecting back on their behaviour women perceive their 'acceptance' of their male partners' behaviour as 'foolish' rather than seeing how little space they were given within which to act. At the time 'acceptance' is the most rational response, in view of his greater physical strength/capability to inflict harm on her, and bearing in mind that she has to think about the impact on the children and the family as well as herself, as Janice says (see also Chapter 3).

> *I took it, like a damned fool, like a damned fool I took it. I'd fight back and I'd rebel back, but what annoyed me so much were, my weakest point were, I will not argue in front of the kids. And he always, he always had to argue in front of the kids.*

Being abused in front of the children, family, friends or neighbours was described by women as particularly shaming:

> *Yes, oh yes. I think the worst thing he used to do, would pull me down in front of me mum and dad ... I mean there's times, I mean [two female neighbours] across the road, it was pouring down with rain and I've walked out and he literally dragged me back in this house and I hated all the neighbours seeing it, but it did happen, yeah* (Jill).

Shame played a large part in the complex emotional dynamics of domestic violence and particularly in terms of the interaction between women and their wider social networks. For this reason I will look in more detail at the emotion of shame, and its connection with blame, when women are attempting to get support and help from sources outside the relationship.

Shame and blame

One of the difficulties women face when they do turn to informal supporters or agencies for help is that uninformed responses can turn the responsibility for the abusive relationship back onto women. This is perhaps not entirely surprising since as we have already seen, it is a cultural norm that women are seen as responsible for the emotional health of a relationship and of the family more widely. This cultural norm is tapped into when people respond as they did to Jill: *I mean they talked to me about it, how can* **you** *do it? How can* **you** *live with him? People used to say to me, how can* **you** *let* **him** *do that to your daughter?* (her emphases) The implications underlying such comments are that the woman has no pride or self-respect and that *she* should sort the relationship out, rather than to question why the man is behaving in this way.

Women may also be told even more directly that what is happening is their fault (it is *their* choice of man that is to blame) and internalise this reason and blame themselves rather than the man concerned:

> *You just seem to pick the same men all over again,* ***that's what I've been told*** (Rachel, my emphasis).

As we saw in the previous section women already feel ambivalence about what is happening, and ashamed of the abuse, because of their sense of personal failure in having been unable to stop the abuse, and problematic responses from their potential supporters are likely to intensify these feelings of shame, and of being to blame for the abuse and violence. These feelings impact greatly on women's ability to tell others; in the case of informal supporters there is an added level of not wanting to upset family members or friends, and with social agency workers, like doctors, there is the fear of reliving 'shameful' experiences through having to reveal very personal details to an outsider; *I just felt as if you were going in there and having to, I couldn't sit there and say to a stranger you know everything* (Christine). The sense of shame that women feel extends beyond an individual shame and self-blame, which I term 'shame-blame', to feeling ashamed of the male partner, and feeling shame on behalf of the family as a whole:

> *I was so used to hearing people say, you know 'you've made your bed you must lie in it!' I think* ***more than that I were ashamed of what he'd done*** (Janice, my emphasis).

The impact of 'shame-blame' varies for women but having tried and failed to end the violence themselves and then, when they turn to others for help, if responsibility is reflected back to themselves, some women tend to turn their feelings inwards. This means that depression is a not uncommon response and for a small number of women, like Mandy and Betty, this may deepen into suicidal feelings:

> *I was ever so depressed, really bad depression I used to get. And I used to sit there and roar [cry] and think, oh God where did I go wrong? And* ***were it my fault, because everybody said it were my fault?*** *And I used to get really down, and sometimes I used to sit with the kids and used to think oh God I might just as well take an overdose and just finish us all off. And I know one day I were really down and we always used to have a drink of Ovaltine before we went to bed, and I got, took my ...*

> *librium and broke them up in Ovaltine and I thought I'll give 'em kids*
> *and mixed it all up in Ovaltine and only thing that stopped me was the*
> *thought that what if kids die and I don't or if I die and kids don't, and*
> *they'll have to go to their dad* (Betty, my emphasis).

Mandy became so deeply distressed that she describes a complete dead-
ening of her emotions such that she did not even feel love for her children at this point. Hitting rock bottom was, however, a turning point
for Mandy:

> *I didn't want kids near me. I didn't want to hurt 'em or owt but I just,*
> *I hadn't got anything left for them … and they were in foster care for*
> *about eight week, I mean I used to go up and see em and phone up and*
> *make sure they were alright, but you know when I went to see em and*
> *I mean he were only little, if they were on me knee, if you can understand*
> *this, me body were holding em but there were nowt in here … there were*
> *nothing, I'd got nothing, I just didn't care no more … but like as I had*
> *explained to me by the doctor it were an emotional breakdown and like*
> *you lose it and you've got to regain something back for yourself, do you*
> *know like get your balance back* (Mandy).

Women experienced different turning points in taking the difficult
decision to leave their husband/partner. This was quite often linked
with abuse/violence being turned against the children, or carried out in
front of them (see Chapter 3), or a point came where women realised
they had tried everything and nothing had worked. Rebelling and
growing stronger after particular turning points was recounted by
several women, such as Christine who left shortly after the incident
described below:

> *I sat down one day and I thought, well I've done this, and I've done that*
> *right, and I've done everything else and I've been in this now for several*
> *years erm this was after a particular time where he'd come in drunk, and*
> *before I'd always been calm, to keep the peace, be calm, don't shout at*
> *him, don't get him too angry, but this time I just thought I've had enough*
> *and I was shouting. And so we had a fight … and I can always remember*
> *picking the crash helmet up and whacking him with it, you know, he*
> *didn't like that … Yeah, and that was when he told me to get out of the*
> *house and I wasn't going to walk out the house and leave the two children*
> *with him, who was drunk! I said, 'no, you go, you go', and he was saying,*
> *'I'm not going nowhere', but I think he was starting to get a bit worried*

then because I was shouting back, you know, I wasn't just being calm and reasonable and I'm saying, 'I'm going to phone the police, I'm going to phone the police', and I tried getting the phone and he pulled the phone out of the socket and he sat with the phone on his knee all night. Sat in the chair with the phone on his knee all night! So I didn't have any choice, I went up to bed (Christine).

All the women in this study found the strength and courage to ultimately leave their violent relationships even in the bleakest of contexts and it was through courage, the support and bonds with their children and other key supporters, but additionally their irrepressible ability to laugh at the many situations they found themselves in:

I've been followed by his friends in cars as well, that were best laugh I've ever had that were (laughs). You've got to have a good sense of humour when this sort, if you don't laugh you would lose your head ... I think he were called [name] his friend and he'd got this car, and we were looking for cars, it were when I were in refuge actually, he'd got one headlight dimmer than the other, and you could see this car a mile off following us ... and he'd been following us for ages and we took it all over and then we went round this island four times and then I think he gathered that we'd seen him, I really enjoyed that! (Sally).

Writers have found a form of 'gallows humour' operating in violent and war scenarios and certainly the women retained, where possible, a sense of humour and ability to laugh at themselves and with others. The importance of a sense of humour has seldom been explored in the literature looking at how women survive domestic violence. In this study it seemed to be one important way in which women maintained a sense of the reality of their own interpretation of events (despite doubts and ambivalence) and ultimately a sense of self-respect so important for their future lives.

Looking to the future

Women looking to the future had different assessments of what this would hold. The ways in which they thought about the future clearly made a difference to their outlook. The differences partly related to their experiences of life in childhood and partly on what they had wanted (or still wanted) to achieve as individuals. Janice and Jill passionately wanted good, well paid jobs so that they could carve out independent careers for themselves. Janice had continued to do paid work during the abusive relationship and continued to do so. Jill's lack of training and the narrow range of jobs in the area made her relatively embittered about her future prospects, which she felt had been spoiled by her ex-husband's controlling behaviour. Moreover, as she was still in touch with her ex-husband, she remained (to some degree) emotionally caught up in the relationship through her children (see Chapter 3) and this undermined her self-confidence to the extent that she still tended to blame herself for what had happened: *I still think I'm a victim. I still think I'm a victim of meself, not of him, of meself …Yes, because of what we've been through, I'm still a victim … still frightened what he's going to say and, stupid really, I still haven't got enough confidence to say, to turn around and say well it's nowt to do with you.*

Lucy and Mandy had different ambitions which revolved far more around their children and wanting to feel settled in their family lives, as did the rest of the women. Lucy saw herself in a pragmatic way as not being that unusual as a single mother coping without a husband/partner and her children were crucially important to her: *I felt upset yes, I felt upset, sometimes I used to feel lonely, but I've been through it that many times that I thought, well, I used to think in me head, well there's lots of girls out there that's on their own, I mean like there's people, there's husbands dying, and stuff like that, and I used to think well they've got to live rest of their life on their own … I mean the children help a great deal.* Mandy, too, had a pragmatic approach looking forward to a more peaceful, settled life in her new home: *Me, I just want to be settled, in a house where I can decorate it and be able to say yeah I'm here and I'm here for good.* Christine took a different route. Like Jill she strongly wanted to build an independent career for herself, she had fewer children (two as compared with Jill's four) and was able to attend a local community college, which had a subsidised crèche. Through this route she was able to progress in further education to higher education, gaining a degree, and ultimately, after several years, a career in the social care field.

Overall, women drew on their own inner strengths and sense of humour to overcome a situation where their emotional lives had been severely tested, but they also drew vastly on the strengths and support of others, of their own children (see Chapter 3), on their family and friends (see Chapter 6), and (potentially), the wider community and support group (see Chapter 7). Being able to express their emotions in such contexts was a vital way of starting to come to terms with the consequences of the abusive relationship.

Conclusion

In drawing conclusions to this chapter on emotional dynamics and domestic violence I use the three strands of argument, outlined in the introduction. The first strand is that women continue to be constructed as responsible for emotions and caring in the heterosexual family and that this has concrete effects on women's lives.

Half of the women in the present study worked in the public sphere, but their jobs would mostly be termed 'female' jobs and were part-time, low paid and insecure (see Chapter 5). Marginalised from the labour market women participants sought to enhance their identities in culturally normative ways in the private sphere as mothers, carers and 'managers of emotions'. Women took these roles very seriously, constantly taking action to try and effect change both in practical aspects to do with the family and in the emotional dynamics of the family. However, the women were at the same time acutely aware of *changing* gendered relations and all had expected their male partners to take a far greater part in these responsibilities than they actually did. Feeling overburdened with responsibilities women tried constantly to negotiate for a sharing of tasks around childcare and in the household, as well as to try to talk with their male partners about emotional issues.

Women expressed bewilderment in the responses received from their male partners; typical responses which caused women consternation were: male partners 'blanking them out' and refusing to respond, and/or responding with abusive and violent actions. Their male partners kept emotional expression to a minimum, expressing emotions viewed as culturally 'acceptable' for men (anger, pride and contempt) and in so doing sought to maintain traditionally polarised gender identities. Women's traditionally ascribed association with love and care through the emotions of warmth and empathy was manipulated by men to their advantage in these abusive relationships.

The second strand is the importance of addressing the emotions of shame and blame experienced by women. The emotional abuse directed at women focused around issues fundamental to their identity; their appearance as women, their roles as mothers and/or wives, and their domestic roles in the home. At the same time women started out in their relationships with strong beliefs in their own capabilities, in discussing and dealing with emotional issues. This meant that women spent a long time believing that they would be able to solve the problems they faced in their relationships.

Over time, with continued failure in this respect, and with men's abusive and violent practices continuing (and in some cases intensifying) women felt a deep and complex sense of shame. Acts of abuse and violence were in themselves shameful impacting *on* the body at the time, and reverberations inhered *in* the body over time. Having to talk about abuse and violence to others opened women up to reliving these feelings of shame and to having to admit 'failure' in managing the emotional health of the relationship and wider family. Moreover, as we have seen, women felt a sense of blame and guilt about this. Partly, women thought the violence deserved through having been told by their male partners that they were responsible. Partly, women themselves thought that they might be responsible as they were the ones who usually took action to discuss problematic issues. As a result there was a confusing ambivalence for women around feeling guilty and/or not guilty.

Outside sources could reinforce (or challenge) the message of responsibility and guilt, both spontaneously and in responding to women's specific help-seeking. Challenging women's felt emotions of shame and blame was vital since otherwise women found it very difficult to speak about their experiences and further delayed their efforts to seek support in effecting change.

The third strand is that although it may help to understand the meaning of love in the couple relationships, women were clearly *not* only absorbed in this relationship; they also had other interests. The feeling of doing the right thing, of being responsible for emotional management in the family (and feeling skilled in this respect), of being 'soft', caring and empathic, all formed an important part of the gendered emotional dynamics underpinning these heterosexual relationships. In some cases these feelings were upheld by responses from others, as seen in Mandy's friend's account that violent men can suddenly change and become ideal partners. In other cases they were challenged as when family members gave women temporary accommodation. Narratives of 'love', however, although present, did not predominate in the women's accounts, but women made constant references to their children and there was a sense that being married/partnered was doing the right thing, especially as far as children were concerned (see Chapter 3).

In Chapter 1 I highlighted the complexity for women of recognising and naming men's actions as abusive in the 'coercive-consensus' context that is domestic violence, whilst at the same time stressing women's continued level of agency and resistance. In this chapter looking at the emotional dynamics of domestic violence identified further constraints on women's actions but here again I have focused on women's agency, on their repeated attempts to understand and get through to their male partners: by sitting and listening, by talking, by negotiating and by asking them to get support elsewhere with little success. Clearly, over this time women were constantly drawing on their own resources, their inner strengths, their sense of humour and so forth, but from their accounts it was also crystal clear that women had other important issues occupying their minds and actions and primary amongst these was their children.

3
Mothers and Children

I thought I were really clever, because I didn't crack up, I thought I were cracking up many a time but I didn't, I mean if it hadn't have been for the kids I would have done, I mean I really would have cracked up but for them (Betty).

Introduction

Women's experiences as mothers of children are focal to this study as children feature strongly when looking at agency (and its enhancement) for women experiencing domestic violence. The roles and attitudes of women in society *are* changing but gendered patterns of domestic work and caring in the family remain relatively static with children primarily cared for by mothers, and fathers primarily seen as economic providers. A new emphasis on fathering in state discourse has not (at least so far) been enthusiastically adopted by men.

So in this chapter I consider the value of motherhood and the value of children to mothers experiencing domestic violence, mapping continuity and change in these key areas. I argue that children's experiences of domestic violence are often gendered, as they are for women. It has been recognised that children have different experiences of abuse and violence (even in the same family) due to their age (Mullender et al., 2002) but different experiences of abuse due to gender has been less well recognised and is important in assessing the impact on children and their relationships with their mothers.

I start by reviewing the extent of change and continuity in gender roles vis à vis parenting. I then examine the mother-child relationship when experiencing domestic violence, taking up the following themes: *Gendered attitudes and practices, Violence around pregnancy, Violence in infancy, The impact of violence on children.* Moving on, I turn to look at the mother-child relationship in connection with ending a violent relationship, taking up the following themes: *Thinking about leaving, Temporary accommodation, Moving into a new home or having the abusive partner leave, Safety issues, Gender issues.* Finally, I attempt to capture something of the significance, in terms of agency, of children to the women participants.

Change and continuity in gender roles: mothering and fathering

It is crucial to an holistic understanding of domestic violence to look not only at the gendered dynamics of the labour market (see Chapter 5), but also the gendered dynamics of, mostly unpaid, care and domestic work in the home. This means looking (briefly in this case) at the state and its discourses as well as gendered experiences in everyday life. Women's relationship with the welfare state is a contradictory one and feminists have theorised the state's contribution to the gender order, for example through interventions in the economy and the patterning of welfare benefits, and how such interventions and discourses can construct norms for 'good' mothering (see for example Holter, 1984; Sainsbury, 1999; Daly and Rake, 2003).

In the UK recent attention has been paid to encouraging new patterns of male responsibility in the home (in Chapter 2 we saw how problematic this was in contexts of domestic violence) to complement women's changing socioeconomic roles. A particular focus is the part that fathers play in bringing up children; underpinning which is the idea that 'fathers have a crucial role to play in their children's upbringing' (Home Office, 1998, sections 6.6 and 6.7). Flexible working has been proposed as one possible way of encouraging a greater role for fathers.[1] The state also wants to enable mothers to transfer a proportion of their maternity leave and pay to fathers, 'to give parents more choice about caring for their children during the first year of life and to respond to the growing number of fathers who want to take a more active role in bringing up their children' (Department of Trade and Industry, 2005, p. 7). Without wishing to be unduly critical of such efforts, the picture on the ground is rather different with a minority of men taking up these opportunities. Most men avoid parenting programmes (Lewis, 2000) and only 12 per cent of eligible fathers have so far requested flexible working (Unison, 2005).

Fathers on average earn two-thirds of family incomes and although fathers' involvement in the home has been increasing (Lewis, 2000) time use studies in Great Britain reveal distributions of domestic work remain largely traditionally gendered. For example, women spend two hours 18 minutes a day as compared with men's 45 minutes a day on cooking and routine housework; and on caring for and playing with their children, women spend 36 minutes a day as compared with men's 13 minutes a day (Office for National Statistics, 1999). I am not arguing that fathers should not share or take responsibility for child-care, however, where children continue to be primarily cared for by their mothers, linked with women's lesser power in society, differences in mother–child as opposed to father–child dynamics are highly likely (Brody, 1999; Benjamin, 1990; Chodorow, 1978). McMahon's study *'Engendering motherhood'* found gendered experiences of parenting not simply around differing domestic work loads but also around 'gendered consciousness, gendered feelings of responsibility, and men's perceived greater ability to compartmentalize and segregate parts of themselves from their children' (1995, p. 233). In my study women overwhelmingly prioritised the needs and well-being of their children, and described their male partners as having been far less involved.

Women find themselves in a contradictory social context where public discourse encourages them to enter the labour force to become economically independent but when and if they do so, many find themselves in lowly and low paid jobs. Simultaneously, public discourse proclaims changes in fathers' involvement with their children but women discover that on the ground this is not necessarily the case. There are many such gaps between public discourse and the lived realities of women's lives and these mirror the gaps between women's evolving consciousness of themselves as becoming, if not equal to men, at least more equal, and the constant undermining of this belief by male partners in abusive relationships. It is in this gendered context that I look at the ongoing male practices of control and how they impact on women as mothers, as well as on children, and women's possibilities for 'acting otherwise' (Giddens, 1984).

Mothers and children living in an abusive relationship

The children help a great deal (Lucy).

North American researchers were the first to recognise that domestic violence has both immediate and long-term detrimental effects on children; which can take internalised forms such as withdrawal and depression and/or externalised forms such as aggressiveness, argumentativeness and hyperactivity (e.g. Wolfe et al., 1985; Jaffe et al., 1990; Peled et al., 1995). In the UK, Mullender and Morley (1994) and Abrahams (1994) carried out early studies in this area. Interviewing children (as opposed to mothers) about their experiences and understandings of domestic violence is a relatively new research focus but there are now studies from the UK (McGee, 2000; Mullender et al., 2002 [interviewed children *and* mothers], Stalford, Baker and Beveridge, 2003; Gorin, 2004), Denmark, Finland and Sweden (see Kallstrom Cater, 2004), Canada (Peled et al., 1995) and the US (Peled et al., 1995). This is vital work but should not of course make it any the less important to *also* continue to listen to mothers' perspectives. There are significant insights to be drawn from the ways that children interact with their mothers and vice versa for the understanding of domestic violence as a process; also mothers play key roles in mediating relationships between children and fathers (see Backett, 1987; Ribbens, 1994; Silva and Smart, 1999; Mullender et al., 2002).

In relation to mothering: the extent to which mothering is undermined by domestic violence is contested, but this study supports feminist writers' suggestion that women's efforts to resist abuse and to protect their children are often underestimated (Radford and Hester, 2001 cited in Jaffe et al., 2003). In relation to children: the dominant construction of children's relationship with domestic violence in the literature characterises them as *witnessing* or *overhearing* violence (Hoff, 1990; Abrahams, 1994; Kolbo et al., 1996). This is misleading firstly because it conceives of children as passive rather than active agents and secondly because it puts a distance between children and the abuse/violence being experienced. Children are in fact actively *living in/with* and *responding to* domestic violence just as much as their mothers are. As Mullender et al. (2002) found in interviews with mothers and children, 'both sides are involved in negotiating emotional minefields, with patterns of avoidance and protection existing alongside openness, honesty and challenge' (2002, p. 156). Children themselves can also be the *focus* of incidents of male violence with many children able to describe abusive and violent attacks in detail (Hilton, 1992; Jaffe, Wolfe and Wilson, 1990, p. 21; Mullender et al., 2002, p. 183). The conceptualisation of children as in some way *distanced* from the abuse and violence can also be drawn on by women themselves mistakenly to reassure themselves that their children are less harmed by remaining in the relationship than ending it.

The women participants in the present study all had children and most of the women in the support group also had children. As we saw in Chapter 1 all the women had their social lives severely restricted by their male abuser, gaining limited access to family, friends and the wider community. This was so much the case that their children often become the primary concern in their lives. Statutory service workers interviewed in previous research have said: '… the children for a lot of these people are the only things they live for …' (cited in Warner and Pantling, 2002, p. 122). Eva Lundgren has talked perceptively about women's lives being gradually narrowed down and the ways in which violence is continued through a process of normalisation (1995, 1998). It is important, however, to hold onto the fact that women *can* and often *do* act, even in constrained circumstances, and the majority of the women in this study managed (with difficulty) to retain contact with one or two key family members or friends who gave support of various kinds and/or helped them to get support (see Chapter 6).

Children were central in the women's lives, 'the emotions mothers have for their children may be as deep and powerful as any emotions women know' (Ribbens, 1994, p. 37); seen as unique individuals, who more often than not supported their mothers. This is not to romanticise motherhood since the frustrations, as well as the emotional depth, in experiences of mothering came through time and time again in both the interviews and the support group; and the extent to which women identified themselves primarily as mothers varied. For Betty children were focal to her identity: *Even when I were really depressed, because when I've got kids around me I'm as right as rain, I can work through me depression as long as I've got kids, yeah*, whereas Christine was clear that she did not want to be seen only as a mother.

Gendered attitudes and practices

The majority of women said that their male partners put responsibility for looking after the children and home onto them (see Chapter 2). Whilst not wishing to reduce their own family responsibilities, women tried to encourage their male partners to take a greater part in activities with their children (as Ribbens also found in her study of non-violent relationships 1994, p. 71) but for the most part this proved impossible:

Yeah, yeah, er I mean he used to throw it in me face that er they were my kids … why should he stay in day after day looking after them? He could never go out where he wants to go out, he could never do what he wanted to do, and I'd stand there and say, 'you've got car outside what's wrong with just sticking kids in car, using a bit of bloody common sense and just going out' and [he would say] 'where have I got to go?' … It were just banging your head up against brick wall every time (Janice, her emphasis).

Male partners saw childcare as the mother's domain whilst they were free to come and go at will, thus extending social patterns established as single men and perpetuating the traditionally gendered public/ private divide. Aware of women's changing social roles, over time women participants became more and more angered by this. Lucy's laugh in the quotation below revealed her anger and her comments were spoken in a tone of bitterness:

He wanted me to stop in this house with my children and him go out whenever he wanted to. **It doesn't quite work like that does it!** *(laughs) … I mean I don't like stopping out late anyway 'cause like I want to get back for kids, but* **he loves stopping out!** (her emphases)

The men expected their wives/partners to exercise control over the children's behaviour in general, however, when at home they expected to have ultimate control. Children themselves often triggered male controlling practices due to men's limited tolerance of noisy and/or boisterous behaviour: *… the kids had to go to their bedroom, they always had to be in their bedroom when he got in. Yeah always had* to (Catherine). In Lucy's case, whilst she was expected to bear the majority of the responsibility for childcare, when her partner came home he assumed authority and was prepared to use physical punishment *… when he's not around I just used to let them riot, it doesn't bother me noise, I mean that's what kids are for, but as soon as he walks in, I mean if he's been out all day and they've been playing around and everything, as soon as he walks in [he says] 'shut up!'… er but he'll just start and if they don't do as they're told he'll smack 'em.*

As the children start to grow up the patterns of coercion, punctuated by incidents of physical violence, continued and women described a range of abusive and violent behaviour directed against their children (see also McGee, 2000, pp. 48–57; Humphreys and Thiara, 2002, p. 31; Mullender et al., 2002; pp. 182–7). Examples of direct violence from abusive male partners against children, whilst they remained in the relationship, included emotional abuse and/or physical assault, and in two cases (both girls) sexual abuse:

But he's even threatened to set me house afire, even when little uns are listening. And oldest one's had nightmares because he thinks house is

> *going to be on fire when he's asleep. ... He went to threaten [son] when he were here [son] saw him hitting me and he said, 'Dad, I want you to go now, please go' and he said ' you, you little' – can I swear? 'you, you little bastard. I wish you were dead and don't think you're getting any Christmas presents off me because you're not'* (Sally).

> *Er he whipped 'em [children]... mm yeah wi' a curtain wire ... They scratched his sunglasses* (Mandy).

> *The very last time, he'd beaten me up bad, beaten me up, he'd abused little 'un [younger daughter]... and [daughter], she took it right bad with what happened to her [sexual abuse], you know* (Betty).

It was not uncommon either for abusive male partners to kidnap children (Mullender et al., 2002) holding them hostage for varying lengths of time to punish their female partners for perceived wrongdoing or attempt to get their own way/impose their will:

> *this time a year ago, that were when [husband] hit me in telephone box. He took [younger son] off me which he'd done quite a few times. He took him off me at Christmas when he were one and I had to get him back. I think I got him back on 6th January* (Sally).

In the present study not only were there clearly differentiated gendered parenting activities, differently gendered attitudes and ways of relating with/to children, but importantly in terms of the abuse and violence suffered by children, this too was often gendered. Emotional abuses directed at daughters focused on aspects of 'appropriate femininity', such as their appearance, their weight, or sexual morality, as happened with Jill's daughter:

> *And virtually from walking in he started on her, about weight, you know, and she's too fat and it's going to take you a lot of time to get that weight off, she's about a size fourteen, ah but it's one down from sixteen, not one up from twelve, one down from sixteen, yeah* (Jill).

Emotional abuse directed at sons often focused on (in)appropriate forms/displays of hegemonic heterosexual masculinity. In Sally's case, for example, her husband assumed he had the right to name their younger son without her consent: *And he went and named him. He went, I had to phone registry office and find out what he'd called him,* and named him after a famous boxer. The older son would also have been named after a boxer if Sally had not managed to stop him. Her older son was a quiet, shy and nervous child and he was bullied on account of this by her husband in the mistaken belief this would encourage him to be more 'masculine'.

> *No, all I remember is him threatening me and … he also threatened our [older son] as well, so I mean, when it got to threatening kids as well… [older son's] got eczema and that fetched it out wi' all the worry of what he did and [older son] gets frightened when his dad comes near. In fact I felt like killing him sometimes when [older son] got frightened* (Sally).

In this study control and violence were also gendered experiences to the extent that they occurred around the biologically and socially gendered phase of pregnancy, when physically, emotionally and financially women were most dependent on their male partner and I look at this aspect next.

Violence around pregnancy

In the UK a recent survey by the Royal College of Midwives found that one in five midwives know at least one of their expectant mothers is a victim of domestic violence, one in five midwives also see at least one woman a week who they *suspect* is a victim of domestic violence, with one in ten midwives believing pregnancy to be the trigger of abuse (*Nursing Standard,* 2004, p. 4).

Evidence as to violence around pregnancy is variable; some studies find pregnancy a time of particular risk (Department of Health, 2000a; Stanko et al., 1998); others that abuse and violence starts or intensifies during pregnancy (Department of Health, 2000a). Yet others argue that although there is some correlation between pregnancy and domestic violence it may be due to younger women (who are more likely to become pregnant) having a higher risk of domestic violence (Walby and Myhill, 2000, p. 2).

I argue that conception and pregnancy are periods of heightened gender difference which can make abuse and violence more likely. Pregnancy is a time when women are more dependent on their male partners, and hence more vulnerable to control. In the present study for example control was exercised by male partners around 'decision-making' on having children, and abuses included 'forcing' women to become pregnant (or not), making them miscarry and abusing women when pregnant.

Where Ribbens (1994) found parents in non-violent relationships to be ambiguous about describing conception as a 'decision', often describing it as 'a natural progression', women in this study were unambiguous in their view that it was their male partners who took decisions:

He were the one who decided we were going to have kids er and not me, it was his doing, he were one who said, you know, 'maybe we ought to have kids', never talked about it, never discussed it, he just took it [the decision], you know (Janice).

I love kids mm, mm, he didn't want er he weren't too bothered about our [son], he didn't want our [daughter], I mean I'm not saying he didn't want her, but he didn't want me to get pregnant again. But funny enough when we were splitting up he wanted another family, he wanted some more family, but I said I know why that were, because of keeping me in house again (Jill).

It is noticeable in Jill's case how her husband switched between not wanting children during the relationship and then wanting more children when he thought this would prevent Jill from pursuing activities outside the home. It was common for husbands/partners not to want the child on being told about a pregnancy: *Er he never wanted me to have kids in first place, he told me to get an abortion with both of them, which is heart breaking* (Sally). Goodwin et al. (2000 cited in Jaskinski, 2004, p. 54) found that abuse was greater when the male partner did not want the baby. Janice's husband also wanted her to have an abortion and yet, when he discovered he had fathered twins, changed his mind seeing this as proof of his virility. Jaskinski (2001 cited in Jaskinski, 2004, p. 54) found abuse was more likely when the male partner perceived that the pregnancy had occurred sooner than intended. In summary, conceiving and having children (or not) became yet another context of male control.

For the majority of women in this study pregnancy was an especially dangerous time. A range of emotional and physical abuses were reported during pregnancy, damaging to women mentally and physically as well as to the unborn child. Betty experienced violence during pregnancy: *I got married in September by time it got to Christmas they [violent incidents] were getting regular then. Then I were pregnant with [daughter] and he broke my jaw, broke my jaw bone here. And I were pregnant with her then,* and later two miscarriages due to violence. Mandy, likewise, describes her pregnancy characterising the violence as part of his jealousy of other men:

> *I mean all the way through the pregnancy like [abusive partner] were like the boyfriend from hell … if someone come to door and I opened door I'd get a pasting because I were messing wi' 'em … all way through, all the time I were pregnant with him, I were badly all the way through, worst pregnancy I've ever had. I mean I got pneumonia, I had influenza, and then him forever battering me, I were in hospital twice with threatened miscarriages after he'd kicked me all o'er, I had no energy at all when I were pregnant, I mean like I were on labour table having him, and he punched me clean in me face[2] (laughs)* (Mandy).

Rachel had had two abusive male partners and in each case the violence against her started in pregnancy and she had one miscarriage as a result. She said of her first husband: … *once we started moving into the house that's when he started bashing me, he'd kick me in the stomach while I were having babby, and he'd do owt, he'd just hit me.* Of her second husband she told me: '*Same again, I thought. It didn't start like until I were pregnant … and er then he used to belt me and I used to end up in hospital all the time … and he kicked me in the stomach while I were pregnant and water come out all over the place, and he didn't care, just went off drinking.*

Research on the incidence of abuse and violence amongst pregnant women supports the need for action (which is starting to happen) to tackle this serious problem; for example, midwives are being recruited to give women support; guidelines on identifying and helping women experiencing domestic abuse have recently been produced by the Royal College of Midwives (Mahony, 1997).

Violence in infancy

The pattern of male control and violence continued in infancy. Much of this abuse seemed to be triggered by male demands for attention from wives/partners, in competition with the infant. Incidents arose in particular over breastfeeding, dislike of the disruption and crying that infants bring, more general violent outbursts aimed at the mother when the child was in his/her mother's arms, direct violence aimed at the infant, and kidnapping of the child/ren (as mentioned earlier):

> *When he were, how old were he, when he were ten days old he smacked him across face because he were crying, he'd only got wind all he had to do was pick him up and pat his back, but he didn't like to hear him crying* (Louise).

I mean one day I had babby in me arms while I were bathing him and he just kicked me literally in the stomach, and you know how you feel sick, I nearly dropped me new born babby in bath. It were horrible (Rachel).

We had like a big massive argument in town and he took [youngest son] and I mean he were only like, I think he were about two weeks old then, and I were scared stiff. ... So I went to the police station and I reported him (Mandy).

Researching the impact of violence on infants' physical/mental health is now starting to be carried out (Smither, 2001; Williams, 2004; Palusci et al., 2005). At its worst we know that violence can lead to infant mortality as other research shows; Florida Governor's Task Force on Domestic and Sexual Violence for instance found that when children are killed during a domestic dispute, 56 per cent are under age two (1997, p. 51, Table 28); further research is clearly needed into this aspect of domestic violence.

The impact of violence on children

I mean our [younger son] once turned round to me and said. 'Don't you wish daddy were kind mummy, I know I do?' (Janice).

Studies of violent men often fail to look at their understandings of the impact of violence on their children, even when it is clear that they are fathers (Mullender et al., 2002). However, Hearn says his interviewees (all perpetrators) rarely commented on how their violent behaviour might have affected their children; 'Almost all ... did not appear to see violence towards women as child abuse, or vice versa' (1998, p. 93). Koepping finds that perpetrators in anti-violence programmes after separation frequently have problems in empathising with their children's point of view (2003, p. 286). Male abusers are in fact more likely to use their children as one aspect of their control over women as shown in the Duluth 'power and control wheel' (Pence and Paymar, 1990). These points reinforce my argument about differentially gendered attitudes towards children/parenting.

A finding of this study is that *incidents of abuse* against children tend to be differently gendered, and so there are likely to be different effects on girls and boys (I pursue this point further in the section entitled '*Gender issues*' below). However, research evidence is inconclusive on this point and the women were not aware of different outcomes by gender. Some researchers report externalising behaviours as being more characteristic of boys with internalising behaviours more characteristic of girls (Jaffe et al., 1986) but others report boys as having greater difficulties (Stagg, Wills and Howell, 1989). Hester, Pearson and Harwin have commented that, 'While domestic violence can clearly have adverse effects on both boys and girls, it would be wrong to assume that responses can be presumed to follow some "given" or "pre-determined" gender pattern' (2000, p. 52).

All the women expressed deep concern over the impact of the father's violence on their children. However, ambivalence about their own possible role in this may have made it difficult at times for them to talk about it, as evidenced by pauses and hesitancy in their speech patterns. Louise illustrates this and her hesitancies are likely to indicate some level of continuing uncertainty and possibly shame in this matter:

Paula: *Do you feel that your son was affected by the violence that happened in your marriage?*

Louise: *Er (breathes out slowly) er I don't know. I think he just resented his father for what he were I think er he were frightened of him then, but he's not now. I think it made him feel insecure, very insecure, even now sometimes, he feels insecure er.*

The majority believed at first that they would be doing their best to protect their children by keeping the family together, by keeping the violence secret and maintaining silence over what they were all going through (Warner and Pantling, 2002). At times the women diminished the impact of the violence and at other times showed acute awareness of its potential for harm for instance by trying to keep children out of harm's way and out of sight.

No he didn't see that much of it, but he must have heard us rowing sometimes when he were in bed. And er I think usually when he did used to hit me I think me son were out of way, out playing, in bed or whatever (Louise).

Although me husband, he never actually hit me when the kids were around, but I think he [son] did actually see it at one point when he came downstairs, listening to the shouting and screaming, so I don't know if that is somewhere in the back of his mind (Christine).

Over time, women became more aware of the negative impacts on their children of growing up experiencing an emotionally and physically abusive father. This had two strands to it, one aspect being fear of the so-called 'cycle of violence' effect; women were scared that their sons might also grow up to be violent and their daughters might become victims of violence (see Hester, Pearson and Harwin, 2000, p. 52 for a discussion on this) and women did not want violence, of any kind, to become a central part of their children's lives.

> *Yeah he's the kind that went badger digging and fox hunting, you know, that kind of thing, and that is one of the reasons, I don't want my kids to be like him, I don't want them to think that violence is everything* (Sally).

Once women found they were unable to get their male partners to stop the abuse and violence against them, and their partners were abusive in front of and to the children,[3] their belief that keeping the family together was the best course of action for the children wavered and they started to seek support. Indeed, direct abuse and violence to their children, or in front of their children, was a transition point for most women:

> *He must have asked me a million times a year, let's try again, let's try again, and I've given in to him, but I just couldn't stand any more of it. Not when he started getting violent in front of the kids* (Jill).

> *… when our [younger son] were 6 days old he also threatened our [older son] as well, so I mean when it got to threatening kids as well* (Sally).

As others have found, the safety and well-being of children acted as a catalyst for the women in deciding to leave their violent partners, or have their partners leave (Henderson, 1990; Hilton, 1992; Syers-McNairy, 1990; Kurz, 1996). The important point here is that women were/are able to act, to leave or take other action in order to protect their children, even given the extreme constraints women experienced in this study, as we shall see.

Mothers and children leaving an abusive relationship

Thinking about ending the relationship

When considering whether or not to end an abusive heterosexual relationship women are confronted by cultural norms which stress that children need fathers and that *mothers* are responsible for keeping the family together. Women in the present study were acutely aware of, and largely responsive to, these cultural messages. Moreover, women also faced a constellation of realistic and practical concerns about their own and their children's future, should they end the relationship. For women to decide on the 'right' course of action to protect their children's well-being in such a cultural climate, when they are experiencing abusive and violent practices (Chapter 1), linked with the emotional dynamics inherent in the relationship (Chapter 2), attachment to the home (Chapter 4), compounded by the structural constraints around work and money (Chapter 5), can seem virtually impossible.

As seen above, some women believe children can be protected from the negative effects of domestic violence through keeping children away from the abuse and violence (Warner and Pantling, 2002). Other women may decide that, despite the violence, it is less traumatic for the children to remain in their home, with their mother and father, and their familiar social network of family, friends and community (see Hague and Wilson, 1996; Mullender, 1996), than to leave. However, they also recognise that this may be at the cost of failing to protect their children from the inevitably adverse effects of experiencing male abusive and violent acts (Warner and Pantling, 2002).

Women also have a realistic fear that ending the relationship may mean leaving the home and that their children will experience increased isolation if they are removed from their social networks (see Stalford, Baker and Beveridge, 2003). Having the abusive male partner removed from the family home remains relatively rare although improving (there were only two in this study). A further deep concern women have is of outside intervention by social agencies; previous research on non-violent families revealed that '... to resort to outside advice ... was somehow an admission of failure' (Backett, 1982, p. 102) and women in violent relationships are fearful that their children might be taken away (Abrahams, 1994) which is a real barrier to help-seeking on their part (Humphreys, 2000, p. 28).

Moreover, abusive men play on this fear by telling them, for example, that they are inadequate mothers: Mandy was told by her partner *'you're not a good enough mother to be near my son'*. Some men are even prepared to contact agencies deploying knowledge of a 'mother's role', should women break their silence over his violence: *But while the police were looking for him, he'd phoned the police up to tell them that I'd gone, I'd took a load of drugs with me, and that I was suicidal, I weren't fit to look after kids* (Betty). As Warner and Pantling (2002,

p. 123) reveal minoritised communities are at greater risk from outside intervention as there are higher rates of non-white children taken into care; in my research Mandy, who had children of mixed ethnicity, was most fearful of this and she and Rachel (who had mental health problems and lost custody of all her three children) were the women who experienced the highest level of intervention from social agencies (see Chapter 7).

Leaving without their children was almost inconceivable unless there were exceptional circumstances: *Wherever I went, they went. The kids go with me, the kids went with me, that's way it's always been, that's how it should be and that's how it always is* (Janice). A minority of women fleeing violence leave without their children either to save their lives and/or because their mental distress is such that they feel unable to look after their child/ren at this point. This was the case for two women interviewed and another woman in the support group; one at the end of her tether needed a short breathing space, another had to leave her child behind due to a mental breakdown and the other lost custody of her child. Having to leave without the kids, even for a very short period, was described as being the worst occasion of leaving by Jill: *But I'd never leave me kids I've often said, I've always said, I'd never leave me kids but I just had to leave them that day and er it was horrible... I just, I couldn't be without me kids* (her emphasis).

The emotional distress and stigma attached to living apart from their children was felt deeply by the women, as Jackson found '... being separated from children is experienced by mothers as being no option at all. None of them particularly wants to be without their children on a permanent basis but they are compelled to get away from the intolerable circumstances that are the context of their mothering' (1994, p. 100). At the same time there is the ever-present pressure to conform to an ideal of motherhood which stresses never leaving the children. Even when women felt they were at rock bottom,[4] and seriously considering leaving, they revealed concern for their children's relationship with their father:

> ... *it were a bit before then that I sort of like thought well, you know, what's it going to be. I mean I honestly thought death was the only way out. I couldn't go anywhere, I couldn't do anything, it were, I honestly felt like it were a crime to breathe! I didn't, I wasn't, I wasn't living. I just lived there. I existed. That's what it got like. So I decided I would start and save up some money, **let him have Christmas with kids** and then I'd go* (Janice, my emphasis).

At the very point of leaving, women remained acutely av removing the children from their home and of the difficu trying to explain *why* they were leaving and *where* they were going to go.

Having taken one of the most difficult decisions of their lives, leaving for the majority of women (having tried staying with informal supporters, see Chapter 6) involved fleeing to a Women's Aid refuge, a local authority hostel or in one case bed and breakfast accommodation (two women had their male partners leave) so I now turn to look further at the experience of leaving with children.

Temporary accommodation

Living in refuges or hostels offers women positive support in terms of living with women and children who have had similar experiences: *I went back, I went back to the refuge and they all, you know, they made like a little party because it was my little boy's birthday ... and bought him a present and everything and it were right lovely. And then I decided I were stopping there no way were I coming back to [city], no chance* (Betty). However, communal living also creates tensions due to inappropriate and/or crowded living conditions and the inevitable distress women and children are feeling. This has been an ongoing problem for refuges from the start (see Binney, Harkell and Nixon, 1981) and whilst overcrowding could be ameliorated by secure and adequate levels of funding/resourcing, communal living is something few people are accustomed to.

Facilities offered for children varied greatly from none at all (in local authority hostels) to a range of work with children (in refuges). The needs of children who have experienced domestic violence have been recognised in refuges through providing children's workers, although children's outreach has developed more slowly (Humphreys and Thiara, 2002). Refuges can be problematic for children in that confidentiality policies make it difficult for children to spend time with other children except in school; '... difficult to sustain new friendships when they couldn't go out freely or invite their friends back to the refuge' (Stalford, Baker and Beveridge, 2003, p. 26). Children, therefore, usually made friends within the refuge. It is a very difficult time for mothers and their children, however, having been uprooted from their home, familiar surroundings and routines to find themselves living communally, in a relatively confined space, with other women and children in similar emotional states:

... your kids are obviously upset they're going to be like, disturbed, they're going to be disruptive, so you're like having to like contend with kids, and you've got your own feelings and your own emotions. You're shoving your own emotions down because if you let your own emotions [go], what're you going to do? (Mandy)

So whilst refuges present potential opportunities for women and children to make close friendships and gain support, at the same time they also, inevitably, present women and children with difficult challenges.

Moving into a new home or having the abusive partner leave

I wish I were a psychiatrist (laughs) I do honestly, I've been saying to [friend] today, I'm sick of worrying about my kids (Jill).

Once women have followed through their decision to leave, being re-housed in a new community or, in a small minority of cases, getting the violent partner to leave, an initial response from children (as with women) was relief at no longer having to cope with the abusive behaviour. Jill's children had been hugely restricted in what they could and could not eat for example: '*... and when he went, my kids said, we can have chicken, we can have chicken!*' Women also talked about positive improvements in their children's demeanour and emotional well-being: '*So I said to him like 'look at the moment your dad's in prison', he knows where he is and he's pleased about it, when I told him, he jumped up and down (laughs). Well, he's six next week and he jumped up and down' yeah, yeah, we can have some peace and quiet'* (Sally).

However, there were also difficulties to be confronted and women struggled to balance their needs with those of their children. Two key issues at this point were: coping with their own and their children's emotional issues and ensuring continuing safety for themselves and their children. From children's perspectives Mullender et al. (2002, pp. 107–9) found similar themes of 'safety' and 'loss of familiar' were dominant. Children were not surprisingly resentful at having had to leave their home, possessions, pets and friends in order to be safe when they themselves had done nothing wrong (see also Hague and Malos, 1994). At the same time some children were asking about their fathers; most women found it difficult responding to such questions: *Yes, that's it, learning to cope, to be on your own when you've been with someone five years, and you've got your kids asking about their dad*

(Catherine). Jill realises the pressure she is under and is aware of how easy it is to take this out on the children: *'We all got on, we used to play games, you know, doing the normal family things, but as soon as he went all I was doing was shouting, perhaps it were me, I don't know, whether me patience was slowly running out ... but all I'm doing now is shouting at them* (Jill).

Whilst women were unsure which of their children's behaviours might be attributable to the abuse experienced, they all expressed concern over one or more behavioural pattern. Research shows that the impact of abuse on children will vary, partly as a result of the different responses of children, and partly because of differences in terms of their relationship with each parent, wider sources of social support and the duration and nature of domestic violence suffered (Warner and Pantling, 2002, p. 125). Nevertheless, in the majority of cases here children had had to leave their homes very abruptly, with no time to say goodbye to friends, leaving beloved pets behind,[5] and often not knowing why they were leaving. As a result of leaving they lost their friendship network (as mothers feared) and had to start making new friends; Stalford, Baker and Beveridge found this too: 'Penny talked about how difficult this was for her and her sister, "It hurt me when I had to leave all my friends behind"' (2003, p. 25). This may be particularly difficult for older children in terms of making new friends at school; Kahn (2003) found widespread evidence of bullying of children who had experienced domestic violence, whilst Stalford, Baker and Beveridge found only two of 19 children reported having been bullied (2003, p. 28).

Children's safety at school is clearly threatened by the bullying of other children but safety factors are also crucial issues for children and mothers in relation to the abusive ex-partner since this time has been identified as especially dangerous for some women, so I now turn to examine these factors.

Safety issues

Research shows that after separation violence is more likely to continue and may even escalate (Binney, Harkell and Nixon, 1981; Okun, 1986; Smith, 1990; Stark and Flitcraft, 1991; Hester and Radford, 1992; Dobash and Dobash, 1992; Kirkwood, 1993; Rodgers, 1994; Johnson, 1995; Kurz, 1996; Radford et al., 1997). Research in the UK found that violence was committed by an ex-partner in a third of cases (Kelly, 1999, p. 17; Wilcox, 2000a, pp. 40–2). In the most extreme scenarios women are killed by their partners (Bean, 1992; Campbell, 1992).

Women reported that after leaving they experienced wide-ranging fears for the safety of their children. Partly this was due to fear of being found by the violent ex-partner but there was also a more generalised fear generated by the abuse suffered, with the belief that if children's own father could hurt them then anyone might do so. Women aimed, therefore, to keep their new address secret from their ex-partner, but not always successfully. Abusive partners actively sought out women's new addresses: feigning concern for the woman or wanting to see the children, asking friends, following friends or relatives or asking the children.

Children's safety was a priority therefore and most women made arrangements with school staff and/or the police to take care/watch over the children:

We had to tell them, police, went and told them, first that nobody at all could pick kids up except me, and if I weren't going to pick them up, I'd got to tell them in morning that me mum were going to pick them up, but no-one else could pick them up at all. And they couldn't even come out of class, like other kids used to, they had to sit in class and wait for me to get there. And when first they went back to school, after I'd come out of battered wives, police watched school at playtimes and dinner times. So that were good, and teachers watched right careful, watched them right careful (Betty).

Mostly women did allow the children contact with their fathers, but as previous research has found there are huge safety issues attached to contact with violent ex-partners and access arrangements were frequently abused by them (Hester and Radford, 1992; Hester et al., 1994; Hester, Pearson and Harwin, 2000; Humphreys, 2003; Humphreys and Thiara, 2003):

I don't think he had access because he wanted to have the children ... No, it was to maintain a contact with me erm yeah, I mean because [son] would turn up and I'd say what have you done today? And he's probably been left with the grandparents for hours and his dad had probably spent an hour with him, or something like that. So it wasn't because he wanted to be with the children (Christine).

Abusive men also frequently used their knowledge of woman's emotional attachment to the children in order to re-contact and to try and reinstate their relationship with their ex-partner, for example by bringing the children gifts. The children in this way became yet another tool of control used by abusive male partners against the women:

> *And then two weeks later, like he used to come up all the time to see kids, cause he wanted me back and like I didn't want him ... and it were [youngest son's] birthday and I didn't expect anything from him for [youngest son], and he come up on his birthday and brought him a big massive car, and er I thought, well he's never done that before I mean he's never ever bought any of his kids anything* (Lucy).

Contact often becomes a key site for continued abuse and violence where abusive partners can use the laws governing child welfare to continue abusing and exerting control over women through contact with the children, even where this may mean increased risk to the mother. For women, grappling with contact issues was another huge mental struggle (as Sally above) was it being selfish or protective to their children to refuse contact? Wallbank makes a similar point that mothers are seen as implacably hostile if they refuse contact, even in cases of domestic violence (2001). Often, it is only over time that women realise that the *protective* step is to stop the children seeing their father:

> *I stopped kids seeing him altogether. They said, that welfare place, you know, at the court, they said he had to see them once a week for half an hour and we used to go down to that centre ... Social worker used to take me down and fetch me back home and I used to see him there. Well then I used to say 'he's upsetting kids, seeing him they get, they're starting being right bad, and they're wetting the bed and everything'. So I went back to court and they said that he couldn't see them any more* (Betty).

As Betty explains she had to cope with the negative emotional after-effects of contact on her children and she had to make the effort to go back to court in order to ensure that they did not have to continue to suffer such abuse. The whole area of child contact is highly complex and contested and I do not have the space to do it justice here, suffice to say that in this study (as others) contact became another arena to abuse women and children (see Hester and Radford, 1992; Hester et al., 1994; Hester and Radford, 1996; Hester, Pearson and Harwin, 2000; Aris, Harrison and Humphreys, 2002; Radford and Sayer, 2002; Jaffe, Lemon and Poisson, 2003).

Gendered issues

In this study, examining the outcome of domestic violence on children with a gendered lens reveals that some boys did relate positively to their father, felt sorry for him, and went to live with him; some became more aggressive; others were the opposite not wanting anything to do with their father. Some daughters turned away from their father completely, others tried to retain contact. Some children will pointedly behave in a way that is diametrically opposed to the behaviour of their father: *That is one thing with my kids, I don't know if it's with him drinking and everything, but not one of me kids drinks* (Betty).

Looking at the visible impacts on sons which are likely to be due to abuse and violence, the range of behaviours reported included: fear, insecurity, nervousness, stuttering, bed wetting, bullying at school, anger, aggression/violence, non-aggression, emotional withdrawal, stubborn and disruptive behaviour, general illness such as sickness and diarrhoea. In other words behaviour patterns are not necessarily stereotypically gendered.

> *[older son] he's such a nervous child, he's very, very nervous, he stutters a little bit … Yeah, there's been a lot of bullying, he's been bullied a lot at school, but every time I've mentioned it it's been sorted out, although he's started to wee bed a little bit [elder son] and he's six now so … I don't know about this little one because he's got a temper on him, but haven't we all, but, but [elder son] he wouldn't hit anybody back if they hit him* (Sally).

> *And my kids [sons] are aggressive kids anyway they're more violent than normal kids* (Mandy).

For some older boys (12+) there do seem to be tensions around identifying as masculine and either identifying, or not identifying, with their fathers and their relationship with their mothers: *I mean he [elder son] lives with his dad … and he says 'I feel sorry for me dad, I want to come home but I feel sorry for me dad', but if that's the way he feels that it's his responsibility, he's took a lot on his shoulders, our [son's name], and I think he's too young to have that responsibility and I think it's screwing him up basically* (Jill).

A further gendered issue for some mothers is how to respond to their son's/sons' behaviour. Women guard against responding to sons as they would have done with their partner/husband, especially when a son is similar to the former partner. Jill confronts this issue both within herself and from her mother: *But even now me mother'll say 'oh he's getting too much like [ex-partner]', you know, it's really, horrible, 'you're getting too much like your dad you'. Like I say, there is, sometimes I think he is too like his dad, but I still love him.* Children who have had a close relationship with their father may blame their mother if, or when, the relationship breaks up; *I think me eldest son blames me because he's the only one who's really close to [ex partner]. So I think he blamed me and he put me through hell, and he's still putting me through hell now, you know* (Jill).

The impacts on daughters are less visible in the reports of the women interviewed than are the impacts on the sons. It may be that mothers are more aware of the contested 'cycle of violence' theory and, connecting this with cultural links between masculinity and violence, are more concerned about the possibility of their sons becoming violent. On the other hand, it may be that daughters are more likely to internalise their emotions hiding them from their mothers and hence mothers assume that their daughters have suffered less; further research would be needed to determine this. The range of girls' behaviours reported in this study includes: anger, ambivalence, emotional withdrawal from the father, hatred of the father, insecurity and clinginess.

> *She hates him, there is no other word about it, she hates him… well we did go over Christmas Eve, because he had kids Christmas Eve, because I was having them Christmas Day, well he said 'will you come down for your tea?' so I said 'yes, I'll tell our [elder daughter]', and she weren't very pleased … So she says, I went down that day, and she just refuses point blank to go down any more … so she can't stand him, she hates him. er [younger daughter] she doesn't like school, she got very, very clingy (telephone rings, call from ex-husband re child and school) … I've been worried about our [younger daughter] on and off* (Jill).

However, there is often a reluctance to pinpoint the cause of physical or mental harm as domestic violence (Department of Health, 2000a, p. 5) and it would be interesting to research further the extent to which consequences are visible or hidden.

Children can and do have different reactions, even within the same family, which may (or may not) be along stereotypically gendered lines and this may relate to the kinds of abuse suffered. This in turn raises complex dilemmas for mothers: e.g. in Jill's case her elder daughter suffered emotional abuse and gendered comments on her appearance and weight and now wants nothing to do with her father whereas the elder son chooses to live with his father and blames his mother for the break up of the relationship. This creates a huge rift between mother and son and mother and daughter. Whilst Jill is trying to maintain an 'amicable' relationship with her former violent partner, for the sake of her elder son, when she does this her elder daughter is extremely angry. The emotional abuse suffered has incurred her rage and I agree with McGee (2000, p. 74) here that girls' aggression may be directed at their fathers, and also more widely at boys and men.

Her younger daughter had been very withdrawn and clingy during the relationship, but since her father left Jill describes her as *'coming out of her shell and becoming more confident than before'*. Her elder son (13) had gone to live with his father because he 'feels sorry for him' and Jill worries very much about this and the responsibilities he is taking on by in effect 'looking after his dad'. Whilst Jill's younger son is causing a good deal of concern; as she describes it *'he is being very naughty, often refusing to go to school and finding it difficult to concentrate at school, he is going through a trauma at moment'*. At the same time Jill's ex-partner remains intrusive in her life. I interviewed her twice and on the first occasion he drove by the house and pipped the car horn to let her know he was passing and on the second occasion he telephoned her whilst I was in the house.

At the same time women who leave domestic violence have to contend with wider cultural attitudes on the family and those who ultimately refuse to allow the children to see their father perceive themselves to be thought of as 'selfish' women; women in this study were acutely aware of this damning social censure both before: *'On their [children's] behalf, yes, yeah, so I wasn't being selfish or anything, from their point of view [in leaving]* (Janice) and after leaving. Sally, for example, had to struggle with her feelings about refusing contact between her son and his father as she felt wider society condemned her as being 'selfish' without even finding out about the abuse and violence she and her children had suffered. This was gendered too as she felt she was particularly criticised by men, and highlighted her new boyfriend as having this attitude:

> *I tell you what I hate more than anything else is to be, I don't know what word for it is, er, typecast I think is only word I can think for it ... but everybody sees you as this person, they've had an **argument** with their husband so they're not going to let kids see, see their partner you see, and I hate being in that category, being put in that category, yeah, yeah. And*

everybody seems to, especially men, even my [new] boyfriend (Sally, her emphasis).

Conclusion

The centrality to women (who are mothers) of their day-to-day experiences with their children cannot be overstated and these were closely connected to women's sense of self and feelings of intimacy. Interacting with children brought rich rewards to women's lives even in the context of abuse. The gendered nature of childcare, and the continuing centrality to women of motherhood and children, was clear. What this meant in contexts of domestic violence (where contact with other people may be relatively limited) is that the children often became women's main or primary concern. Thinking about ending the relationship for women meant considering their children's futures in tandem with their own. Agency for women was constructed in connection with others, in this case their children, and it was simply not possible for women participants to see themselves as the 'individual actors' of rational action theory (Kovalainen, 2004, p. 163). Concern for their children was a significant factor of constraint which tended to prolong the abusive relationship. Having said this when women became convinced that their children *were* being harmed by the abuse and violence then it became a spur to ending the relationship.

Research, policy and practice on the impact of abuse and violence on children is still at a relatively early stage in the west. We do know that domestic violence has *adverse* effects on children and from children's perspectives we know that 'children do not think that they or other children should have to live with domestic violence' (Mullender et al., 2002, p. 230). Women participants revealed their uncertainty and lack of knowledge about the impact of abuse and violence on their children. They drew on a model of children as being 'safe' from abuse and violence, so long as they did not witness violence or 'only' overheard violence. This model is indirectly supported by the literature which conceptualises children as 'witnessing' or 'overhearing' violence as opposed to recognising that children are intimately involved *in* and *with* the violence. The former model must be challenged in future and research findings on the adverse impacts of domestic violence on children need to be widely disseminated. It is essential that mothers (and fathers) realise that their children *are actively involved* in any abusive and violent practices in the family.

This chapter (building on Chapters 1 and 2) has demonstrated the need for continuing gendered analyses for the following reasons: abuse and violence were gendered experiences occurring around pregnancy (a time of gender polarity when physically, emotionally and financially women were most dependent on their male partner); women experienced controlling male actions in getting (or not getting) pregnant, 'punishments' for being (or not being) pregnant, 'punishments' for not being good enough mothers, for not making sure the children were quiet (or not seen) or for attending to the children rather than the male partner. The abuse against children was also gendered in that emotional abuse against daughters focused on aspects of their appearance/femininity and against sons focusing on the extent to which they achieved (or failed to achieve) accepted norms of dominant, heterosexual masculinity.

The women in the present study identified the resourcefulness and strength shown by children experiencing domestic violence as previous research reveals (Jaffe et al., 1990; McGee, 2000; Mullender et al., 2002). Children are often characterised as support receivers, this research has revealed children as important support givers. For children what matters most is the quality of their relationships with those who care for them at home and with their peers in their wider social networks. Children, whose fathers are violent to their mothers, experience confused and insecure relationships often with both parents. As they grow up, immersed on a day-to-day basis in contexts of domestic violence, they learn a model of gender relations where male practices of violence and control are commonplace. They learn to see their mothers as subordinate to their fathers, and that their mothers are not always able to protect them from their father's violence. Girls and boys will be reflective on what they have experienced and will be active in taking up, adapting and/or rejecting such a model. What they all have in common is the experience of a negative and traumatic model of a heterosexual relationship which will impact in a variety of adverse ways on them in their future lives. This is, therefore, an absolutely vital area where much more research is needed; '... we are still not listening sufficiently to children or ensuring that they have someone to talk to who can understand and help them' (Mullender et al., 2002, p. 231).

4
Home and Security

Oh the house, that were horrible, I'd never seen nothing like it in all
me bloody life to tell you the truth, because er when I came with the
woman from the hostel, when we first came to look round it, she
said, 'I wouldn't move in here', she said, 'but it's the one and only
offer that you're going to get, you'll have to take it' (Catherine).

Introduction

This chapter provides a further window into women's agency in the
face of constraints in contexts of domestic violence focusing on home
and security. In order to escape her violent relationship Catherine
found shelter in two refuges and several months later was re-housed in
a community 70 miles from her own hometown. A severe constraint
faced by Catherine was the local authority 'rule' whereby homeless
people are made one offer of a house only and in her case the house
was in so many ways inappropriate for someone fleeing domestic
violence. I pursue this point in more detail later in the chapter.

As seen throughout this book domestic violence is a context for gender
relations in which men seek to maintain and enforce traditional relationships and privileges. Home is integral to this process since domestic
violence largely takes place in the home and I argue that an exploration
of the meanings of home to women may be as important as practical
housing issues if we are to fully grasp the dilemmas women confront
when considering what they should do in an abusive and violent relationship. Chapman has argued that people's investment in their homes
is extremely significant for the project and realisation of self-identity;
however, '... the sheer familiarity of home makes it difficult for people to
recognise the depth of meaning it represents' (1999, p. 133).

Home is not only a physical arrangement of space but an expression of social meanings and identities for human beings (Dovey, 1985). It is not surprising then that the concept of home has been passionately alluded to in literature and poetry. Home provides a focal point in most people's lives whether for better, for worse, or more likely for both at different times; it fosters an orientation in the world, a way of being and relating to others (Douglas, 1991). We assume that our homes will be relatively permanent and that we have control in them (more so than in other sites). These assumptions give us a sense of security and stability in our lives. Domestic violence disrupts both of these assumptions. However, as we shall see, women do maintain positive feelings and attachments to their homes in contexts of domestic violence making it as, if not more, difficult to contend with an abusive relationship. In this chapter I explore how the social meanings attached to home can persist for women in the face of an abusive relationship, the dilemmas this poses for women and why leaving their home is, therefore, a last resort (Levison and Harwin, 2001).

In the existing gender order women retain responsibility for actively producing stability in the home for men and children through attending to their emotional and practical needs (Lee, 2001). Women also have primary responsibility for childcare whilst men continue to spend less time with children retaining, for the most part, the 'head of household' role in a position of authority and control over women and children. We, therefore, need accounts and better understandings of the nature of home for women experiencing abusive heterosexual relationships. And since all too often when women attempt to leave an abusive relationship, they face the loss of their home and community, we need better understandings of women's experiences of leaving and the meanings they read into the processes involved. How is home/not home gendered and how does gender impact on processes of support (sought and given) and finally on the policies and processes involved for women in accessing refuge and re-housing?

What I attempt to do in this chapter, therefore, is to explore women's ideas of home/not home in the context of ending abuse and becoming lone mothers, against the backdrop of gendered cultural, economic and political systems which 'privilege unbroken two-parent families' (Somerville, 1990, p. 536). I will start by briefly summarising significant research and theorising on gender and home before turning to look at these issues in relation to domestic violence. I then highlight women's perspectives on home whilst in the violent relationship before examining their perceptions when thinking about leaving.

Finally, I attempt to capture something of the process women went through in being re-housed (this was the case for all but two women) and how this impacted on women's feelings of safety and security.

Gender and home

> For women and men alike, home is where the heart is, but love means unpaid caring and labour for women, whereas for men it means emotional stability and gratification (Somerville, 1990, p. 535).

Home (linked to 'family') is a potent site in which gender-differentiated meanings, relationships and practices are produced, reinforced and potentially can be changed. Where other vertical hierarchies (of class, ethnicity and 'race') frequently entail spatial segregation (Giddens, 1984, pp. 91–2) this is not the case for gendered relationships in heterosexual couples where women and men (usually) share the same spatial location in the home.

In modernity home was conceptualised by white, heterosexual, middle class, men, largely as a sanctuary away from the competition, struggles and dangers of the public sphere. Such modernist beliefs and discourses have been influential in shaping social practices in the west. As Witz and Marshall (2004) argue masculinist social scientists have actively constructed theories of sex differences and conceptualised the home (located in the private sphere) as opposed to work (located in the public sphere) and binary oppositions of woman/man were linked to this home/work dichotomy.

Structural functionalists such as Parsons, Bales and Shils (1953) saw women and men as having complementary roles in the home and at work. They conceptualised the family as a subsystem of society, serving the needs of both children and society. The husband-father was identified as the primary 'task-leader' of the subsystem, differentiated from the wife-mother by his commitments **outside** the family/home which precluded his taking certain responsibilities inside the family. The wife-mother was differentiated from the husband-father by her skilful management of the emotional problems of family members '... obviously the primary traditional focus of the feminine role' (ibid., pp. 267–8). This view of gender complementary roles and practices, within the home for women and outside the home for men, constructed an idealistic view of home and family as working without conflict or tension and implicitly endorsed male dominance (Chapman, 1999, p. 166). Middle class social practices tended to make such a view of gender roles both common-place and respectable and helped to shape patriarchal relations to/with/in the home.

> For much of the twentieth century, it has generally been accepted that the home *is* the woman's domain – the place where women can nurture their young, satisfy the domestic and personal needs of a husband and exercise their own creative energies. In popular songs, films, novels and television programmes, this view of the home has been constantly – *relentlessly* – reinforced (Chapman, 1999, p. 165).

Second wave feminists critiqued this traditional view of the family arguing that the home was a key site of women's oppression, uncovering how notions of 'home as sanctuary' and 'safe haven' applied to husbands rather than wives. For women, particularly working class and minoritised women, 'home' has always presented far more complex realities; as places of caring/work, of dependence, interdependence and intimate interrelationship which may result in love and intimacy and/or stresses and strains.

> Among the working class the wife makes the home … The working man's wife is also his housekeeper, cook and several other single domestics rolled into one; and on her being a managing or mismanaging woman depends whether a dwelling will be a home proper, or a house which is not a home (Thomas Wright, engineer, 1868, cited in Cockburn, 1983, p. 34).

Historically (and today) working class and minoritised women have usually worked outside as well as inside the home; and minoritised women were seen 'primarily as workers rather than as members of family groups, [minority] women labored to maintain, sustain, stabilise and reproduce their families while working in both the public (productive) and private (reproductive) spheres' (Thornton Dill, 1988, p. 428).

If we look, for example, at unpaid work in the home, the majority of childcare, house care, relationship care and maintenance is still carried out by women in all cultures (although to differing degrees and in different ways). Women remain by and large the primary caregivers of children, regardless of whether they work outside the home or not (see Chapter 3). Women spend nearly three hours a day on average on house care (excluding shopping and childcare) compared with one hour 40 minutes spent by men (UK 2000 *Time Use Survey*).

Women, by and large, invest more emotional and physical energy in caring for and maintaining the home, in sustaining and nurturing family relationships (see Chapter 2) and in caring for their children (Duncombe and Marsden, 1993, 1996, 1998). This kind of work also often extends beyond the family to local community networks in areas of deprivation and poverty (see for example Stack, 1974; Belle, 1983; Campbell, 1993). Studies suggest that traditional gender roles are more likely to become entrenched after the arrival of children (Ribbens, 1994) and that the domestic division of labour remains largely unequal with women continuing to make larger contributions, although the increase in men's participation should be regarded as significant (Benjamin, 1999; Sullivan, 2000). At the same time men continue to have long working hours in the public sphere (Fagan, 2000).

Women spend more time interacting within the home and mediating between the home and the outside world and as a result are more likely to experience a connected relational sense of self. This has important implications for women's ways-of-being in and around the home and their ways of conceptualising 'home'. So while men largely continue to claim an identity assumed from their position in the public sphere work hierarchy, women, and particularly those in poverty, continue to see themselves as being connected with others and claim their identity as part of a web of relationships (Gilligan, 1982).

Feminist theoretical analyses of the family also critiqued the dichotomy of instrumental and expressive tasks in the home (as argued for example by Parsons, Bales and Shils, 1953) which ignores the organisational and managerial components of domestic work (Finch and Mason, 1993; Jamieson, 1998), as well as the division between the public and the private, that forms the basis of many policies and services, rather than seeing the interpellation of the two. As Bourdieu argues, 'The public vision ... is deeply involved in our vision of domestic things, and our most private behaviours themselves depend on public actions, such as housing policy, or more directly, family policy' (1996, p. 25). These insights are pertinent to a gendered analysis of domestic violence and are developed throughout this book.

Despite feminist challenges to dominant constructions, home continues to be widely associated with femininity in the sense that assumed feminine principles of 'boundedness, physicality and nurturance' (Wardhaugh, 1999, p. 97) are commonly linked with notions of home. It is also women who are usually seen as homemakers and who are often expected to carry out the day-to-day running and maintenance of the home. Today the idea of home as somewhere to relax away from the stresses and strains of the public world still holds more validity for men than for women (Darke, 1994).

Feminist research challenged notions of the complementary nature of gendered relations in the home, revealing the home to be a place of conflicting meanings, and potentially a place of anxiety and danger for women and children due to male physical, sexual and emotional violence (Dobash and Dobash, 1979; Borkowski et al., 1983; Hanmer and Saunders, 1984; Walker, 1984; Stanko, 1985, 1995, 1998; Maynard, 1985; Pleck, 1987; Mama, 1989; Richie, 1996). As Wardhaugh argues the tensions between binary opposites such as risk/safety, fear/security, invasion/privacy, conventionally seen to fall either side of the public/ private divide, for many women and children exist *within* the home (1999, p. 93).

Domestic violence, gender and home

> The importance of housing cannot be overestimated. Along with economic independence and viability, it ranks as one of the crucial factors affecting women's ability to find viable alternatives to a violent relationship (Dobash and Dobash, 2000, pp. 199–200).

There is a paucity of literature specifically on housing and domestic violence (Levison and Harwin, 2000) and what exists has focused (unsurprisingly) on women's urgent need for safe temporary and permanent housing rather than looking at the meanings of 'home' for women (see for example Schechter, 1982; Clifton, 1985; Pahl, 1985; Ferraro, 1989; Bull, 1993; Malos and Hague, 1993, 1997; Charles, 1994). Research shows us that obtaining appropriate help from housing agencies has often been difficult for women who have ended a violent relationship and has frequently involved contacting large numbers of different organisations (Binney, Harkell and Nixon, 1981; Homer et al., 1984; Rai and Thiara, 1997).

In most cases women have to find alternative housing away from the abusive relationship and more rarely women have remained in their homes and had the perpetrator of violence leave/be removed. Access to independent, safe housing is a key factor in women being able to leave domestic violence (Morley, 2000). Humphreys and Thiara (2002) found that 64 per cent of their sample had contacted their local authority Housing Department and women reported varied responses, pinpointing especially important issues as being taken seriously/believed and so accepted as homeless, and being re-housed quickly. Batsleer et al.'s study of minoritised women found their experiences of housing allocation to be 'largely distressing and substandard'; housing was often reported to be in an 'appalling state' and also 'in dangerous areas' (2002, p. 81). Davis (2003) researched local authority and housing association responses to domestic violence (the latter are becoming increasingly important as providers of social housing). As others, she highlights the varied practice that exists in this area towards women and children made homeless by domestic violence and the use of discretion (Malos and Hague, 1993; Humphreys and Thiara, 2002; Davis, 2003).

There are still many gaps in our knowledge about the relationships with/to home of women who stay in abusive relationships and those who leave; about which housing options work and how they work; and about service responses to women in this context. For women in abusive relationships (as for everyone) home is a powerful site of significant attachment/s, of hoped-for happiness and hoped-for positive, intimate relationships. Home and family stand in a 'reciprocal relationship' to one another (Gubrium and Holstein, 1990, cited in Ribbens, 1994, p. 60). Moreover, for women who are mothers, investment in the home is likely to be especially significant since investment in their children and childcare overlaps with caring for the home environment; 'Ideas of motherhood may be *bound up with* attitudes towards the house as a physical space' says Ribbens (1994, p. 61, emphasis in original).

For women experiencing abuse, home is also a site of emphasised constraint and threat to their, and their children's, security and safety. Despite this, such intense individual and cultural significance is invested in both home and family that women are (more often than not) incredibly tenacious in trying to hold both together, even in the face of ongoing controlling and abusive behaviour. As Gurney (1990, cited in Somerville, 1990) recognises it is possible for women to have strong and positive attachments to the home even in situations of exploitation and oppression. However, for women, such as those in this study, continued (and sometimes escalating) abuse becomes no longer bearable and results in their fleeing the family home and seeking alternative housing elsewhere (or have the abuser leave).

I now turn to look at women's accounts of their differing relationships with, and attachment to, home as compared with their male partners, revealing how male controlling action around home constrains women's freedom, threatens women and children's safety and disrupts meanings of home. I then unpick what it is like for women thinking about leaving, leaving and returning to the family home (often several times) and the difficulties in finding alternative accommodation. Finally, I look at the complex processes women go through in ultimately setting up new homes when they flee their homes and communities.

Women, attachment and home

Home as site of hoped-for 'ideal' heterosexual relationship/ romance

The heterosexual relationship is the most valued and celebrated relationship in our culture (Cockburn, 2004, p. 30) and as already seen all the women started out thinking that the early days of their relationships were 'wonderful' (Richie, 1996, p. 70). However, it became clear from the outset that gendered ideologies and identities shaped their expectations and formed the context within which male authority and dominance was often seen as 'what you do'. The women were understandably keen for their relationships to be successful and the experience of abusive actions of violence were quite unexpected and shocking. Women tried to find ways to rationalise why it had happened, and frequently asked the questions of themselves, 'why me?' and 'am I responsible for his behaviour in some way?' One of the most extreme examples of violation of the meaning of home as the base for the hoped-for romantic, heterosexual relationship was recounted by Betty, whose husband would bring other women back to their home, in total violation of the meaning of home as the locus of an intimate, caring relationship as we saw in Chapter 2. Initially, and for some time, women do not want to admit to any failings in their relationship and try to deal with the abuse/violence themselves.

As the heterosexual relationship (and especially marriage) is valued culturally over and above all other relationships it is, therefore, something to be embraced and striven for. Moreover, women seem to have a need for a confidante, a person in whom to confide and seek love, comfort and companionship. Here cultural and personal forces interact in powerful ways such that the threatened loss of this kind of close relationship (whether sexual or not) raises deep anxieties. Women expend massive efforts of will power and emotional energy, in their attempt to hold onto having a close confidante and a socially valued heterosexual relationship, even when the reality of that relationship fails to live up to the ideal. Moreover, for women who have had children with their partner, there is another level of physical and emotional investment in the partnership through having a child/ren together, caring for a child/ren and the creativity involved in making a hoped-for 'ideal family' (as seen in Chapter 3).

Home as site of hoped-for 'ideal' family relationship

Home, heterosexual relationship, nuclear family – form a powerful symbolic and actual triumvirate, which has been constructed as the core of social organisation in 'western' society, and where children are raised. Women remain by and large the primary caregivers of children, regardless of whether they work outside the home or not. In Britain in 2000–2001 women living in a couple and working full time spent on average nearly four and a half hours on childcare on a weekday; for men in the same circumstances the comparable figure was just over three and a half hours (Office for National Statistics Labour Force Survey, 2003). All the women in this study were mothers and the home was where they and their partners brought their newborn baby/ ies back to. For those women who suffered abuse/violence during pregnancy and during the child's infancy (see Chapter 3) this was clearly a spoiled experience, but the home was, all the same, the site of caring for the baby, of child rearing and of children growing up. Over and above the problematic heterosexual relationship then, all the mothers were highly conscious that the home was their children's home, as much as their own home. The home was where mothering took place and where their children formed friendships, often through the mediation of mothers, linking the home with the outside world of nursery, childminder, school and friends' homes. Additionally, most women held strong views on the importance of the children's relationships with their fathers over and above the abusive relationship.

Women perceived their male partners as having a different, less attached relationship with the home and family. Whereas Ribbens' middle class mothers 'expressed resentment at how far the worlds of work took their husbands away from "the family"' (1994, p. 65). In this study the male partners were also often away from the home but more often as a matter of leisure rather than work patterns:

> *I think even a whole year went by when everything was O.K. but even then I was left on my own a lot because he'd always go seeing his family. I don't think he could cope with having come from a big family and then just sort of [being on our own]... And I kept trying to say, you know, 'you don't need to do that all the time'. It was every day he was going to his family, 'you don't need to do that every day, you know'. But it was a real*

job of persuasion to try and get him to stay at home, so, but then I think it just got worse after a year, he'd just keep taking off at all times (Christine).

In relation to the home women said their male partners exercised a far greater degree of freedom in relation to being at home/away from home. In this way they demonstrated their felt lesser sense of responsibility for home and childcare, as compared with their female partners. This freedom to come and go from the home at will was exercised at the cost of their wives'/partners' freedom. The women recounted the various ways in which their freedoms were restricted by their male partners; both in terms of where they could go **outside** of the home and who they could see **inside** the home (see Chapter 1 and below). This practice of male control was linked with the men's view of the home as the woman's domain, as the site of her home-making and childcare.

Home as site of home-making and domestic labour

The majority of home-making and domestic labour is carried out by women in all cultures. As noted above, caring for the home for women overlaps with caring for children, although at times these are in conflict. Many women saw both as contributing towards building a healthy and safe family. For instance, allowing the children to be untidy and to make noise in the house was described by some women as an important aspect of good mothering (as also Ribbens, 1994) which the men tended not to endorse: *'when he's not around I just used to let them riot, it doesn't bother me noise, I mean that's what kids are for'* (Lucy) whereas for other women *'an orderly house'* indicated good mothering (Ribbens, 1994, p. 61).

Caring work in the home remains hard work, unpaid, invisible and isolating, as second wave feminists argued (Oakley, 1974a and b; Deem, 1986). However, caring for children and creating a home also have deep, emotional meanings for women in addition to being physical labour; indeed the significance of women's domestic lives needs to be recognised as central to the 'real' issues of society (to paraphrase Ribbens McCarthy and Edwards, 2001, p. 766) without seeing such domestic caring work as exclusive to women. It may be also that women exercise some power in the domestic sphere through their 'expertise' (Martin, 1984 cited in Chapman, 1999) and women may also play a part in the fact that they do more work in the home than men do (Chapman, 1999). However, the extent to which domestic lives for women retain elements of 'compulsory altruism' (Land and Rose, 1985) women will perceive them as complex and ambivalent. What is clear from this research is that currently domestic lives and work remain gendered.

How far is the home perceived as 'women's domain'?

This study demonstrates how women's perceptions of changed and changing gendered relations clashed with their male partners' unchanged perceptions. We can see the extent to which male partners had more traditional views, constructing the home as women's domain (in certain respects) and how different these are from how women now see themselves:

> *It were more or less a case of I'd got to stop in the home. They were my kids, my dogs* (Janice).

> *Stay at home, typical stereotype, you know, cooking a meal and having babies* (Mandy).

Women no longer saw themselves as fitting this stereotyped view of gender roles and found it frustrating and unfair having to take on virtually sole responsibility, for the home, for feeding the family, for childcare and so forth. They were adamantly against the view of the 'stay at home wife' and found the limitations placed on their freedom by their male partners intolerable.

However, the home was in certain other respects decidedly **not** seen by the male partners as the woman's domain. For example, who was allowed to visit the house when he was at home was seen by the men as very much in their gift. According to the women's accounts the men in this study assumed overall authority and control in the home when they were at home. This applied both to what happened in the home, how children were to behave, and who was allowed to come into the home. Betty talked about this aspect of male controlling practices saying:

> *I couldn't have any friends at all. Only time I could see [friend] was when he went out. She knew what days he went out and she come up on them days …*
> *And I used to talk to women but I daren't ask anybody back to the house, he'd have killed me. He would have really throttled me, I daren't do that … He's [describing a friend's husband] a bit like our old feller were,*

I can't go to his, their house when he's in, he don't like women coming to see her, so I just go when he isn't in! (laughs) (Betty)

Women did find subversive ways to see friends and family, but this was not always straightforward. Friends and family may not suspect that the man is abusive since some appear as 'normal' other men in public and only reveal their abusive practices 'back stage' (Goffman, 1959). However, other men in this study did reveal publicly, if not abuse, at least very rude behaviour to their female partner's friends and family. When this happened, friends and relatives were more likely to take evasive action, such as not coming to the house, rather than confronting the abusive behaviour (see Chapter 6).

The meanings of home were, therefore, problematised for women through male domination and control when he was at home, but as we have seen male partners were often not at home. On these occasions women were able to run the home as they wanted, to care for the children in their own way/s and as a result relationships and identities were built around these times (see Chapter 3). There were also good times at home for women with their partners, as well as home being the venue and locus of abuse and control.

Home as the venue and locus of abuse and control

Control and abuse of the women in this study frequently revolved around the home and home-based issues. As seen above male partners saw it as the woman's role to do the housework, take care of the children and cook the food for the family. When arguments happened husbands felt they had the authority to 'punish' women and negative sanctions were often home-related, for instance rejecting or destroying food a woman had cooked for him/the family:

I think he had such a quick temper and he always wanted his own way erm and when we used to have arguments and, he weren't violent, he just used to go off for hours and hours on end. And when he came back he wouldn't tell me where he'd been, or he just didn't speak to me for about three weeks, just ignored me, if I made him a drink he'd just pour it down sink, he wouldn't eat meals I cooked for him (laughs) (Louise).

Indeed, the fabric of the home itself, and objects within the home, were also attacked at times, with furniture, doors and other items around the house being destroyed. As Sally described her husband attacking her and then destroying their fireplace: '*He took me fireplace down, that fireplace were right up to there [indicates height]*'. Treasured, and often irreplaceable, objects can be associated with self-identity and when these are destroyed this can have a powerful impact on women's 'deeply rooted sense of security and place' (just as Chapman 1999 describes in relation to similar losses in burglary). This applied to significant possessions but also to family pets which could be injured or even killed.

Home as a sense of independence and freedom?

As referred to earlier the liberty of the husband/male partner seems to be achieved at the expense of the women's liberty, revealing differently gendered relationships to home: *No, I could not go out. He could go out wherever he wanted to. I mean even if I had a big bust up with him he'd still walk out, but more times than not if I wanted to go out he'd lock door so I couldn't get out and he'd take keys with him so I couldn't get 'em off him. So I'd be locked in me own home!* (Lucy)

Betty was often pushed out of her own home and made to walk the streets by her husband. Betty reveals clearly below how her feelings of safety were shaped during the abusive relationship by fear of being in the home and how this changed when she moved out:

> *Yeah, I just had to walk around until he decided to let me back in (laughs) God it were right bad. And then, I weren't frightened, I had to go walking round streets, and round the back streets and everything and I weren't a bit frightened, but now I daren't leave house, once it gets to, once it's like night, if I forgot something from shop [new husband] has to go to shop and I daren't go out. I'm frightened to death now, I never used to be. When I were at [place name] I never had me door locked I **had this fear of being locked in**, yet now I have door locked nearly all day* (Betty).

The men's seeming ability to walk out of the house and away from taxing situations was something the women commonly identified as a major problem. At the same time no woman felt able to do this and most led constrained lives. For women in these circumstances the home becomes less of a castle than a cage (Oakley, 1974a; Roberts, 1991; Darke, 1994; Goldsack, 1999):

> *Oh I couldn't have me own life whatsoever... in fact when we first got married I was virtually a recluse, I never used to go out anywhere and er when I was breast feeding my children I put weight and weight and weight on because I just couldn't stop eating, because I was sat in the house all day, virtually all day* (Jill).

Women's dilemmas in thinking about leaving home

Despite all the difficulties and disruptions around the home and home-related activities women retained deep attachments to their home (and community) as the place where they and their children belonged, as discussed above. The decision to flee their home (and community) was one of the most difficult things they had ever done. For most women thinking about and leaving home is the last resort, after prolonged efforts to stop the abuse, and as a result of an ongoing and cumulative personal crisis. Were there other factors which made leaving so difficult?

Home as stable and permanent?

When we 'set up home' with a partner the assumption is that the relationship will last. The idea of a 'family home' evokes notions of assumed stability and permanence. These ideas are disrupted when women started to think about leaving as a result of abuse and violence over time from their partners. As suggested above this pattern of behaviour has cumulative effects which become increasingly unbearable such that women start to think more and more about leaving. Not only does violence disrupt the assumption of safe space within the home (as opposed to the assumed dangerous world outside) but also it disrupts the assumption that both parents will provide security in the home for their child/ren. Mothers become increasingly aware of the risk to their own safety and of their own inability to provide their children with security. Thoughts about leaving are nevertheless fraught with deep and disorienting anxieties since leaving home entails massive changes in identity for the mother and her children and raises immense financial and material questions about economic survival. Moreover, leaving involves huge changes for children too, taking them away from their homes, upsetting their social networks and disrupting their schooling. Christine said that fear over her children was one of the worst feelings in leaving (see also Chapter 3):

> So that's what I did [left the home], but that feeling, that seemed to be one of the worst feelings, taking the children away from their home, you know, it doesn't matter what the house is like, what you have got, what you haven't got, **it's still their home** and you're responsible for, you're changing their life in one move basically you know (Christine, her emphasis).

The difficulties of finding alternative accommodation

When at the end of their tether, and/or when the abuse was directed specifically towards the children, these women decided that they had to leave the home, for the sake of their, and their children's, safety and sanity, for them there was no other alternative. Deciding to end the relationship, however, was not necessarily the end of the story, Jill, for instance, stayed on with her abusive partner for many years (see also Bull, 1993) as it proved impossible to find alternative accommodation: '*I mean, I'm not being funny about social workers, 'you've got to do something, leave him', but where could I go with four kids?*'. Jill, as most women, turned initially to her family to put her up, but as seen below, this proved extremely problematic, and Jill (unusually) eventually succeeded in getting her husband to move out of the family home.

Back home with your birth family

In this study all of the women moved out at some point to stay with family members, just as Dobash and Dobash (1979) found, women were more likely to approach their birth family for help if their partner was violent. However, three quarters of the women had also used temporary agency accommodation of one sort or another.

Where women had families to turn to most attempted to provide women with accommodation; five women were accommodated, usually for short periods, by their families when trying to make the break it was, however, a contradictory experience. In order to approach their family members for help women had to overcome intense feelings of shame, reticence and self blame (see Chapter 2). In most cases women initially approached their mothers for informal advice and as the violence got worse they were more likely to approach their parents for temporary accommodation, but only if they thought they had a chance of getting the help needed (as Davis, 2003, p. 127).

One woman, Sally, who had had a difficult relationship with her mother, left her partner 17 times and stayed at her parents on nine occasions. Although she was grateful for this help she found it difficult to share accommodation with two small children and her parents, both for practical and emotional reasons. She felt guilty about putting extra burdens on her mother:

Sally: *Because she likes her own space and we were getting on her nerves and things, it were awful.*

Paula: *How long did you stay with her the first time you left?*

Sally: *A couple of weeks sometimes and like I knew me mum were getting fed up with me being there and he is saying 'I want you back' and this that and other and so you went back because it's easier. I were hurting me mum everything I did. It was selfish.*

Betty stayed at her parents' flat for a while to flee the violence but her partner was constantly coming around harassing her: *And he were round all the time. He used to wait until me mum had gone to the shops and then come and try and break the door down ... and I felt well it's not fair on me mum and dad so I will just go back.*

Daughters are acutely aware that it is their mothers who do most of the domestic and caring work in the family and so they realise that staying with their family puts a further burden on, and hurts, their mothers. However, unless they can get their own accommodation they are in a no-win situation since returning to their abuser also hurts their mothers. A few women turned to female friends for accommodation whilst pursuing re-housing, like Louise:

Well before I left him erm I rung a friend up and asked could I come and stop with her till I found somewhere else to live and she said that I could. So I stopped with her for about six weeks ... I went and stayed with her, and then straight away I went to Housing and said I'm living with a friend and it were crowded she'd only got two bedrooms, and I were sleeping on settee and so they gave me a flat.

Women stayed with relatives, often on more than one occasion, but usually for short periods of time (see also Office of the Deputy Prime Minister, 2002, p. 43), since staying with families posed many difficulties; for example lack of space, lack of resources, personality clashes, further harassment (see Chapter 6) as Betty who stayed with her parents describes:

And me mum lived in flats, and one day he were kicking front door in and me brother had to jump over gang landing at back, how ever he didn't break his legs, and run for police, it were police at [area in city] because me mum lived there. And he said, 'oh well really it's a domestic, it's nothing to do with us'. He was taking me, when they used to come they used to say,' just go lad, just let her calm down she'll come to her senses'. Me come to me bloody senses!

The women in this study who finally left the relationship for good at a later stage then turned to refuges/shelters and local authority housing departments for both temporary, and later on permanent, accommodation.

At the point of leaving home

The way in which women left their homes was typically extremely sudden and abrupt, even though some planned it mentally in advance and others did not. Women often simply took their opportunity as and when it arose, with no clear idea or prior thoughts about where they would go or where they would be re-housed:

> *And then I started to plan to get away. And he must have known because he went out every day but at this point he stayed in all day, he stayed in the house all day. And I'm saying, 'Are you not going to your mum's today?' you know, 'No, no' he said 'I don't think so' ... and he stayed in for about three days. And so then he must have thought 'Oh she's not doing anything here' and because we were at [estate] then and his mother lived at the other end of town, when he did go I knew he'd be gone at least an hour, to get there. So I phoned the Samaritans and said, 'I have to get out' and she said, 'Right, get some clothes together, what you can, get in a taxi and come to such and such a place'. Oh, but that feeling, going rushing round the house, thinking 'what do I need, what shall I take', and shoving stuff in, I managed to take two suitcases, but the panic, you know, half of you is wanting to remember everything, because you're thinking 'I'm not coming back here, I'm not coming back'* (Christine).

The women and children had to abandon their home, prized possessions, favourite toys and neither had any time to say 'goodbye' to friends or family. The feeling of rushing around the house in a panic is well remembered by Christine above. Most women had already tried unsuccessfully to leave before, staying with family members, and now turned to refuges/shelters, and local authority hostels to make their getaway.

A refuge/shelter or hostel is not home

As found in previous research (Bull, 1993, p. 18) most women fled to a refuge or hostel the last time of leaving having tried unsuccessfully staying with family previously, a few women went to friends' houses and two women were able to stay in their own homes. Moving more than once was the pattern for all the women who fled to a refuge or hostel, which was both disruptive and disturbing for the women and their children.

Women faced difficulties in finding refuge spaces and after this in gaining permanent housing. In general, women were more positive about refuges than other forms of temporary housing, and many comments were made about feeling safe and secure and about the support gained by being with others who were in the same position (which supports findings in other research). The main difficulties encountered were: overcrowding, sharing amenities, poor standards of hygiene, lack of privacy, behaviour of other residents (including children), the lack of provision for women with older male children and the need for staff to be available 24 hours a day (see also Office of the Deputy Prime Minister, 2002, pp. 49–50). The women did not know what to expect on going into a refuge/shelter and they had never lived in a communal way before and so not surprisingly this seemed alien at first, especially having just left their own homes:

> And going into the refuge[1], and got to the refuge aaargh just thought, 'oh god it's horrible' ... and I can remember walking in, there was just kids everywhere and I think I burst into tears, just walking through door. And then they show you to your rooms. It was the noise, as you walked in, it was so noisy... there must have been about 20 [women], because it was full, and there just has to be one woman who has three kids, you know and half a dozen mothers and that's it, there's kids everywhere. You're just sort of shown to your room though and that's it then, there was no support (Christine).

For most women going into a refuge/shelter was viewed as a step down in status, a loss of independence and autonomy. They felt fearful and terrified of taking this step into the unknown and all the time dreading that they might be found by their abuser. When I interviewed Mandy she was staying in bed and breakfast accommodation, considered unsuitable for women leaving abusive relationships, and she explains some of the reasons for this. Mandy had also stayed in various other refuges/shelters some of which she considered excellent and others poor:

Paula: *Can you say a bit about that place [the refuge], your impressions.*

Mandy: *It were a dump, it were loppy [dirty]. Me and kids got a stomach bug after like one day I were out on there and it's like a lot of other places you go to, they show you a room, that's your set of rules and close door on you, so then you might have like just come out after having a good hiding or some mental*

headache and you're stuck in a room ... you're thinking, well
no, I'm going home, I'd sooner have him on me back, at least
it's like me own.

Paula: *It's your own home rather than someone else's?*

Mandy: *Yeah, yeah. I mean a lot of these bed and breakfasts, I mean*
really you're lucky here that they let you go in kitchen, majority
of 'em don't.

Paula: *You've just got to live and eat in one room.*

Mandy: *Well you've got to eat from shop. How can you give your kids*
proper meals? And plus your money's not going to go far when
you go to shop to buy [food]. And you think like chippy [fish
and chip shop], you're talking a fiver, no, it's rubbish.

Paula: *So what about the other places you were in, were any of the*
other refuges any better?

Mandy: *[name of hostel] is brilliant, but that's a council one, that's*
really good, now that is made out for families, you know, that
is a good un they should all be like that ... it's in middle of
fields, they've put swings up, a slide up, a climbing frame for
kids, you've got a laundry room there, a big kitchen, you've all
got your own fridge, your own cooker ... because I've got three
kids, I were in two rooms, so I could have one like a little
sitting room and one were a bedroom. I'd got a table and
chairs in there and two easy chairs.

It is important to stress at this point that the support received by
women on going into shelter does vary depending on whether it is a
Women's Aid refuge or Local Authority hostel, on staffing and resource
levels. For the most part refuges have been run on pitifully small
amounts of money, and volunteer labour, and hence they have not
always been able to provide the level of support needed. Even where
refuges/shelters are well funded, I agree with Somerville who says that
'although they [women's refuges/shelters] can provide the essential
"safe" house, they can rarely restore the wider experience of home
which the women have lost' (1990, p. 535).

Finding security: a more permanent alternative home

Most of the women in this study had to leave their homes and communities to find safety, but as mentioned above, Jill, and also Lucy,
managed to stay in their homes and to have their male partner leave
the family home. Indeed Lucy had never put his name on her Local
Authority tenancy agreement:

> *I mean I've got one advantage like it's my home and his name's not on it at all. So I mean he kept saying to me 'why don't you put my name on rent book?' and everything, but I'd never ever do that, not unless we were going to get married, and then it'd have to go on, but until that day it's my home, mine and me kids, that is it.*

This quote is interesting in that on the one hand Lucy reveals a clear awareness of the advantage and degree of independence she gains through the home belonging to her and the children in keeping his name off the tenancy agreement. Yet, at the same time, we can also see gendered expectations at work in her remark that **if they were married** then **his name would have to be on the tenancy agreement**. Security is not guaranteed, however, by having the woman's name on the tenancy agreement, and it can be used as a means of trying to ensure that a woman does not leave, as Sally found out:

Paula:　*And had you got a house there?*
Sally:　*Yeah, he'd actually signed it over to me to make me stay, you know, so 'you've got some security now, you can't go', but he still managed it!*

Humphreys and Thiara (2002, p. 73) found in their research that 64 per cent of women (most with children) had contact with their local authority housing department; of these 42 per cent were accepted as homeless, 20 per cent were refused and 18 per cent had difficulties in proving they had suffered domestic violence.

After ending the relationship and/or leaving home for the last time

> *I were frightened more than anything, frightened of the future, of being on me own and having four kids and being lonely* (Jill).

Women who have been forced to relocate from several to many miles from their own home and community have particular needs for support in finding their way around a new area and in terms of setting up new homes. All the women had lost a close relationship and the process of getting back on their feet again took time, energy and courage. Leaving a relationship after years of violence, having to flee rapidly and secretly, having to remove their children from their homes, and finally, often after months in a refuge, having to cope with being re-housed in a new community as a single mother/woman was a daunting prospect. Clearly there were emotional difficulties to be grappled with, alongside practical problems.

The first emotion most women felt, however, was a relief to be in their own home again, and out of the refuge, despite all the positive things about refuges, and to have some peace, quiet and hoped-for security. There were two women who described feeling both relief and a sense of freedom at breaking free, which feelings persisted for them – they were just so glad to be out of the relationship and pleased to be able to start again:

> **Paula:** *So how did you see yourself at that point?*
>
> **Janice:** *Free! (laughs) I don't know, like I said I never analysed it, I just felt that once I'd got over the hurt, I just felt free to do what I wanted to do.*

The fear that women felt fell broadly into three main categories – fear of further violence (after being found by their former partner), fear of the future and fears caused by the environment they had been re-housed into. Fear of being found and suffering further violence was expressed by many women; and this fear was both for their own and their children's safety. Such fear was found to be justified where two thirds of the women interviewed experienced continued violence and/or harassment; and many women from the support group told me of similar experiences of violence over the course of the fieldwork.

In my study all the woman were white but two women had children of a different cultural heritage and one woman, Mandy, had to face racism on top of all the other difficulties of leaving:

> **Mandy:** *Well first house they offered me, right ... I went to see it and they told [son's name] to 'fuck off you black bastard' so I phoned [name of housing officer] up I went, 'I'm not taking that, this is, my little boy's been told, you know, fuck off you black bastard'. He went, 'you'll have to take it'. I went, 'I'm not if there's racialism around here' I went, 'I'm not'. He went 'you'll take it', he says 'or we'll throw you off our housing list!' I went 'I am not taking it'. He went 'take it and then sort out the problem when you move in, phone the police', I went 'I'm not', he went 'well either take it or we'll not re-house you at all', so I thought well now! ... I phoned Racial Equalities Board, they put me in touch with top homeless lawyer going,*

> *then somebody from London from CRE got in touch with me,*
> *so there were like loads of them got in touch with North East*
> *Derbyshire Council, that [housing officer] got carpeted, you*
> *know what I mean. He phoned me up, he went, 'erm I've*
> *reconsidered and decided I will offer you somewhere else',*
> *I went, 'that's nice seeing as you know so and so's phoned you*
> *and you've nearly lost your job' (laughs). They offered me a*
> *house a mile down road! A mile down road!*

Paula: *So did you take it then [Mandy]?*

Mandy: *I took it because I did feel pressured by them taking me up to*
> *see it and everything er when health visitor came up to see me*
> *she said, 'you shouldn't have been moved there', she says 'just*
> *across motorway is British National Party's headquarters'!*
> *(laughs) Will you imagine that, that's [name of place] District*
> *Council!*

Carol, who I quoted at the start of this Chapter, had been re-housed into a house that was completely inappropriate for a woman fleeing domestic violence. It was in extremely poor condition, with a garden that was unsafe for children and in a dangerous area. Batsleer et al. (2002, pp. 81–2) found that African and African-Caribbean women reported being given similar houses; as they argue whilst recognising that choices are currently limited with the reduction in social housing stock, nevertheless, inappropriate housing can mean that women go back to the abusive relationship and it is likely they will have to be re-housed again at some later date.

Setting up and furnishing a new home

> *Even though I might be in debt, or whatever, it's me, you know and*
> *I know I'm not being lied to, you're in control of your own situation*
> (Christine).

Leaving the family home and being re-housed raised particularly thorny problems for women to do with money and debt and much of this revolved around the financial costs of establishing a new home for themselves and their children. Apart from the difficulties in securing a suitable new home for themselves and their children, which have been well documented elsewhere (see e.g. Charles, 1994) another major financial issue most women faced, once they moved into their new community, was the costs incurred in setting up a new home (Wilcox, 2000b). Most of the women had been forced to leave all their furniture behind and were faced, therefore, with furnishing a house in its entirety. Many women were too afraid to return to their former homes and of those who did so most found that their furniture was gone or had been 'trashed'. Furnishing a house is a very large financial outlay at the best of times but the women studied had to attempt to do this, after experiencing years of violence and abuse, and on minute incomes and with debt and rent arrears incurred during the violent relationship.

Home alone

None of the women I interviewed had lived on their own before so this was a huge change for them: *'you're on your own and you know you're on your own'* (Jill). However, it was not just the physical and practical challenges posed, although these were difficult, but coming to terms over being without a male partner and the social and economic difference this implied in terms of gendered expectations of male financial support and the socially approved status within the heterosexual family:

> *Just coming to terms with it I think. I think that were main problem. Yeah, I think that were main problem, just coming to terms with it, just getting used to living on me own, because I'd never lived on me own before. I know me son were there, but like **I ain't got a man to support me any more** (Louise, my emphasis).*

Women described having very strong feelings of loneliness, especially for the first six months to a year and cited this as one reason why they and other women were more likely to return to their abusive partners.

> *I were lonely. Because sometimes I can understand why women go back really, because I think if it hadn't been for, with the kids I'd have gone back again, because I were totally lost. I were just totally lost (Betty).*

Women said they often felt very lost and empty at first, which reinforces the finding of Kirkwood's study where the women she researched described an initial feeling of numbness or shock (1993, p. 108). Women described the difficult mix of feelings; of not wanting their violent partner to be there and yet missing him, feelings of emptiness or upset and an inevitable sense of mourning for what has been left behind and the loss of the relationship:

> *For the first year I'd still got this empty feeling inside, and I suppose it were, I were used to living with him and he weren't there no more, even*

though I didn't want him, so maybe that's why I felt empty because he weren't there any more (Louise).

To say I had good friends and good neighbours and a good family, you still feel alone, you've still got to come back here and sit here on your own at night time er and they say loneliness goes after so long and you feel better, you enjoy living on your own, O.K. you enjoy living on your own after a bit, but the loneliness doesn't go away, there's a difference. There's a lot of difference and I say to my boyfriend now when he's on nights, I say 'I hate it' and he'll say, 'Well what did you do before?' and I say, 'I used to smoke!' ... I were on me own for quite a bit, about eight or ten months ... and you do get used to it but you've still got to come home on your own and kids are in bed and it's not a nice feeling (laughs). No, you feel as though nobody cares and things like that (Sally).

Security in the new home?

Most of the women gave mixed responses when asked about how safe they felt having been re-housed or having their male partner move out of the house. Like Christine there was a decided improvement in how safe they felt and yet they still felt nervous; not surprisingly as they had lived for several/many years with feelings of anticipatory anxiety.

Paula:	*Right O.K. Can I just ask you a few bits about how safe you felt, your security? Did you feel safe in that house after you moved out of the refuge?*
Christine:	*Initially, yes, I felt safe but then when my husband was wanting access. At first we arranged to meet somewhere away from the house, but then I, I let him know where I was, for him to come and pick the kids up, yeah, erm and so when access fell apart basically, then I started to worry about him turning up, so I didn't feel safe really ...*
Paula:	*And what about psychologically?*
Christine:	*Erm, I think still quite nervous erm but it was just nothing as compared to when I was in it [the relationship].*

The two women who stayed in their original homes were confronted more regularly with the possibility of seeing their abusive partner but the women who had travelled longer distances were also fearful and this depended very much on the level and range of support responses received from informal supporters and social agencies, and I look at these issues in Chapter 6 and Chapter 7.

Conclusion

Domestic violence provided the context for men to maintain their relationships with home as quite different from those of their wives/partners. Hence, home in this study held significantly different meanings for women and men. Women participants experienced close ties to their homes; homes were places where emotional bonds were formed and a crucial part of this was creating and building a home for their children. As a result I found that for many women feelings of safety and security were closely tied to 'home'. This did not mean that home was seen as a haven or as static, singular and bounded (Massey, 1994, p. 172). There were important differences in men's and women's experiences of home, teased out in this study, which resulted in differentiated meanings and experiences of home.

The meanings of home for women were complex, tied in with the birth, and memories of, bringing up their children, with creating and making a home, and a sense of attachment to home. These positive meanings were clearly disrupted by the abuse and violence suffered but not totally crushed. In confronting an abusive and violent relationship, women experienced an ongoing consciousness of constraint and threat. There was a sense of endurance, of having to 'put up' with their situation in order to maintain the family relationships, but at the same time women were actively trying a range of strategies to effect change in their male partner and in the relationship as a whole (as seen in the book so far).

It may be helpful to try and distinguish which meanings of home were disrupted by violence and which meanings women were able to maintain. To do this I have adapted Kenyon's (1999) findings on the meanings of home for young people (see Table 4.1). I stress that these are my interpretations and it would be necessary in future research to ask women to what extent this matches their perceptions.

As we can see from Table 4.1 there are meanings of 'home' which women could maintain even in an abusive relationship. Women were able, for instance, to hold onto a sense of belonging in a home where significant others were located (particularly their children) and of developing a personalised space containing meaningful possessions. Aspects of home most disrupted for women by violence were the thoughts of home as supportive and comfortable (although it is impor-

Table 4.1 **Meanings of home for women in abusive relationships**

	Maintained	Disrupted
Personal home	• Home is meaningful • Home is a personalised space • Home is a sense of belonging • Home is memories	• Home is a sense of independence and freedom
Temporal home	• Home has the potential to be familiar and lasting	• Home is stable and permanent
Social home	• Home is made up of significant others • Home is a friendly neighbourhood (?)	• Home is a supportive atmosphere
Physical home	• Home is a single household dwelling • Home is made up of meaningful possessions	• Home is a comfortable environment

Source: Adapted from Kenyon (1999, p. 87)

tant to remember the support that children often gave to women), however, feelings of independence were also threatened, since as we saw in Chapter 1 women's social contacts were severely curtailed. Once women started to think about ending the relationship then thoughts of home as stable and permanent were also threatened. Home as a friendly neighbourhood was something that might or might not be threatened depending on the response women received from neighbours and the wider community (see Chapter 7).

Ending the relationship and, in most cases, leaving home, meant breaking away from the intimate partner as well as the small web of relationships which women had nurtured over several/many years. It was also tied up with women's sense of self and identity and ironically with the loss of security and safety in the home, and also a strong sense of deviating from the norm. Moreover, it meant taking their children away from their father and their own web of friendships. Hence, ending the relationship and/or leaving home was a traumatic decision both to consider and ultimately to carry out. It was only as women's experiences in the home became increasingly dangerous, and threatened their children, that women considered making themselves (and their children) homeless a safer option than staying.

5
Work and Money

I think that was all part of me putting me foot down and saying I'm damned if I'm going to be the one that's got to stay in the house all the time, I need time to myself too ... I want a job, I want to work towards a career and I'm not going to have no bloke stop me ... I mean it's erm you just like, you're rebelling all the time, you're rebelling all the time (Janice).

Introduction

The potential negative impact of domestic violence on women's financial and employment prospects seem to have been more readily recognised as a serious problem in developing countries. Uganda is one such example where women participating in poverty alleviation programmes identified gender-based violence as one of the major contributing factors to their poverty. Projects such as the Mifumi[1] Domestic Violence Intervention Project was set up with two aims: to empower women economically and to protect women from male violence. There is much we can learn in the west by looking at the links between domestic violence and women's poverty and these links are now starting to be researched (see for example Kirkwood, 1993; Tolman and Raphael, 2000; Wilcox, 2000b; Humphreys and Thiara, 2002; Lyon, 2002; Meisel et al., 2003).[2] Studies that have investigated the prevalence of domestic violence have found that over half of the women receiving welfare had suffered physical abuse. Derr and Taylor's (2004) recent study of 280 women who were long-term welfare recipients found that 81 per cent lived in a physically violent relationship as an adult.[3] Historically, however, there has been relatively little research on the relationship between lone motherhood, domestic violence and

109

poverty or the relationship between women's employment and domestic violence. In the UK research on lone parents suggests abuse or violence may be a significant factor in marital breakdown; Bradshaw and Millar (1991) report 13–20 per cent of lone parents; Ford et al. (1995) report 40 per cent of lone parents; but the potential impact of such violence on employment and living standards has scarcely been addressed (Wilcox, 2000b). In the US there has been some attention to the impact of domestic violence on women's employment (see Shepard and Pence, 1988; Murphy, 1993; Lloyd, 1997) but in the UK research on women's employment often overlooks domestic violence as a factor; Kingsmill's review *'Women's employment and pay'* (2003) is a recent example. At the same time, studies on domestic violence have tended not to focus on structural economic factors; the government strategy document *'Domestic violence: a national report'* (Home Office, 2005) for instance does not address policy on women's employment or finances.

Awareness of women who deserve individualised attention because of their difficult circumstances has come recently from the US and Australia mainly in relation to New Deal and Welfare to Work programmes where it was found that women's mental and/or physical health problems may be linked to domestic abuse. In Australia, for example, the Personal Support Programme identifies domestic violence as one of several 'difficult circumstances' which merit individualised attention as a significant barrier to participation in employment (www.workplace.gov.au). Research in the US on the Temporary Aid to Needy Families Program (TANF) revealed that when women experience domestic violence this may stop them working altogether or women risk continued abuse if they continue to work (Raphael and Tolman, 1997; Tolman, 1999; Tolman and Raphael, 2000). In 1996, Congress adopted an amendment to the Personal Responsibility and Work Opportunity and Reconciliation Act, the Family Violence Option (FVO), which recognised that people fleeing domestic violence would need more flexibility in making the transition to work than allowed for under the welfare guidelines, which require most recipients to work. The FVO allows States to temporarily waive work requirements and increase services to families facing domestic violence. According to the Family Violence Prevention Fund of San Francisco, 50 to 60 per cent of adult heads of families receiving welfare (90 per cent of whom are female) have suffered domestic violence at some point in their adult lives, compared with 22 per cent of the general population[4] (Tjaden and Thoennes, 1998).

Literature on the economic aspects of domestic violence is, therefore, at an early stage of development and addresses two main areas: (1) the potential disruption of women's patterns of employment and (2) the possibility of financial impoverishment. The latter can be further divided into (a) poverty associated with the onset of domestic violence; (b) poverty associated with leaving a violent relationship and (c) poverty as a 'risk marker' for 'domestic violence' (a more recent development). The majority of studies draw on quantitative data and at present there is a paucity of qualitative research on the lived, day-to-day material realities of poverty which may be associated with domestic violence (during and after leaving the relationship).

In this chapter I continue to analyse the gendered aspects of women's economic situation and how this intersects with domestic violence. As the group of women studied were living in impoverished circumstances during the abusive relationship this raises the issue of poverty in an especially stark way and the extent to which poverty is an exacerbating factor in provoking abuse, as well as it being an outcome of the abuse is also an issue to be considered. I will address this issue by looking at the following key areas: domestic violence and women's employment patterns and domestic violence and poverty. This will involve an examination of debt during the relationship, the legacy of debt after leaving, extra expenses after leaving, income levels, setting up and maintaining a new home and finally social exclusion.

Women's employment patterns

It is in the area of paid employment that significant shifts in the gender order have taken place. Women are increasingly being employed in the public sector, are increasingly represented in government and are increasingly visible in the visual media. These transitions, happening in many industrialised countries, are seen by Walby (2002) as a movement from a domestic to a public 'gender regime' with varying outcomes in terms of gender in/equality.

In the UK, for example, the wages gap between women and men has been steadily reducing for those in full-time work, however, the gap between women and men remains large for those in part-time work, and women part-time workers make up 44 per cent of all employees (Office for National Statistics Labour Force Survey, 2004). In terms of income, for couples with children, women's median total weekly income from 1996 to 2002 was £146 whereas for men it was £410[5] (Women and Equality Unit, 2003). The presence of young children under school age reduces women's participation in employment, especially for women in a lower social class (Walby, 2002, p. 22) and whilst there have been improvements in registered childcare outside the home, in 2002 there were still 4.5 children for each place in these types of provision.[6] Women, therefore, continue to face structural disadvantages in the labour market; in particular those women in a lower social class and/or with few or no qualifications.

The latter point applies to the women participants in this study who had left school at the age of either 15 or 16-years-old having relatively limited academic qualifications and skill sets. All except Lucy had employment prior to the abusive relationship and five women worked during the relationship: Catherine was a cleaner, *I had a job on the side, a cleaner, get me out of the house at night time,* Rachel had worked in a factory and ran an Avon agency during the relationship, Jill had been an auxiliary nurse before the relationship and was now a dinner lady, Louise, Sally and Christine worked in a factory, Mandy had been an auxiliary nurse and a clerk, Betty had worked as a chambermaid and Janice worked in a bar during the relationship.

All these jobs reflect both gendered and classed patterns of work in that, with the exception of factory work, they are mostly seen as 'female' jobs, and they are part-time and low paid; as the Women and Work Commission's interim report points out, 'Women working part time tend to be less well educated, are more likely to be married and have young children, and are more likely to work in a narrow range of occupations' (2005, p. 7). Whilst conscious of the changes in terms of women's roles and employment in society these women were located in social contexts where they were least likely to benefit from them, and I now turn to look at how domestic violence impacted on their employment.

Domestic violence and women's employment patterns

In many cases abusive actions by male partners can make it impossible for women to work at all. During the relationship, as found in previous research, about half of the women participants were not employed in the labour market, but were working unpaid at home and looking after the children (Lloyd, 1997). In my study Janice, Jill, Louise, Catherine and Rachel continued with part-time paid work despite the difficulties encountered; the remaining women gave up their jobs (Lucy never worked). Friedman and Couper (1987, cited in Lloyd, 1997) found that 56 per cent of the women they interviewed had lost at least one job due to domestic violence. Lloyd (1997) found that low income women who experienced domestic violence were more likely to have experienced unemployment and to have had more job changes. The British Crime Survey (BCS) 2001 found that 'among employed women who suffered domestic violence in the last year, two per cent lost their jobs' (Walby and Allen, 2004, p. viii). As these statistics and my study reveal domestic violence does not prevent employment for all women, some manage to continue to work although finding it a constant struggle (Raphael, 2000, cited in Tolman and Raphael, 2000).

Women who are physically assaulted feel ashamed to go into work when and if bruises, or other physical injuries, are visible to work colleagues. At the same time domestic violence increases poor health (physically and emotionally)[7] and women may turn to (or be prescribed) drugs[8] to cope, all of which makes it difficult for them to maintain consistent attendance and timekeeping at work. Louise talked about how one physical assault in the evening had left visible results in the form of bruises on her face and she had felt too ashamed to let her co-workers see this: *I didn't go to work for a week after that erm because I didn't want people to see what I'd got* [bruises] (Louise). Catherine was threatened by her ex-partner on her way out to work and found that although it did not stop her going to work she was unable to concentrate on what she was doing: *before I was going to work, he just walked up to me, got his hands round me throat and [threatened her] so I went to work, I couldn't do nowt, me mind wouldn't focus.*

Friedman and Couper (1987, cited in Lloyd, 1997) found that 54 per cent of women reported missing an average of 3 days of work per month due to domestic violence; whilst Shepard and Pence (1988) found that 58 per cent of women they surveyed in refuges/shelters who had been working during their violent relationship said that their work had been disrupted by absenteeism and lateness. The BCS 2001 found that 'among employed women who suffered domestic violence in the last year, 21 per cent took time off work ...' (Walby and Allen, 2004, p. viii).

There are many different ways in which partners interfere with work, as Raphael (2000) found: 'destruction of homework assignments, keeping women up all night with arguments before key tests or job interviews, turning off alarm clocks, destroying clothing, inflicting visible facial injuries before job interviews, deliberately disabling the family car, threatening to kidnap children from child care centres, failing to show up as promised for child care or transportation, and in-person harassment on the job' (cited in Tolman and Raphael, 2000, p. 664). Most of these were also reported in this study by women who trying to hold down a job found that their partners attempted to disrupt their work. When Jill became an unpaid worker at a local community centre she used to worry about the harassment she would get on her return home:

> *I used to have a lot to do with [community centre] and I used to do a lot of voluntary work, so I got me friends through working down there, which I enjoyed, but he tried to put a stop to that ... I used to walk out thinking 'oh God, what am I going to face when I come back' you know, because he always used to play hell when I used to come back* (Jill).

Jill's husband behaved in this way whenever she attempted to have a measure of independent life away from the family; her use of the expression 'play hell', as if to describe a naughty child, is misleading, however, as this abuse affected her physical health to the extent that she was prescribed tranquillisers for depression (see Chapter 2 on women's conceptualisation of male partners as children). Janice managed to hold down a paid job working in a bar, but as quoted at the beginning of this chapter, she had to screw her courage to the limit in order to keep her job as her husband attempted to disrupt her work; for instance by constantly turning up at the premises, or as in this quote by mistreating the children and thus undermining her confidence that they were safe with him:

> *I'd get ready to go to work and he'd purposely upset 'em [children] before I went to work. I'd be standing at work thinking, shall I phone up or shan't I? I hope them kids are alright. It used to worry me, I knew, I mean he'd already had a go at our [son] before* (Janice).

The harassment at work combined with worry over the children made it extremely difficult for Janice to remain in employment and also clearly made it hard for her to focus on her work. As seen in Chapter 3 children may be used by abusive husbands/partners as a means of control and this applies as much if not more to women who attempt to carve independent work lives for themselves as to women who remain at home.

Women participants referred mockingly to their pitiful wage levels as failing to compensate for the work they put into their jobs and moreover referred to the disparagement they suffered at times for being women. Jill, who worked as a dinner lady, for instance refers to the sexist comments and behaviour of some young male pupils. She was so offended by their personal and misogynist nature that she did not wish to repeat the comments in the interview:

Jill: *Last year I had this certain boy and he was really vulgar to me, he were, what he could do with me, I can't, you know, say it, so I reported him to [name of headmaster] and er he had him in office ...*

Paula: *Do you feel you have to put up with a lot?*

Jill: *Yeah, we do put up wi' a lot, you want to talk to all blinking lasses down there to be honest, it's horrendous, and for £15 a week, it's not worth it, but £15 a week's better than a smack in't nose (laughs)!*

Paid work for women can be imbued with gendered and sexualised meanings in this way, as others have pointed out (see for example Adkins, 1995) as well as having structural aspects.

Despite all these drawbacks, when interviewed most of the women said they would like to be working; only one woman said she would not be able to work due to caring for her disabled son; leaving just one woman who said she did not want to work at present. This reflects the findings in the 1991 DSS/PSI survey where 'most of the out of work lone parents said they wanted a job one day' (Ford et al., 1995, p. 10) although there needs to be recognition that some lone parents do not wish to work, particularly in the early years of a child's life (Bell et al., 2005, p. 8).

So the desire to work needs to be set against women's expressed desires to mother their children well, as well as the provision of an appropriate range of childcare options. Despite improvements in this latter area much more needs to be done as seen above (Ofsted, 2003). Moreover, as Yeandle et al. found in their study on living in poverty, mothers said that the 'very limited opportunities they could see in low-paid, low-status work would exacerbate the strains already in their lives. Their main concerns were the need for low cost and available childcare which would improve their access to employment and training alike' (2003, p. 26).

I now turn to look at women's financial arrangements more broadly both during and as a result of leaving the violent relationship, which in this study revolved around the level of poverty women struggled with.

Domestic violence and poverty

Walby and Allen argue that the nature of the links between poverty and the risk of interpersonal violence is unclear and they say; 'it may be that poverty is associated with the onset of domestic violence, or it may be that in fleeing domestic violence women are reduced to poverty' (2004, p. ix). In my study, as we will see, both of these aspects were found to be relevant and poverty also precipitated domestic abuse.

Living in impoverished, resource-poor communities has recently been identified as a risk marker[9] for domestic violence (see e.g. Hotaling and Sugarman, 1990; Walby and Myhill, 2000; Walby and Allen, 2004). Walby and Myhill (2000) found that 'people' living in financially deprived households are more likely to suffer domestic violence (although as they say this does not mean that it does not occur in better off households); 'In the previous year women in households with an income of less than £10,000 were 3.5 times more likely to suffer domestic violence than those living in households with an income of over £20,000, while men were 1.5 times more likely' (Walby and Allen, 2004, p. ix).[10] These statistics need to be treated with caution, however, for a number of reasons. Firstly, the emphasis in the criminal justice system on physical assaults hides a whole range of other controlling behaviours which are found in domestic abuse and which are less likely to be recorded by any agency. Secondly, this finding may be an artefact of increased police presence in certain areas and/or of patterns of reporting of domestic violence. It may be that women in middle class areas are less likely to report domestic violence to the police and are more likely to draw on other resources for support. At present, therefore, it is unwise to state categorically that this is a 'real' difference in terms of the experience of domestic abuse (although it is being accepted as such in some quarters).

Finances during the relationship

The experience of the women participants was that the abuse they experienced impinged on their financial arrangements in multiple ways. It was the women's role to manage the household budget in this study, limited as it was, and this was often a constant struggle. Jill made this point when I asked her who looked after the finances during the relationship:

> *Me, because he's (pause) he likes spending money basically, and we had a lot of rows about that, because he, you know, as soon as he gets his*

wages, it's straight down to electrical shop and all these gadgets, yeah, exactly, so I used to have the money and er I used to budget. Say he got paid on Friday I used to budget on Thursday night and then if I'd got any money then fair enough, but I used to make sure that I got what I wanted for me. I mean when we were married we went without a lot of stuff (Jill).

This finding chimes with Yeandle et al. (2003, p. 7) who describe how one woman accompanied her husband to a cash point machine at 5 a.m. every Friday morning (the earliest time he could draw his wages) to ensure she had adequate housekeeping money. The major problem for most of the women in this study, however, was that they were not always able to keep control of the budget due to the actions of their male partners. Most of the women experienced difficulties in getting their partners/husbands to give them housekeeping money in the first place:

Sometimes he used to take money off me. He wouldn't pay nowt, no bills or nothing. He wouldn't even pay the rent. I was worried all the time. It were making me a bag of nerves. I was going to his mother's like this, shaking, because sometimes he used to fist me at his mother's, chase me round at his mother's [in order to get money] (Rachel).

Women explained how even when they had the housekeeping money it still proved difficult to organise the household budget because of the actions of their partners. For example one of the problems mentioned by a majority of women was that their former partners would often run out of spending money and come back to the women for more, often provoking further abuse. This was the case for most of the women here and is an example of how poverty may exacerbate (but does not cause) abuse as if there was adequate money available for the male partner, as well as the family, then at least this would be one less area where negative conflict can arise:

Well, he wasn't working, so it was benefit, unemployment or income support I can't remember ... Theoretically it seemed O.K. because he'd give me the money, because I did the shopping and everything, and paid the bills. But he'd want some money for whatever, spending money. So he'd have, I don't know, a few quid [Pounds] a week. But then it'd always be, he'd always be wanting more. And you'd say 'Well, no, I can't because this is the money for the gas' or 'this is the money for the electric', or whatever. So he'd just take it ... It wasn't just a one-off, it happened quite often (Christine).

Like Christine, women explained that previous experiences of their partner's controlling behaviours (including the ever-present threat of violence) made it difficult to refuse to hand over money which had been budgeted for food or household items for fear of provoking further abuse/violence. Occasionally women found ways to avoid this but only by being devious with their partners and hiding money, as Jill did for instance:

> ...*when we were married I hid it [money] (laughs) I know I shouldn't have done but ... I'm not saying I was skint all the time, I've always had, I always like had a bit in the bank ...* (Jill).

For most women, however, the outcome of their lack of control over the family finances was an accumulation of debt:

> ... *It was a gradual process really because, you know, bits would just start going missing, of money, and then it would get worse. And when it came to his paying fines and stuff, he always had a fine for whatever, I did, yes, I did get into debt. Because I can remember, was it the bailiffs came round, or someone came round, and said, 'if you don't pay this then he's going to be in prison' sort of thing. And so you just find the money, you know, from somewhere, either borrow it, or whatever, so yeah you would get into debt in the end* (Christine).

In the lives of people in poverty debt is a constant presence as a 'mundane and chronic problem' (Yeandle et al., 2003, p. 8) but in this study women had to deal with their partner's abuse as well as trying to pay the bills and cope with more serious outcomes of debt, such as bailiffs (above) and court cases. In order to survive women said they had no choice but to frequently borrow small amounts of money in order to pay essential bills, such as gas and electricity, to buy food for the children and other necessities. A strong theme in my data is that these loans/gifts were borrowed/given mainly from/by female relatives and occasionally female neighbours would help out too (see Chapter 6 for detail on female support networks).

> *His main problem was if he got any dole money he never used to give me any. Because like he used to get his money in same dole cheque and then he used to go and put it in bandits [gaming machines]. And I used to have to run over to me grandma's and get some food money for the kids. She used to fill a trolley full up and give me some money and all so I could feed kids* (Rachel).

Both the qualitative and quantitative data reveal that one of the major problems for all women studied was the depth of material poverty they had to endure.

Finances after leaving the relationship

All the participants became lone mothers once they left their abusive relationship and all were on welfare benefits, mainly Income Support.[11] In situations where women have fled domestic violence it is very unlikely that such women will receive any maintenance from former partners. Indeed the fear of violence is considered 'good cause' for women not to have to name the father of their child/ren by the Child Support Agency (see e.g. White and Perkins, 1998). Half of the women had taken a drop in income on leaving, but most said they felt they had more in the sense that they had more control over it. This echoes the finding in Rose (1978) that women entering refuges initially feel 'richer' on welfare benefits in comparison to the money they had to manage on when married or in a partnership. It is important to stress nevertheless that all the women said they were almost always short of money and often in debt (see 'Debt' below). They managed to cope by budgeting carefully and with the help of small gifts and loans, *usually* from the family, just as they had during the relationship only now they no longer had to deal with the abuse (see Chapter 6).

> *It's better now because you're in charge of your own money so you decide, even though you've not got enough money, you've never got enough money, but at the end of the day it's up to you, you know, and whereas you know you don't have to think about him, giving him the money, and he used to take the money as well, he used to just take it out of me purse, yeah, for the drink* (Christine).

> *Financially, I get more what I want and I've still got a bit of money in the bank, but ... I mean I could do with more, everybody could do with more* (Jill).

Since their income level had been limited during the violent relationship and remained low after leaving, the majority of the women had no savings at all when they left and none at all at the time of the interview. A minority had none when they left but a very small amount when interviewed. The women in this study, therefore, had no financial resources to fall back on in case of a large expense or emergency. Women often took refuge in humour and laughed about the occasions when they got so sick of this effort that they blew some money on a 'luxury' item; one woman bought herself a new dress and on arriving at the support group, pointed to the dress announcing *'this is my gas bill!'*

All the women talked about the enormous amount of energy and effort it took to budget every penny, to try and pay off previous debts, such as rent arrears, and to cope with the extra expenses incurred through leaving, such as setting up and maintaining a new home, and so I will look at these aspects next.

Debt after leaving

In my study all of the women experienced debt, and three quarters of them started their new lives in severe debt, which I defined as greater than £700, seven times their weekly income in 1995 (Wilcox, 2000b, p. 179). Humphreys and Thiara (2002, p. 102) found that financial hardship was the biggest difficulty for women in the first six months after leaving (58 per cent). Kirkwood, too, says that '...nearly all the British women and one-half of the US women who had dependent children identified financial hardship as one of the major long term stresses faced after leaving their partners' (Kirkwood, 1993, p. 99). As Marsh says of lone parents, 'They are prone to hardship and form the largest group in Britain among people of working age who live on household incomes below half the national average' (2001, p. 11). Minoritised women, disabled women and women who are asylum seekers experience financial problems leaving violence in especially harsh ways (Humphreys and Thiara, 2002, p. 103).

A typical case from this study is a woman who finally left her abusive husband, after many previous attempts, and who had outstanding telephone, gas bills and catalogue debts in her name as well as being made responsible for rent arrears. Consequently, when she wanted to install a telephone in her new home, she discovered herself to be on a bad debtor list, and was refused a telephone unless she placed a large deposit with British Telecom of £100. She also found that it was impossible to either open a bank account or to obtain credit. The only way she was able to get a telephone (an essential security item for her) was by persuading her mother to have it in her name and then pay her mother. This woman had been paying off her debts regularly every week in small amounts out of her welfare benefit but three years after leaving the violent relationship she still had debts of over £500; £300 owed to a gas company and a £70 council/local tax debt, both incurred during the time with her violent partner and £175 rent arrears incurred whilst she was in a local Women's Aid refuge.

Rent arrears

Local Authority Housing Departments have the option of dealing with rent arrears arising from relationship breakdown in a number of ways depending on both their policy approach and the type of tenancy involved. Where there is a joint tenancy, which was the case for the majority of women in this study, they could either divide arrears equally between partners, or collect the full amount from the 'remaining' partner or apportion arrears according to financial circumstances or ability to pay. With a sole tenancy in the name of the person leaving then that person is legally responsible for the debt.

The finding of this study chimed with Department of the Environment research which found that with joint tenancies 'where the other partner was not traceable the full arrears were collected from the remaining partner, often the woman with the dependent children ... [this was] often felt to result in women bearing the burden of debts they had no control over in the relationship' (Bull, 1993, p. 42). This was the most common occurrence for women in this study too, and in a minority of cases there were also varying degrees of prohibition on re-housing or transfer of tenancy where there were outstanding rent arrears, as this woman's case reveals:

> I mean I'd been in battered wives [refuge/shelter] altogether nine months, and he hadn't paid no rent, so me rent arrears were nearly £1,000. I went down and they said that I'd got seven days to pay this else they were evicting me. I went down to the Social. Social said 'You can't expect us to pay for two places at one time, battered wives and your house', and I just didn't know which way to turn. Anyway me dad sold all his insurance policies and everything and he went down and paid it off. He went down and paid all lot off so I could stop in house (Betty).

As seen in the above case, existing household debts were frequently compounded as a result of leaving the violent relationship through the incurrence of rent arrears for the period of time spent in refuges and hostels. Betty thought she would have been evicted from her house if her father had not cashed in his insurance policies to pay 'her' debt thus putting himself and his wife in a financially precarious position.

Another woman had rent arrears of just under £1,000 and this bill was forwarded to her as she moved from a refuge in Wales to another refuge in a Northern city. Her financial position was such that she was unable to pay it. Yet another woman had fled violence from one Northern city to a neighbouring town where her violent ex-partner had found her. She therefore decided to try and get her former home back in the city and was told that she owed £390 in rent arrears. The only way she could pay this was by borrowing from her mother; *I mean I ended up being in debt to me mother for about £500 by the time I'd finished paying for the move.*

In this study two-thirds of the women participants were bearing the brunt of rent arrears incurred whilst fleeing violence. Their ex-partners meanwhile were untraceable, having possibly also left the former family house to stay with friends or relatives. The women obviously had no choice but to find alternative housing for themselves and their children, and it was at this point that their former Local Authority was able to trace them and charged them with the outstanding rent due on their former homes. This practice of some local authority housing departments penalised women leaving violent relationships and further undermined their ability to build violence-free lives for themselves and their children. To the women in this study it felt as though they were being penalised for their partner's violence. This is one example of where the implementation of seemingly gender neutral policy has differently gendered impacts; in this case impacting negatively on women leaving domestic abuse.

Expenses incurred through leaving

When women left and had overcome the first hurdle of getting themselves a new home, or in rare cases getting the abuser to move out,[12] they were still faced with many organisational problems. Even in cases where their former partners had done little if anything to help, women said there was a qualitative difference in the realisation that there was now no-one at all to turn to in the home, from now on they had sole responsibility for everything. For those women who had, in effect, been forced to migrate to a different part of the country there was the additional stress of having to find their way around a new city and to adapt to a new cultural environment.

At this stage women found that they had to spend a lot of their time dealing with social agencies. Some of them had support in dealing with housing agencies at the refuge/hostel, but there was still much more to be sorted out; the legal aspects of the separation from the violent partner for example, such things as injunctions, divorce proceedings, custody proceedings, contact arrangements and the like. Also their children's education had to be dealt with; getting children settled into new schools, and all this entailed (e.g. talking to teachers about the violence and its impact on the children, whether specific safety precautions were necessary and so on) and dealing with essential amenities (water, gas and electricity). There were also health issues (theirs and the children's) resulting from the years of violence and abuse which involved frequent visits to, and communications with, a range of social agencies all of which resulted in large increases in women's expenditure:

> *Yeah, and you've got to remember: keep papers, do this, phone this, and your bills! Your phone bills go up and bus fares! I know it sounds stupid but your bus fares go up, and when you're a single mum you can't afford things like that. And having to go to court, and getting someone to look after your kids, all that! It's probably frightening someone into staying now isn't it!* (Sally)

Dealing with agencies at this point in time was a difficult task for women whose self confidence and self esteem had been damaged by years of abuse. Women, understandably, often felt vulnerable and under threat of (and experienced) further violence at this time. Women were not always able to 'fight their own cause' as effectively as they would have done under normal circumstances, and consequently there was a real need for emotional, practical and importantly financial support. As one woman said about this time: *[it was] another part of all the real hassle you have to go through! It's not just over when you get them out of your life! No, it isn't, No!* The extra costs incurred and the stress of reorganising their lives applied to all the woman studied, with the exception of two women who managed to stay in their own homes and got their ex-partners to leave the house. This was achieved with the support of friends, colleagues and outside agencies but brought its own problems (see Chapter 7).

Much expense was incurred, for example, on legal aspects of the separation. Even if women were entitled to legal aid, which was the case for all of the women in this study, numerous visits to solicitors' offices meant increased bus fares and/or taxi fares. It is important to bear in mind the physical and mental health of women is likely to be fragile and fear of further violence high. Women often said they had taken taxis to different agencies, through fear of further violence and through health problems. Women also found it essential to phone their solicitor fairly frequently with obvious increased costs. The majority of women said that their bus fares had doubled over this period, as had the telephone bills (for women who had a telephone).

Another outcome of having to flee the family home was that many women did not have with them all their relevant documents, such as birth and marriage certificates. This in itself incurred extra expense in having to get copies made. If this is then compounded by inefficiency on the part of a professional member of staff, possibly even further expense, as one woman explained:

> *He wanted a divorce from me, I wanted the divorce, but I thought I'd let him go through it you know, so they gave my marriage certificate to his solicitor and now they can't get it back because it's into [place name] Court or something, and they expect me to buy another marriage certificate. I know it sounds stupid but £5 or £6 is a lot of money to me ... I've paid for one, I paid for that one and they gave it to his solicitor, I can't go round keep getting £5 for a marriage certificate every time and I refused to do it* (Sally).

Costs were obviously increased also by the number of children in the family. Most could not afford the cost of employing a childminder to look after their children whilst making essential visits, but had extra bus fares to pay instead. Sorting out all the many issues to do with the separation and the violent ex-partner's contact with the children was distressing and often the site of continued abuse; at the same time there were many other practical issues to organise. For the women studied this had to be survived with most support coming from family and friends; there was a distinct lack of agency support relating to employment and financial issues (see Chapter 7).

Setting up and maintaining a new home

Apart from the difficulties in securing a suitable new home for themselves and their children, which have been well documented elsewhere (see for example Charles, 1994 and Chapter 4) another major financial issue most women faced, once they moved into their new community, was the cost incurred in setting up a new home. Most of the women had been forced to leave all their furniture behind and were faced, therefore, with furnishing a house in its entirety. Many women were too afraid to return to their former homes and of those who did so most found that their furniture was gone or had been 'trashed':

> *Because he drank a lot, he was probably selling stuff for money for the drink, so there was very little left in the house ... I think I got [son's] bed and [daughter's] cot, but t.v. and video had gone as well, so he'd obvi-*

ously sold those, yeah, stuff he could get money for were gone, so it was just what bits you could get together from family really (Christine).

Furnishing a house was a very large financial outlay and the women who contributed to this study had to attempt to do this, after fleeing years of violence and abuse, and on an income of less than £100 per week. In this study the finding was that the majority of women were reliant on charities or car boot sales, on borrowing or being given items by family, friends and/or neighbours, as exemplified by Sally:

If I can take you round my room and tell you what I paid for what. The table £2, next door neighbour's carpet, you know I've had this carpet nearly two and a half year now, settee somebody gave me. That over there [chair] next door neighbour gave me; me mum bought me dogs [china]. You know everything belonged to somebody else beforehand, yeah. Even me video were me boyfriend's. Just everything you know, only little things, like I bought the plant, and that ornament there, others I bought for £1 and pictures, you know things like that. It's hard to get a room together …When I moved in here really all I'd brought were carpets and curtains, that were it you know.

As seen here most charities were not able to provide a whole house full of furniture so women tended to have to get bits from here, there and everywhere. The women who had the most difficulty in setting up a new home were, not surprisingly, those who had moved considerable distances away from their hometowns who were less able to rely on the help of family and friends and were consequently more dependent on charities. Catherine, who had moved the furthest from her home and community, put it like this:

*Well, St Vincent de Paul I got some beds from them, yeah I got some beds from there. Cooker from St Vincent de Paul which is on its last legs, going out! I never had no three piece suite when I moved in here. I got that and that sideboard. And then when they came to deliver this stuff they had a settee on it [van] and erm it was a brown leather **thing**, and I said 'Oh I'll have that if it's nobody's, and so I had that, and then it was ripped and all that lot. And then we went to Nomad [homeless charity] and there was a green **thing** and then [woman from the support group] said 'Me daughter's got this one if you want it' (her emphases).*

The mixture of shame and disgust in the woman's voice as she talked about her furniture as 'a green thing' or 'a brown thing' was clear and she evidently felt (as others did) very humiliated by the experience. Virtually everything she had was from a charity, and it was, as she said, difficult to ask any friends back to the house because she felt ashamed of the shabbiness of both the house and furniture.

By the time I interviewed this woman she had had her telephone cut off as she had been unable to pay the 'phone bill. In this study a third of the women were unable to afford a telephone due to the extent of their poverty and were therefore in a more vulnerable and fearful situation than those women with a telephone. A telephone was a vital item of security hardware for women who left violent relationships since it linked them with their informal support network and, as importantly, with the emergency services. (In this study one third of the women experienced continued violence and harassment after leaving their violent relationship).

House maintenance costs were a further financial headache. More often than not the house women moved into needed a good deal of work on it in terms of both repairs and decoration. This aspect of setting up and maintaining a new home was yet another expense that women had difficulty coping with. Some women also had additional one-off expenses to do with the new house in addition to repairs and decorating costs. One woman, for example, had a major expense which she had to save for on moving into her new house. This was due to the fact that the kitchen lacked a gas pipe for a gas cooker. The Housing Department insisted that there was a gas pipe installed and refused to come out to check this and, subsequently, to pay for it:

> So I had to pay £40 to have the Gas Board to come out and put a pipe in. He said 'There isn't one here, there's no connection for no cooker or nothing'. Yeah. I couldn't cook. I couldn't cook for about a month, I had to borrow someone's deep fat fryer from the hostel and was living on chips and sausages all the time. Yes, because it was going to cost me £40 to have it [gas pipe] done ... (Catherine).

This was a large expense for a single mother on welfare benefit and this incident obviously put yet further strain on her finances, and on her own and her children's health.

Social exclusion

Poverty and debt were major contributory factors in constructing women who left domestic violence as a particularly social excluded group. The depth of poverty experienced prevented one third of the women from being connected to the telephone network, which would have helped them obtain a degree of support and security (Wilcox, 2000b). Some of the women were too embarrassed to invite others back to their new home because of the shabbiness of their home and its furnishings. Women were rarely able to afford to go out socially due to the expense, not only of the evening's entertainment, but also of childcare. During the day time women's social lives tended to be restricted to the house, taking children to school and back, and the shops. At night women said they felt like prisoners in their own homes; *'after the children are in bed it's just you and the telly'* and holidays were an impossibility (unless paid for by someone else, such as a relative). A few women took advantage of adult education classes and community groups based at the local adult education centre where a crèche was provided (for a very small charge) but even so as one woman said to me, *You don't always want to be doing something educational you just want to enjoy yourself from time to time.* There was a dearth of work in the area and with children to care for these women could not afford to travel far afield, and the work that was available was poorly paid.

A lack of economic resources was the situation all the women in this study found themselves in regardless of whether they did paid work or not, both during and after leaving the abusive relationship. This is even more the case for women and children who are ineligible for public income, such as female refugees or asylum seekers. A survey entitled *'Trapped in violence'* (2000) from Immigrant Women's Speakout Association Domestic Violence Team (New South Wales, Australia) for example, found that such women often did not have access to income support, others were faced with threats of deportation and in the face of such threats many had returned to their abusing partners due to the lack of financial assistance. The lack of economic resources made it harder for them to leave their violent partner (Walby and Myhill, 2000) but all did eventually leave with support from others (see Chapter 7).

Conclusion

It seems clear from the evidence in this study that domestic violence impacts both directly and indirectly on women's pattern of employment and their financial situations contributing both to the impoverishment of women and of the family. In the present study women's ability to participate in paid and unpaid work outside the home was made deeply problematic by male partners' actions in disrupting their efforts to do so. In the US there is increasing attention to the impact of domestic violence on women's employment but in the UK this has yet to be fully recognised.

In relation to women in poverty, and particularly those on welfare benefits, US research shows the prevalence of domestic violence to be higher amongst female welfare recipients than the general population. In the UK one study found that women in poverty were over three times more likely to suffer domestic violence than those living in wealthier households (Walby and Allen, 2004, p. ix). However, as noted earlier these statistics need to be treated with caution, since differences may be (at least partially) a factor of patterns of reporting.

Much greater recognition and research is needed on the links between domestic violence and employment and between domestic violence and poverty. Important too is the need for further qualitative research on the lived, day-to-day material realities of poverty associated with domestic violence (during and after ending a relationship). This study found women experienced severe levels of financial hardship during the violent relationship, and this was exacerbated by the particular constellation of issues they faced having left. This involved having to establish a new home (for the majority), increased travel costs, communication costs, legal fees and other expenses. During the relationship poverty exacerbated abusive practices from male partners. The advantage of taking an holistic, gendered approach to the study of domestic violence is that it clarifies how much more significant than being in poverty were the roles played by the gender order, gendered regimes and individual gendered interactions in contexts of domestic violence, seen throughout this book.

The gender regime of employment, for example, still reproduces differently gendered outcomes for men and women; women continue to face structural disadvantages in the labour market and particularly women in a lower social class and/or with few or no qualifications, as the women participants. 'Gender-neutral' policies can generate gendered outcomes, as for example the housing policy on reclaiming housing debt which resulted in women who had fled domestic violence facing large rent arrears incurred during the violent relationship and whilst they were temporarily housed in refuges/shelters.

Again, however, it is necessary and important to stress women's agency; the resourcefulness of women in managing the household finances, of dealing with debt (in and out of the relationship) and the significant role played by the wider supportive networks of female relatives and friends. These women provided gifts, money, loans, help with bills, food and so on, all of which played a huge part in enabling these women to survive in these difficult circumstances of abuse and poverty (see Chapter 7). These supportive responses were essential for women in surviving domestic violence.

6
Family and Friends

> *It's me mother and me nanan [who have given support]. Me mother and me nanan, they're only two, oh and me mate [name], she's been good, but me mum and me nanan, I turn to them for everything ... I have got a good family there, there's only a few on them, but they are, they're really good. I couldn't cope wi'out em, I really couldn't* (Mandy).

Introduction

Domestic violence does not occur in isolation, it is embedded in webs of personal and other relationships surrounding the heterosexual couple. The people in a woman's social network will display behaviours, and express different views, towards the woman and her marriage/partnership over time. Such views and behaviours may challenge, or be supportive of, male violence, or they may be inconsistent and it is important to recognise the ways in which the gender order impacts on support responses. Support (or the lack of it) is therefore highly significant to the future well-being, and safety of women and children in abusive relationships.

Domestic violence occurs in particular spatial locations. Whilst the home is the most frequent locale for abuse (see Chapter 4) it also spills out into other more public contexts in the community. Sometimes abuse/violence is witnessed or overheard by family, friends or neighbours, sometimes signs of physical abuse may be noticed on women's bodies and sometimes signs of emotional abuse may become noticeable in women's behaviour with their partners.[1] In kinship, friendship, neighbourhood and/or workplace networks, there is usually someone, other than the couple, who knows about or suspects that abuse is taking place. There is, therefore, the potential for spontaneous positive, negative and/or inconsistent support responses in domestic violence contexts, in addition to women's own active help-seeking efforts.

Our knowledge of informal support for women experiencing male abuse remains relatively limited as activists and policy makers have focused on social agency responses. However, we do know that most women garner more support over the long term from informal than formal networks (Kelly, 1999; Wilcox, 2000a) and some women make no contact with formal social agencies (Fine and Weis, 2000). Nevertheless, women[2] do actively seek support after having tried and failed to deal with the abuse/violence themselves (see Chapter 1) usually turning first to (mainly female) friends and relatives (Cavanagh, 1978; McGibbbon, Cooper and Kelly, 1989; Mooney, 1994; Hanmer, 1995; Kelly, 1996; Wilcox, 2000a and b) before turning to social agencies (see Chapter 7). Women's need for positive agency support should be borne in mind throughout this chapter, despite the fact that my focus is on informal support since I am not suggesting any diversion of attention from research or policy initiatives on agency support, nor am I arguing that the responsibility for addressing domestic violence should be transferred onto families, friends or the wider community. Rather, I argue that we need to be moving towards a situation where *all* potential support sources are activated into working towards the outcome of enabling women and children to lead violence-free lives.

Support interactions form a complex and dynamic matrix, difficult to express in a linear format in print. Indeed, separating out support responses of family members, from those of friends and from those in the wider community, does inevitable injustice to the complexity of interactions at any one point in time. However, for analytical purposes, it is helpful to examine how support responses from different groups may vary or be the same.

Turning to look at support from family members, knowledge of the history of a woman's support within her family is helpful, prior to, as well as during, the abusive partnership. Support histories are important because of their role in shaping future support responses and I addressed this by asking for women's accounts of family support when growing up, to assess possible links with experiences of support during and after leaving the abusive relationship. Individual biographical and situational support histories do not, of course, give us the entire support context of women experiencing violence, we also need awareness of the material and cultural resources available (or not) to women (as seen in Chapters 3, 4 and 5).

In this chapter I focus on women's perceptions of interactions (supportive or otherwise) with their family and friends. I highlight the core issues which are involved in support for women from such family and friends, and attempt to capture some of the complexity of this subject by addressing the following themes: Women's support in their family of origin; women's support during the relationship (*family support, friends' support*); women's support after ending the relationship: support contexts (*the neighbourhood, the depletion of women's support networks, family support after leaving, friends' support after leaving*).

Women's support in their family of origin

Women found it difficult to talk about support they may or may not have received when growing up. As Jill says when asked about this: *(pause) You've gobsmacked me there! (longer pause) I was close to me dad, but I were never close to me mother ... right up to being thirteen, I thought I were, I didn't even belong in family.* The difficulties women had in talking about support for themselves illustrates one aspect of the gendered nature of relations of social support; that women can find the idea of being supported a strange one. Benjamin asked what care mothers got and received a rather confused reply from one woman: 'someone taking care of me? ... I'm the mother, I'm the one, I take care of him!' (1990, p. 214).

Drawing on biographical accounts seven of the women referred to one or other problematic aspect of support when growing up, whereas three talked only in positive terms about family support. The women who experienced supportive family contexts whilst growing up (for the most part) found their families helpful to them both during and after leaving the abusive relationship. Two main themes emerging from these discussions were: relationships with mothers (sometimes fathers) and how parent/s related to their daughter's chosen spouse/partner.

Four of the women talked about their mothers; Louise's mother, for instance, had died when she was 15-years-old and she, therefore, had no mother to turn to during or after the abusive relationship. Both Sally and Jill had conflicted relationships with their mothers who they perceived as dominant: *But mother, phew, never got on, me mother used to go into long silences, you know, instead of telling us what we'd done wrong, she used to go into long silences for a couple of weeks and you never knew what you'd done wrong, because she used to just clam up* (Jill). Rachel's mother had learning difficulties and was unable to provide a stable background for her children; she had been married three times and had two other boyfriends. Having a conflicted relationship with mothers was a factor affecting women's future support. Some women perceived it as hastening their departure from the family home; four women said they wanted to leave home as soon as possible; Betty, Sally, Rachel experienced conflict with their mothers, and Christine with her stepfather, and left home for the relationship in their late teens: *I'd left home as soon as I could because I never had a good relationship with me father, well step-father actually, you know, I was always rowing and everything. So I left as soon as I could.*

Conflict with parents made it more difficult for women to disclose the abuse they were experiencing to their mothers (or fathers). These women were also young women in their late teens or early twenties and it may also be that younger women are less likely to confide in family members (however further research would be needed to confirm this). Disclosing violence to professionals was even more difficult and this protracted the process of help-seeking.

Mandy was in a similar situation in that she had a difficult relationship with her mother (she had been in care). However, when she finally disclosed the abuse to her mother, it was her mother who provided her with vital material, financial and practical support: *Oh, we [mother] don't have a very good relationship now to be honest, we're forever arguing, but at end of day I'm her daughter!* whilst her grandmother provided emotional support.

Most of the women said that their fathers were less directly involved in support responses and this would fit stereotypically gendered expectations of fathering. Betty, Sally, Jill and Louise reported that they felt closer to their fathers when growing up: *Mmm it's a long time ago now. I don't know, he was always there, you know, when I needed him. He used to take us on walks, and if he could afford it buy us things what we needed* (Louise).

Local authority care had been a key experience for three of the women; Rachel, Lucy and Mandy. The experience of care is often one of stress and anxiety for children and young people and can lead to a loss of self-esteem in adulthood. Rachel had the most difficult family background of all the women since her mother had learning difficulties, her father was largely absent, and for much of her childhood she was looked after by her grandparents. However, her grandfather was physically abusive and so she was also placed in three foster care families.

The second key theme was the relationship of one or both parents to their daughter's chosen partner/spouse. Over half of the women's parents openly expressed dislike for the future partner/spouse. Sally's parents were against her marriage to the extent that her father refused to attend the wedding. Jill, Mandy and Christine's mothers disliked their partners: *I didn't tell me mum ... she never liked him* (Christine). Louise's family had not liked her husband at all right from the start. These emotions inevitably impacted upon future support interactions. Betty's parents felt the same way and her father tried to persuade her not to marry him on the way to the wedding:

> *Me mum and dad never liked him. Me dad used to be able to see through people, you know, the first time he met them, he knew if he liked them, but he didn't like him at all ... even the morning I got married, and me dad said, 'don't love', he said, 'don't get married' ..., and I were nearly an hour late at the church because he kept telling the driver to ride round and round, thinking I'd change me mind, ohhh* (Betty).

We know how difficult it is for women to disclose abuse and both Sally and Betty admitted to being especially defensive about their relationship due to their parents' dislike of their chosen partner, and so felt even less able to disclose abuse.

In summary, where there has been a history of conflict with one or both parents in the past, where the woman's parents were hostile to her new partner/spouse and where there was no parental support for other reasons (for example death, mental health problems) then women started out with negative support contexts, a constraint which contributed towards them remaining in the relationship for longer periods.

Women's support during the relationship

> *I weren't allowed to have any friends. Only friend I were allowed to have were his friends' wives. Whether I liked them or not, it didn't make any difference* (Sally).

Previous research has shown that women *do* turn to friends and relatives for support during the abusive relationship (Cavanagh, 1978; McGibbbon, Cooper and Kelly, 1989; Hoff, 1990; Mooney, 1994; Hanmer, 1995; Kelly, 1996; Wilcox, 2000a). The interrelationship of informal and formal support was also important and I explore this aspect in Chapter 7.

Family Support

There is little research that directly asks family members for their perceptions of and responses to the abusive relationship and who, if anyone, *they* turn to for support (however see Hoff, 1990, Chapters 5 and 7). This was beyond the scope of my study but I did map women's potential supporters and ask them who provided which kinds of support. A common response from relatives was to ignore the abuse altogether or to say nothing at the time, and then later on talk to the woman about his behaviour:

> **Paula:**   *So did you find most people just didn't do anything?*
> **Jill:**   *Just ignored it, ignored it. I mean they talked to me about it. 'How can you do it? How can you live with him?'*

Women found this particularly unsupportive as not only did it fail to address the man's abuse, but this response was perceived as in essence transferring responsibility onto the woman to deal with his behaviour.

As noted above women who *were* in contact with their parents found it difficult to talk to them about the abuse; they felt ashamed and varying degrees of responsibility and guilt (see Chapter 2). Women said they had not wanted to upset parents, they felt ashamed of their unsuccessful marriage/relationship and were frightened of further abuse/violence: *Beatings just got worse, I mean he's dislocated my hip, he's fractured my skull twice, he's broken me ribs ... I were always at hospital. I used to think they [parents] must think I were demented 'cause I was always 'falling down stairs' or summat, and I daren't tell anybody I wouldn't have dared tell, I didn't even tell me mum.* Here Betty highlights the importance of women's closeness to their mothers in emphasising that she didn't *even* tell her mother.

As we saw in Chapter 2, due to male coercive control some women were unable to maintain much contact with their family, rather they were expected to fit in with *his* family. During this stage women attempted to maintain a front of normality: *...but no-one to really talk about it to because I think you try and pretend to other people that everything's O.K. really. And I think with being on the tranquillisers at the time didn't help* (Christine). Having disclosed the abuse to their mothers (usually), and where women did have their positive support, this was found to be a crucial factor in providing emotional and practical support. Importantly, too, mothers mediated between their daughters and social agencies, encouraging their daughters to go to the police, the doctor, the solicitor or whoever might be appropriate, and often accompanied them on such visits.

Mothers (and in some cases fathers) also provided one means of accessing alternative accommodation and similar practical help, such as childcare, small loans of money and gifts (see Chapters 4 and 5). It is important to note, however, that although support from mothers (and some fathers) was crucial, giving support was far from straightforward. Women said that their parents could not understand why they stayed with their violent partners, reflecting the commonly held viewpoint epitomised in the question 'why do women stay?' Parents who know that their daughter is being abused are likely to be unaware of the full extent of the abuse/violence. Also they suffer complex and ambivalent feelings (as does their daughter) around the social desirability of keeping the family intact whilst not wanting their daughter (or grand-children) to be hurt.

Women described their mothers as becoming more upset and angry as time went on, expressing increasing frustration at their daughters for not leaving, or for leaving and then returning to the abuser. This raised thorny issues for the daughter/mother relationship around control and autonomy with some mothers attempting to tell their daughters what to do. For women who were suffering high degrees of non-autonomy in their marriage/partnerships this was experienced as adding insult to injury. Such difficult emotions were compounded by mothers' increasingly feeling powerless to change the situation. In some cases the frustration and anger became so great that parents decided they wanted nothing more to do with their daughter. Breaks in contact with the family happened especially when women either went back to their partner or had him back:

> *I can remember once when he left and me mum and dad were sort of alright with me, because they were never happy that I was with him, they never liked him. And then after a period of time he'd come back ... and when they knew I was back with him, they more or less didn't speak to me either (wry laugh). You know, I can remember one particular Christmas they didn't even send me a Christmas card! You know they couldn't understand why I, why I wanted to live with somebody like that* (Christine).

Once rifts occurred with their families it was more difficult for women to turn to them for accommodation and if they wanted to leave they then had no alternative but to turn to social agencies for support through Local Authority housing services.

Women rarely went to their fathers for emotional support; Louise, for example, when asked if she could talk to her father about things said; *Not really no ... I don't know, we were close in one way but not in another. He loved me and I loved him but we never showed it and we never said it, but we knew we loved each other.* It seems that fathers tend to get less entangled in the emotional frustrations of the ongoing abusive situation than mothers do. However, this is not to say that fathers were unsupportive, Betty's father, for example, provided a wide range of different positive support responses once he was aware of the situation (and he had tried to dissuade her from marrying this particular man) and also mediated between her and social agencies, in this case a solicitor: *Oh me dad's getting me straight to solicitor's again but it didn't make no difference and he used to give me money and he used to say, 'go out and buy the kids summat, go on, go and buy yourself some clothes' ... and he used to take us away for the day in car, have days off work and take us away for day.*

Indeed, because fathers were more likely to maintain some emotional distance women sometimes perceived them as being more helpful than their mother, as Sally says: *I think I can only remember one incident where he was just talking really calm 'What do you want to go back for he is only going to hurt you again' sort of thing. 'Your mum's only trying to help you, she just gets upset about it', that sort of thing.* Occasionally fathers' support took a more stereotypically gendered form in threatening, or carrying out, retaliatory violence against the violent man. The women interviewed saw this as positive support since it allowed them to feel that they were not to blame for the violence, as well as holding out the promise of punishing the abuser for what he had done. However, in the longer term it failed to offer any real solution to ending the violence and perpetuated a view of dominant male behaviour as including violence.

Other family members, who might also have been potential supporters for women, were often driven away by abusive behaviour, as Jill says about her two brothers: *I mean they wouldn't come down, me brothers wouldn't come down to see me while he were here, people wouldn't come to see me I'd have to go out to see them ... me and me eldest brother were close right up to me marrying and he could never stand him so that's, you know, we had a right big rift.*

There were other members of women's families who did try to be helpful, however, especially female members such as grandmothers: *I used to have to run over to me grandma's and get some food money for the kids. She used to fill a trolley full up and give me some money and all so I could feed kids* (Rachel). However, not all female relatives provided positive support, there were a few cases where older female family members responded with the encouragement to keep the family together, and more rarely still, direct encouragement to put up with violence, as Betty's aunt: *One of me aunties kept saying, 'we know, don't just run away every time you get a little crack' and I thought, 'oh I best go back', and so I went back, and me mum didn't speak to me.* In this case we can see the tensions between two different sources of informal support, pulling against each other, from a mother and an aunt, and by following her aunt's advice Betty alienated her mother and lost her support for some time.

Where violence had been directly witnessed, or families were giving women direct support, such as accommodation, it was not uncommon for family members to be fearful that violence might be turned against them. This indeed happened to Sally's family when her ex-partner went to her parents' house and threatened her mother saying: *'Your family, you can run, run, run but you can't hide, you're like rats, I'll find you wherever you go'* and spat in her face. Sally said, *she's very brave me mum, she is, she hit him and he never hit her back.* Alternatively, family members worry that their intervention might invoke further violence for their daughter/sister: *I remember one time, me brother were there at the time, me son had done or said something wrong and he just stamped on his head, you know. He [brother] were frightened, well I wouldn't say he were frightened of him, but he didn't want to cause any trouble for me, you see, because he thought if he said anything, he, me husband would take it out on me, so me brother didn't say anything.*

Yet other aspects of the complex support matrix were the responses women received from the abusive partner's family and how women themselves reacted to this. In Rachel's case, her abusive partner's mother tended to support her son, as here: *and his mum ... she used to say 'it's your family that's split you and [abusive partner] up, you know'. It's because me grandma took me in when I ran away from him* (Rachel). However, she also told me that occasionally his mother did try and stop him from being violent when he got in 'these fits'. In most cases the abuser's family supported their son and if, as sometimes happened, his family became aware of the violence women often made up an excuse to cover up the violence out of a sense of shame and embarrassment (see Chapter 2).

Friends' Support

In Chapter 1 I looked at the range of strategies abusive men used to control women's contact with potential informal supporters and, as with family, the women in this study reported difficulties in maintaining contact with their *own* friends over the duration of the relationship:

> **Paula:**   *Did you, I was just wondering whether you were able to keep your friends whilst you were married?*
>
> **Louise:**   *A few, a few, but they only used to come when he wasn't there because they didn't like him. Because like he used to walk in and never used to talk to them you know. No, I didn't really have many friends at the time.*

Many women were compelled to make friends with the wives/partners of their male partners' friends and not all friends knew about the violence, as Sally said: *No they didn't know at the time, [wife of one of his friends] who I still see now, they're not friends with [ex-husband], but she, she says that like when, if I were upstairs when they come, he'd say I'd got a little bit of headache and had gone to lie down, and she didn't know, you see, all she knew were what he said.* This made it especially difficult as these friends could not believe that the partner was violent: *Somebody said to me, 'How could you say he's nasty? He speaks to you, he talks to everybody, he's polite'. He just knows definitely how to do it, definitely (laughs) yeah.*

Out of the women interviewed in-depth half had, with difficulty, maintained some contact with one female friend (two in the case of Janice), one woman was friends with her ex-husband, one woman had made friends in the refuge and three women who had no friends at all. In these straitened circumstances what support were friends able to offer during the violent relationship?

It is important to stress that for the majority of the six women their friendships were maintained clandestinely. Women felt that by secretly keeping these friendships alive they had claimed some power back in the relationship, but having to do so secretively (although evidence of women's agency and resistance) was nevertheless to some degree disempowering.

Some women refused to talk about the abuse to their friends for a long time, even those that had witnessed violence: *Oh I never told nobody, I wouldn't tell nobody. Well, me friend knew but she used to ask, 'What's he done?' 'It's nowt to do with you is it, you don't know, you're not married, you don't know what you have to put up with'. And you see I'd got it in me head, he'd drilled it into me head, that it were normal* (Betty); whereas other women talked a lot about what was happening and to female friends in particular:

> **Paula:**   *So that's good, and did you tell any of your friends, I know there was a period when you really didn't see many friends, but*

> were there any friends that you talked to about what was
> happening?
>
> **Jill:** Oh when we were married, yeah, oh yeah, I say they must have
> got sick of hearing me actually, because there was always a
> problem somewhere along line (laughs).

For women's friends (again as with family) giving support is not straightforward as women's support needs changed over time. The process for women of trying out different responses to try and stop their male partners abuse/violence can take a long time (see Chapters 1 and 2). At first it is likely that, although a woman may want to explore how she can get the violence to stop, she may also be looking for validation to stay in the relationship from her friend; whilst at a later stage she is more likely to want support in challenging the behaviour and later still possibly leaving. Friends need to know about the options available to women but also allow a woman to make up her own mind on how to respond, in her own time and as with family members this can be difficult to do.

Like mothers, friends often mediated between the women and social agencies, recommending that their friends speak to social workers, to doctors, to the police, and sometimes accompanying them on visits. Women's female friends seemed to pick up on the problem of abuse/violence even when women had not talked to them about it. They showed concern for the women's health and safety and gave emotional support, especially important was simply 'being there' for the woman and listening to what had happened to her: *Me friend had started showing very deep concern … I mean I never told her. I never, I mean I never told her, but yet she seemed to know for herself. I don't know, I used to say little bits, but nowt much* (Janice). Jill talked a lot to friends made while volunteering at a community centre as she explains:

> **Paula:** And was it helpful to talk to them [friends]?
>
> **Jill:** It was helpful to talk to them as far as I got it off my chest but
> as for in the physical sense, no, no. There was nothing anybody
> looking back, there was nowt else they could do. I'd got to make
> that decision myself. I mean everybody was saying 'Why don't
> you leave him? Why don't you do this, why don't you do that?'
> But I'd got to make that decision meself, yes.

The most common support offered by female friends then was talking and listening to the woman, in other words giving emotional support. This was mentioned by the majority of women. One woman's main informal supporter was her ex-husband and she said that he offered practical support. In these cases the support given fits the gendered expectation of emotional support from women and practical support from men.

As with family support, friends' knowledge of the options available to women, as to where women could go and what they could do, was limited. Only one woman's friend was in a position to offer her accommodation as most of the women's friends had children and were themselves in heterosexual relationships. However, three women's female friends offered positive practical support in addition to emotional support; helping to get women home after an attack in a club, to hospital, to see a solicitor, and to get away.

The process women have to go through before deciding to leave is a long and hard one and particularly due to the relative normalisation of such violence, not only from wider society but from the perpetrator himself. I looked at the problems in relation to leaving home/meanings of home and accessing alternative accommodation in Chapter 4 and the difficulties of economic dependence in Chapter 5. I now turn to examine the process and levels of informal support received after women leave the abusive relationship.

Women's support after ending the relationship: support contexts

What is different about women's support needs after ending an abusive relationship? The answer to this question depends very much on the particular support contexts that women find themselves in after leaving the relationship. Did women have to leave their own homes and communities to find shelter in different neighbourhoods? If so how did they leave and who did they go to for help with accommodation? How far away were they from their original support networks? How robust, depleted and/or conflicted were their support networks? What were the characteristics of the neighbourhood where they had been re-housed? Were there potential meeting spaces for women where new friendships could be made? Did the abusive partner know where the woman was located? If a woman managed to have the abusive partner leave then there were different issues to confront centering on the potential for future harassment.

As with support during the violent relationship, attempting to capture the process of relations of social support is again complex; there are factors which can change a woman's situation overnight and

I am thinking here, for example, of when an ex-partner discovers a woman's new address, which happened to some women in this study. Again, therefore, it is important to visualise support contexts as complex and shifting over time as different 'players' interact with the women and with material, financial and cultural contexts. In order to try and capture something of this complexity I will begin this section with an overview of the support contexts of the women studied at the point of leaving the abusive relationship. I look at the neighbourhood where women were re-housed. I then go on to look at interactions between informal and formal support, followed by an examination of who provided what kinds of support during and after leaving the abusive relationship.

The initial feelings most women had on having been re-housed (or having their partner leave) was relief and a sense of freedom. It was positive to be in their own home again, and to have some peace, quiet and hoped-for security. Despite this sense of relief and freedom most women told me these feelings were mixed with fears about their future. Principally women feared being found by their abuser and being lonely; the latter could be exacerbated by the neighbourhood in which they now found themselves (I discuss this in Chapter 7).

The depletion of women's support networks

The circumstances surrounding women leaving violent relationships, as already seen (poverty, loss of friends, lowered self-confidence, responsibility for children), tended to make most women more reliant on family support. As seen in Table 6.1, however, potential family supporters after women left were few in number. Networks clearly varied for each woman but depended to some extent on the geographical location of family members as well as the nature of women's relationship with their families. Mothers were especially important to women's well-being after leaving a violent relationship because of the gendered expectations of, and support that is often given by mothers; seven of the women had mothers who could potentially support them but two of these women had such conflicted relationships with their mothers that help was not forthcoming.

Turning now to look at friendship networks at the point of leaving violence, again the networks are severely depleted with three women having no friends at all and the rest having maintained one female friend, as seen in Table 6.2:

Half the women interviewed had lost friends during the violence before leaving but some found they lost friends after leaving. On the

Table 6.1   Women's family support network immediately after leaving

Woman	Family	Comments
Betty	Both parents 2 brothers	Live in area, father supportive, brothers' support made difficult due to gender order
Jill	Both parents No other family	Live in area, conflicted relationship, no support
Louise	Father 3 brothers	Father lives too far away to support. Two brothers, one lives c. 5 miles away, the other c. 50 miles away, both provided company and practical support
Lucy	No parental support No other family	In care and no contact with family
Janice	Both parents No other family	Mother – emotional and practical support
Sally	Both parents No other family	Live c. 12 miles away, conflicted relationship but supportive
Mandy	Mother Grandmother	Mother – financial and practical support Grandmother – emotional support
Catherine	No parental support 2 sisters	Sisters – live c. 70 miles away and have childcare responsibilities of own
Christine	Mother, stepfather 2 sisters	Live c. 5 miles away, conflict with stepfather, sisters supportive, one lives in the city the other in London
Rachel	Mother Grandmother	Mother and grandmother live c. 12 miles away, conflicted relationships

Table 6.2   Women's support network of friends immediately after leaving

Woman	Friends
Betty	1 female
Jill	1 female
Louise	1 female
Lucy	Ex-husband
Janice	2 female
Sally	None
Mandy	1 female
Catherine	2 friends made in refuge
Christine	None
Rachel	None

one hand, friends may feel awkward about socialising with a single woman (there may also be pressure here from their husbands/partners) and on the other hand single women can feel awkward socialising with other couples/families: ... *it was me who felt awkward, they'd say, 'oh come out with us', but I thought no I'm not going to be a gooseberry* (Jill). Jill illustrates the difficulties women face being caught in the transition from heterosexual couple to single woman/mother;

Paula: *So you know you said the friends dwindled, did you find, were they treating you differently do you think because you were on your own?*

Jill: *They've not done it, they've not done it consciously, but I just seem to be seeing less and less and less of them ... but I went on holiday with all me friends and it was the most horrendous two weeks of my life ... because they were in groups of families, I was on my own, and like I say it was the worst two weeks, and I would never [go again] ... Yeah, there's only one friend that I've got that I really stick to now, she lives on [estate],* **she's single, but if it weren't for her I'd have gone under a long time ago** (my emphasis).

As seen in Chapter 1 the isolation suffered by women due to the depletion and disruption of their support network makes it particularly important for them to start to build new supportive relationships after leaving (see Chapter 7). Isolating women from relatives, friends and other support services is one of the most common techniques used by abusive men. As Russell says, 'such social isolation greatly facilitates the dependence of these wives on their husbands, causes their social world and concerns for others to shrink, resulting in an intense preoccupation with the narrow and distorted family reality and, as with other torture victims, deprives women of all social support for their ability to resist their husbands' (1995, p. 114). In my study this technique did not isolate women from all social support since most of the women resisted their male partner's control to some degree, two-thirds of the women maintained some contact with their family and at least one female friend, three gave up all contact with their own friends like Christine: *Because all my friends were dropped really when I got married. So I didn't have any friends as such. Yeah I didn't start to build up friendships until I went to College.*

In many cases women had to leave the abusive relationship rapidly and secretly in order to escape violence. Family and friends may not even know where a woman has gone to, and so in the initial weeks after leaving, women, like Catherine, may not be in touch with any of their supporters at all. This makes them heavily reliant for support on the other women and workers in the refuges, shelters or hostels that they flee to: *No, they [sisters] didn't even know where I was going all I did was jump in a taxi and a month later I got in contact with them to tell 'em, I wrote to them to ask them to ring me.*

Making friends through a shelter or hostel can be a positive long-term support factor and in Catherine's case she made several female friends in both places who provided initial support:

Catherine: *I borrowed [female friend's] deep fat fryer and did 'em [children] some chips ... She was in the hostel. She's been in there quite a few times.*
Paula: *So she was the only one really who offered any support in the neighbourhood really.*
Catherine: *Yes, that was it ... well, I had a mate living here [another refuge friend].*

Ultimately Catherine's new friends were relocated to different areas of the city and transport costs made visits prohibitive (see Chapter 5). Distance from potential supporters and transport costs are important factors. Women who were able to maintain direct contact with their support network, like Sally, benefited from a degree of family contact, which brought practical and emotional support. However, visits to her former hometown also brought the risk and reality of being found by her abusive ex-partner and continued harassment and violence.

Extreme distance from potential supporters raised different issues. Indeed, women who had to move far away from their own homes/communities were the most isolated of women and often at greatest risk of returning to their abuser. Catherine, for example, after five years of abuse, left her violent partner in fear for her life, with her ex-partner's threat resounding in her head: *It would be a pleasure being put away to see you dead this weekend, because that is what is going to happen to you, and don't plan on leaving.* Catherine then spent the next four months moving to two refuges in different parts of the country, and then to another hostel and refuge before being re-housed onto the study estate. Catherine, who moved about 70 miles away from her hometown, was grateful for the cessation of abuse but had difficulty in maintaining contact with her family and suffered extreme isolation (see below).

Family support after leaving

Paula:	*O.K. erm so is there anybody at all now by lending you something, it could be small or big, is there somebody who could help you out?*
Christine:	*Financially or other things?*
Paula:	*Both.*
Christine:	*Me mum (laughs) yeah if I'm stuck. With the kids especially, buying them shoes and winter coats.*

Parents, and particularly mothers (where available), proved to be vital in providing support. The support relationship remained complex, however, and all the women were clear about not wanting to upset their parents. This, reinforced by parents' unease in talking openly about what had happened and combined with women's continuing sense of guilt/responsibility for what had happened, made open communication unusual. Mothers, as well as fathers, were then less than helpful to women coming to terms with what had happened to them. However, in lots of other ways mothers provided invaluable support as we shall see.

Betty and Christine, who had mothers living in the same area, received a lot of practical support from them; Jill's mother lived nearby but gave no support at all; mothers who lived further away were unable to offer as much support for logistical reasons but were still important in offering practical support. Louise only had her father alive, but he lived a great distance away. Catherine lost contact with her mother through the violence and did not see her father, so she had no parental support at all. Lucy had been brought up in care and had only occasional telephone contact with her mother. Rachel had been brought up by her grandparents for part of the time, had been in foster care (due to physical abuse from her grandfather) and had a conflicted relationship with her mother. Therefore *only half of the women interviewed received any maternal support.* This is significant because it might be assumed that most women leaving violence would be able to look to mothers (and fathers to a lesser extent) for support and this is clearly not necessarily the case.

In terms of practical and emotional support family members other than parents could be important. Louise, for example, gained company and a lot of practical support from her brothers, who she described as 'being there for her':

Louise:	*I've got three brothers and they all helped me. I didn't have anything only me clothes, yeah all I had were me clothes. Erm*

> so like they helped me with carpets, pots and pans, cutlery and things like that. So I didn't have a stick of furniture, so again they helped me, I got second hand things ...

Paula: Were they [brothers] supportive in similar ways or different ways [to female friend]?

Louise: Erm in different ways, erm I don't know how to explain. They just, they were there for me.

Paula: So did they see you more often?

Louise: Oh yeah, yeah. A lot more often, especially me middle brother at the time, he used to see me nearly every day, and we used to go for walks together and shopping together and things like that.

As seen in Chapter 4 parents were more likely than friends to offer to put women up both during and after leaving, for various periods of time, usually a matter of days, weeks or sometimes months (nine months in one case). This provided desperately needed alternative housing and could be helpful at time but was fraught with difficulties and contradictions for the women concerned, since as we saw above women's relationships with their families came under severe strain over time. Despite this it was women's female relatives in the majority of cases, especially mothers, who provided women with the most support after leaving in terms of accommodation and practical help.

In Christine's case it was mainly her mother, her aunt and her sister who helped her out in a range of practical ways, such as giving her furniture and other small gifts as her ex-partner had taken everything out of the family home. When asked if she had had support after leaving said it was mainly from her mum and aunt: *It was good because you can appreciate that there are so many women who just haven't got anyone at all so if I hadn't of had them [mother and aunt] I don't know what I would have done.*

Christine's sisters also offered support at key moments: *So I can remember having to organise my stay when I was going to go in hospital [having baby daughter] and I had no phone and ... it was me sister in London. I told her the situation, I said, 'I need a telephone', so she sent me the money to have the telephone connected that was it, and I arranged with me other sister to have [son] when I was starting into labour.*

Mandy, as other women, got much support (both emotional and practical) from her female relatives, in this case her mother and grandmother:

Mandy: *Oh no, I mean she [her mother] like really drags on at me, it's financial more than owt ... She's very, very good like that ... Me nanan's the one I'll go to, you know, like if I'm fed up and I can't be bothered to cook.*

Paula: *She'll look after you?*

Mandy: *Yeah, yeah, you know, like runs about after me, do you know, 'do you want a cup of tea?' and things like that and really it should be other way round, know what I mean (laughs). But like I'll trail in me nanan's with all kids, I mean even now, she'll go to [supermarket] on a Thursday and she still gets me me supply bag, every Thursday, she gets a bag full of shopping for me ... me mother's bank and me nanan's, you know, support.*

As seen in Chapter 5 financial support also most often came from mothers, although Betty's father was exceptionally generous financially. Christine's response was more typical: *Oh yeah, me dad never would, you know, he'd sort of say 'you can't manage, why can't you?' He'd never put his hand in his pocket and say go and get some extra groceries or go and get the kids some clothes, or whatever, just never, no.*

Support with childcare was a priority need for all the women (except Louise since her son was 16 when she left and Rachel who had had to leave her child behind) both day-to-day and emergency support. However, the women did not usually identify this need themselves. The problem here is once again the nature of support in a heterosexual society where women are brought up expecting to have to give support to others, in particular to care for children, and so do not expect to get any support with childcare. Therefore when questioned about such support many say, 'Nothing, I can cope'. Asking the question for these women implied calling into question their skills as mothers and their ability to cope. This situation will only change when funds are made available to women for child minding, and/or free childcare is provided, and women become more aware that an important part of being a 'good mother' is about developing themselves as people.

Lack of support with childcare means that women have to turn once again to mothers for such support, thus reinforcing the heterosexual imperative on women's role in childcare, and even though this was not always easy since most of the women's mothers worked and therefore did not have much time to spare (one of the contradictions of late industrial capitalism). For day-to-day help with childcare

Mandy turned to her friend but relied on her mother and grand-mother for emergencies:

> **Paula:**　*And if you had an emergency and had to go somewhere and leave the kids who would you leave them with then?*
> **Mandy:**　*Me mum and me nanan.*

Women who did not have mothers living nearby, or who had had complete rifts with their mothers were especially disadvantaged. Jill, whose mother provided her with little support even though she lived nearby, now turns to her 15-year-old daughter for help with babysitting. Christine is typical of the five women who tend to rely on their mothers for childcare support, when asked how often her mother helped out, said:

> **Christine:**　*Erm it depends really because she works full time, and if I'm desperate, and if I'm stuck, she will help out, she will have them a day, you know if I have something to do.*
> **Paula:**　*So it's not a regular thing?*
> **Christine:**　*No, no …*
> **Paula:**　*Yeah, O.K. and going back then to those days when you first moved out from the refuge, if you had an emergency who would look after the kids?*
> **Christine:**　*It would be me mum yeah.*

Friends' support after leaving

Those women with a woman friend said how important it was to see that friend regularly, but if that friend also had children then they, too, could rarely get out in the evening. Nevertheless, those women who did keep at least one existing woman friend said how much they valued the emotional support they gave, both in the early months and the longer term. The women talked about the different kinds of support women friends could and did give them such as accommodation, visiting regularly, listening and talking, validation, advice, encouragement to go out, shared childcare, accompaniment to agencies, and just being there. Nevertheless, loneliness was something they all felt at different times, particularly Christine who had lost her own friends:

> *I think it is because when you've been with a partner for so long, and like I said I gave up my friends before, when I was with him, and so often is*

the case, your friends are his friends and of course he came from a big
family and erm, which I had a lot of contact with them when I was with
him ... so I was quite isolated, I think the only thing available for you,
what you could have done, was join a 'mother and toddler' group, which
got right up my nose really.

Louise found her friend most helpful in talking about the abusive relationship whilst it was happening, since her friend had experienced an abusive relationship herself, and also later in encouraging her to become more sociable:

Well, she'd been through it all herself before ... but at that time she'd
been married twice, so she knew in which direction to guide me I
suppose, you know. She says, 'Best thing you can do is get a divorce
because things won't get better' ... She used to encourage me to go out. I
didn't want to go out because I'm not a going out person, not to pubs
and things and I went with her to clubs and that, but I didn't enjoy it
because I just weren't in mood. It were like a big upset you know after I
left him, even though it were for the better I didn't think it at the time,
but it were, she used to talk to me about things, er tell me that I would
feel better eventually.

Having ended the abusive relationship women found their female friends were essential to them in providing company, practical and emotional support (Kelly, 1988; Hoff, 1990). It was with their female friends that they were able to talk about and try to make sense of what had happened to them as well as simply to start to socialise again. However, as we saw above, women who had been re-housed into a new neighbourhood or area often had no female friends and they urgently needed support in making contact with other women for potential friendship (see Chapter 7).

Conclusion

Women disclosed domestic violence to family and friends before turning elsewhere for support. However, the informal support women received from family and friends was inconsistent in its helpfulness. This was due to a combination of factors; firstly people wanting the couple to stay together, secondly relatives and friends not knowing what options were open to women and thirdly informal supporters lacking the resources women needed.

Women's social networks on leaving a violent relationship were far smaller in size than those found in studies of other populations (see Phoenix, 1991). Women's networks, although very small, varied somewhat in size and density depending on how far away from their hometown most women had been forced to move in order to feel safe. There was not a straightforward relationship between the size of the network and the support women received since not all potential supporters gave helpful support.

The communities we live in have become more fragmented; for example only five of the ten women interviewed had any maternal support, but it was still women (as individuals) who were expected to bear the brunt of providing support to their relatives. Where women leaving violence had mothers (or other female relatives) living nearby, they provided crucial support in terms of gifts and loans of money and goods, as well as practical help with childcare. However, family emotional support in coming to terms with the violence was limited as most of the time women's family members lacked knowledge of services that could be called upon and were unaware how best to help their daughters. For families, as with the wider public, they found it difficult to understand the complexities of domestic violence and the fears women had over ending the relationship.

Support is embedded in a gendered society and this impacts on the support that is offered and how it is received. Although there is an overlap between practical and emotional support, the women in this study found it more difficult to gain emotional support from their parents and families in terms of dealing with the aftermath of the violent relationship. It is worth pointing out again that for most women in this study relationships with family members had been strained during the violence. Mothers were absolutely crucial supporters for half of the women in this study, for the other half it was other female members of the family and/or female friends who gave support. Fathers on the other hand were not expected to give emotional support and were judged on a lower standard and by different criteria.

Women leaving violent relationships needed longer-term emotional support as well as specialist help to deal with the immediate problems faced on leaving, such as debt and legal issues. Long-term support was mainly provided by women friends (when available) who had some understanding of the situation their friend was in. However, having a lack of friends was common for women in this situation. Also, whether women friends were married or single made a difference; single women friends were able to offer significantly more emotional and practical support since they were not as tied down by the domestic and emotional work involved in heterosexual relationships. Women who had survived a violent relationship themselves were particularly helpful.

7
Community and Safety

Paula: *Do any of them ever help you out with anything like lend*
        you things, or can you borrow stuff off them?
Lucy: *Yeah, yeah, next door, they always like if I'm really, really*
        like skint at weekend then [female neighbour] will lend me
        some money like till Monday ...
Paula: *And do you help them out as well in any way?*
Lucy: *Yes, when she hasn't got nobody to look after the kids*
        cause like they do pools on a Thursday night and it's a bit
        hard taking kids with them, so I watch kids sometimes for
        her.

Introduction

In the last chapter we saw that women disclose domestic violence
to family and friends before turning elsewhere for support. Most
family and friends gave support of some kind but this was inconsistent in its helpfulness. In this chapter I broaden my lens, taking an
overview of the wider community in which women lived their lives
looking at the nature of support in the wider community, from
neighbours and social agencies. Research and practice over the past
decade demonstrates improving responses to domestic violence in
social agencies (although still more needs to be done) but we have
much less knowledge about responses amongst the community-
at-large. Indeed, whilst there has been a resurgence of interest in
community in many fields this has been singularly missing in relation to domestic violence in the UK (Walklate, 2002). Furthermore,
I argue that the dichotomisation of formal from informal support
has hidden the ways in which they intersect. The aims of this

chapter are, therefore, threefold: to look at responses in women's neighbourhoods, to assess agency responses towards women participants and to explore the intersection of informal support with formal support.

Informal support in the community

The neighbourhood

An important factor for the women who had to leave their own homes/communities was the neighbourhood they moved into. The study neighbourhood was located in an area of local authority social housing, of considerable poverty and deprivation; employment was scarce and transport into the city centre expensive. Little neighbourhood infrastructure existed to facilitate women new to the area in making social contacts and friendships. I asked the women to rank the factors they thought important in their new neighbourhood. They ranked as positive: firstly, a quiet and safe area, secondly, good public transport and local shops and thirdly, friendly neighbours. Women wanted to feel safe and to live in an area which had the necessary infrastructure to combat feelings of isolation. They ranked as negative: an unsafe area for children to grow up in.

Neighbourhoods impact significantly on women's prospects for building positive futures for themselves and their children. A safe neighbourhood with good quality housing increases women's sense of safety. Moving to an unsafe neighbourhood, into a house in disrepair, has the opposite effect. In the present study four of the women said they felt unsafe where they had been re-housed, supporting Nicky Charles' contention that housing agencies do not always take safety sufficiently into consideration in offering accommodation to women leaving violence (1994, p. 481). Whilst most of the women were housed in safe neighbourhoods, a significant minority had negative experiences. Lucy and Louise had different experiences on the same estate due to variation at neighbourhood level:

This bit here what I'm on, it's like quiet, I mean it's brilliant on this bit, but further down [estate] it's really, really bad, there's all like drug addicts and taking heroin and I mean no end of times we've been up at school and there's been like needles on school and we have had to move 'em before kids go on 'em and that, but I mean it can be good but there's also like really, really bad points for it (Lucy).

It was horrible, terrible er it's a bad place anyway for drugs, thefts, dogs, it's just a bad area, so I were frightened when I went to live there, but it was nice inside and I wanted me own place anyway. It were just like, just people, environment, that's what were bad about it (Louise).

Housing agencies must consider women's safety a priority as further violence is experienced by one-third of women who end a violent relationship (Kelly, 1999; Wilcox, 2000a); care over choosing neighbourhoods can moreover prevent women from having to be re-housed again in the future. Another housing issue on the estate was that it tended to be a tight-knit community. When I interviewed Mandy (temporarily in bed and breakfast accommodation) she described the estate like this:

It's like me nanan lives up there, me mum lives up there, me mum were born in that house that me nanan's in, I were born in that house that me nanan's in. Me mate [name] her mother's up there, her grandmother's up there, her husband's off there, all her family's up there. [Friend] all her sisters live up there, her brothers live up there, her nan's up there. Everybody knows everybody ... and everybody's married into each other, if you did like a tree of say whole estate, eventually, you'd probably get back to say ten people, know what I mean, that's just how it is up there!

Close networks of family groupings can make a neighbourhood problematic for 'outsiders' to meet and make new friends (so important for women who have left their own homes/communities), as Catherine says of the mothers she met at the school gate: *They don't talk to you, they like stand in a gang round, (drawing in of breath) no, they don't speak.* For two women who had stayed on the estate, however, close networks were partially supportive, in providing friends and neighbours who could help out, as Lucy says:

Lucy: *I went to the solicitors with [neighbour] once and I got an injunction out on him, to stop him from, I went to see her and she got me the injunction like a couple of days after.*

Paula: *Was anyone else helpful?*

Lucy: *Yes, [ex-husband prior to abusive male partner] he took me to the solicitors ... He took me and he phoned them up to make an appointment for me cause I didn't go through wi' it at first ... he knew that I were going for it and he even came along wi' me ... Yeah, he waited outside in court while I were getting it.*

Close-knit neighbourhoods often thrive on gossip, so conversely women who stayed ran the risk of losing friends and having to turn to agencies for support, as Jill says:

I've always had people to talk to about it, but since we split up, I've only had like professional people, like doctors to talk to about it, I haven't had me friends. I mean she'd love me to talk to her, next door neighbour, not next door, but the friend I go out on Sunday with, but I wouldn't because it'd be all round estate, you know that type of thing, so I just keep to myself.

First impressions of the neighbourhood are important and women vividly remembered moving in; who had helped, the condition of the house, immediate impressions of the neighbourhood and neighbours' reactions. For women who came via a refuge/shelter where friends were made, an important consideration was whether their new friends lived nearby. Catherine found to her dismay that three friends made in the refuge were re-housed on the other side of the city. She could rarely afford to visit them and this added to her sense of isolation. Moving in to their new homes was understandably a contradictory experience, one of mixed feelings:

Yeah it was good because, mmm let me, because you were on your own and you didn't, wasn't sort of fixed at worrying about your partner coming backwards and forwards ... you just had yourself to think about and the kids erm, so that was good but also you could feel quite lonely, you know, especially at night when the kids were in bed and then that's it, there's just you and the television sort of thing (Christine).

Informal support from neighbours

Women fleeing violence have had to move (sometimes long distances) due to circumstances beyond their control, so whilst neighbourly relations are rarely chosen, the response of neighbours was even more important to them. The neighbourly relationship is always a delicate one because of the tension between individuals' need for privacy and the need for recognition from others; 'Neighbourliness requires the preservation of a balance between two needs – to be alone and to contribute to the community' (Ball and Ball, 1982, p. 19). Lucy (who remained in her own home) explains this delicate balance (note that her neighbour accompanies her to court, an example of the intersection of informal and formal support, see below):

> *So I mean, she's brilliant, but it just gets a bit (pause) a bit much some-times. Like when we first started seeing each other she used to come like every single night and like we couldn't have us time to us self then but she's like wore off now. I mean don't get me wrong, some nights I love it, you know to be, somebody to talk to, but other nights I just want to be on me own so, she's alright. I mean she'll come, like if I haven't got nobody to go to court with me* (Lucy).

Colin and Mog Ball argue that to feel any sense of belonging to a neighbourhood, a person needs to first settle into an initial layer of neighbourliness, i.e. the visual and aural experience of neighbourhood, which includes what they can see out of their windows, people passing by and basic greetings; 'We cannot emphasise too much how strongly this sense of belonging, of understanding the local patterns and rhythms, was conveyed to us' (Ball and Ball, 1982, p. 26). This can take time because the established community may be wary of newcomers at first and watch them for a while. This may be particularly difficult for women who have left violence moving into an area where they know nobody and are still feeling emotionally fragile.

Women said that the responses of neighbours made a huge difference to how supported/unsupported they felt in their new community. Three women said their neighbours were brilliant, two women said they were alright and two said they had not helped at all and one said that one woman neighbour, who had suffered violence herself, was supportive but the response of the others had been negative.[1] Several women said the neighbours spoke to them on the day they moved in and that this had been positive for them:

> *I saw them the first day I moved in. One, at one side particularly, they were always, although we never went in each other's houses they were always friendly and sort of, 'how are you' and sort of stand and chat for a bit, so that was good yes. And the neighbours at the other side, they also had kids so that was good for my kids. They had other children to play with* (Christine).

The frequency of contact women had with neighbours varied from seeing them almost every day (most women) to hardly seeing them at all (a minority of women): *Some days I can go a week without seeing her and next minute you know we can come in to each other for a cup of tea, it's that sort of thing* (Sally). The degree of contact also varied from verging on friendship, to chatting informally outside the house, to just saying hello. However, it was not the frequency or degree of contact, but the feeling that neighbours would be there if and when needed, that was of paramount importance. For women struggling with the consequences of domestic violence, and with all the extra pressures of living on their own as single mothers, positive responses gave them a feeling of acceptance in the neighbourhood, a sense of belonging. They did not necessarily want a close relationship: *I mean if she's stood at the gate we'll have a chat you know things like that, but we don't socialise* (Jill).

Women who expressed warm feelings about their female neighbours often received material as well as emotional support from them. This material, and occasionally financial, help was very much needed due to the poverty the women experienced (see Chapter 5). Sally, who described her neighbours as exceptional, saw them nearly every day said how much of a difference they made to her life:

> *It's a lovely couple, this side especially, they've really helped me with furniture and everything, anything they don't want. Their daughter runs a second hand clothes shop in [nearby town] and they help me with clothes and things, really brilliant, you couldn't wish for better neighbours. But not everybody I know has got brilliant neighbours like that ... [other side] they keep themselves to themselves, but they're friendly and nice when you see 'em. They don't complain about kids making a noise or anything* (Sally).

Women who have left violent relationships are rarely in a strong position to reciprocate neighbourly support, nevertheless, half of the women did help their neighbours out whenever they could, as the quotation from Lucy at the beginning of this chapter illustrates. Support is a reciprocal arrangement with women giving each other practical support like help with childcare, loans and gifts of items like clothing and/or small amounts of money. It was also sociable on a less close level than friendship. This finding chimes with previous research which has documented the networks of helping between women in poverty inside and outside families (see for example Stack, 1974; Belle, 1983; Fine and Weis, 2000).

The minority of women who had negative experiences of their neighbours painted a starkly different picture of their lives. When Catherine first moved in she got no greeting or support from her neighbours: *That was bad. You expect a bit more support off people when you move in. You do it yourself don't you, you ask them if they're alright, if they want owt, but not these round here.* Louise also had negative experiences with her neighbours when she moved in saying they were 'standoffish' and that one family used to shout through her letter box and push cigarette ends through her keyhole so she could not get her keys in; she never got to know anybody in this neighbourhood and ultimately moved away. Betty had similarly negative responses from her neighbours, experiencing problems due to her lone mother status (see Chapter 6), and because she had a lot of children in the house (four of her own and their friends) experienced racist comments: *They [neighbours] just looked at me as, [pulls face] one of the neighbours, like her next door, she says, 'it's worse than living next to gypsies' living next door to me. So yeah I've always got kids here you see, I've always got loads of kids here ... But I don't know, I don't get on with nobody round here. I talk to them but I wouldn't make a habit of going and sitting in their houses and having a cup of tea and something like that.*

The lack of supportive neighbours made it more difficult for women to assimilate into their neighbourhoods and feel part of the community. It also fed into and compounded feelings of guilt and shame about the violent relationship being somehow their responsibility. Ideally, the women who had negative responses wanted: *Just a friendly chat now and again, or just to say hello but everybody kept themselves to themselves. I think it was because of the area we lived in, it was so bad you know a lot of people were frightened to come out on their own doorstep* (Louise).

After being re-housed women may have to contend with continued abuse and violence from their ex-husbands/partners. The violence is now more public, no longer located *inside* the home. This did not mean that it was totally excluded from the home, however, as abusive men used the telephone to invade women's new homes and/or persuaded women to let them into the house. Social agency support, from criminal justice agencies in particular, is therefore essential in responding to continued violence to preserve women and children's safety.

Agency support in the community

Research demonstrates that women have to consult many agencies in order to get support which is appropriate for them since they receive such varied responses (see Binney et al., 1981; McGibbon et al., 1989; Mooney, 1994; Grace, 1995; Hanmer, 1995; Dominy and Radford,

1996; Stanko et al., 1998; Humphreys and Thiara, 2002; Batsleer et al., 2002). Agency response has been far more widely researched than informal support, so I focus here on key, generic themes rather than looking in-depth at individual agencies.

I draw on examples of agency responses, many from the police/ criminal justice system,[2] since they were identified by women as particularly significant. Moreover, as Humphreys and Thiara say 'the police are the most frequently used front line service responding to domestic violence; it is often the woman's first contact with outside help; it usually occurs at an intensely emotional and fearful time; their protective actions or lack of make a major difference to women's experiences of safety; they are one of the few services that intervene directly with the perpetrator' (2002, p. 49). The present study found that women reported helpful and unhelpful experiences of agency responses.[3] I look at unhelpful responses in *'Denial and minimisation of domestic violence'* and in *'Blaming the victim'*, and helpful responses in *'Challenging domestic violence'*.

Denial and minimisation of domestic violence

Some responses from agency workers minimised domestic violence and we have already seen that women themselves have a tendency to minimise experiences of domestic violence, saying 'nothing really happened' (see Kelly and Radford, 1996). However, as women started to gain a more acute awareness of the dangers of their situation, they turned to social agencies for help. What they required more than anything else was for their reports of domestic violence to be taken seriously. Mandy gives a typical example of how not taking domestic violence seriously can lead to neglectful behaviour on the part of the agency which in turn puts women (and children) at risk of further violence. In Mandy's case a promised alarm was not fitted in her house by the police and a serious physical assault ensued as a result of which she was hospitalised:

> Then when I got into this other house police were going to bell [alarm] it up for me when I moved in, [when she telephoned the police she was told] 'Oh he's off sick, we'll try and sort something out'. **They never did!** So eventually [ex-partner] did find me and I didn't have a panic button in, so I let him in (Mandy, her emphasis).

When I first met Sally she was still living with a considerable level of fear of violence from her ex-partner. Sally talked about the ways in which agencies minimised domestic violence putting her at further risk. In particular Sally was terrified as to what would happen when her violent ex-partner was due to be released from prison. Her fear was clearly due to experience of his violence but was also exacerbated by problematic agency responses:

> *I am absolutely terrified of when he comes out of prison. The thought of him coming out of prison, because policeman told me that he'd threatened me and I didn't know about that. And then he phoned me up from prison and he said, er, I've got it written down somewhere actually but I can't remember er on his last phone call he said 'Enjoy it bitch because when I come out' and I didn't give him chance to say anything else I just put phone down.*

This undermined Sally's feelings of safety in two ways; firstly the probation service allowed her ex-partner unsupervised phone calls during which he verbally abused, threatened and intimidated her in her home; secondly the police said her ex-partner had threatened her from prison, frightening her still further. The police also told Sally she would be informed of his release date and that they would lend her an alarm, however she did not feel reassured by this:

> *All I know is that as soon as he comes out of prison they're going to let me know straight away, police, the courts and me solicitor. Now, will they? That is the point, and I'm thinking to myself, now police tell me that he were in court tomorrow for this other offence, now is he going to be let out, can another judge let him out, or does he have to apply to the same judge? Er everything, will he be in a bit longer, and you phone up and you ask and **you feel as though you're intruding** ... All I end up wi' is er not the solicitor himself but his er what is it? clerk, and **that's all I ever get you see, and I've had so many that one didn't know what other one did**, that's why one solicitor's clerk, or whatever, didn't know that I'd got a warrant out for [ex-partner's] arrest* (my emphases).

Sally's lack of confidence in agency support is rooted in her previous experiences of domestic violence not being taken seriously; for example at the solicitors her case is dealt with by many different clerks who are unaware of the case-history. When she tries to clarify the situation (taking an agentic stance) as to exactly what will happen, she is made to feel that she is intruding on professionals' valuable time. This contributes further to undermining feelings of safety. Legal processes are complex, but this is an argument for careful and detailed communication with women like Sally so they are clear exactly what is going to happen and when, rather than leaving women in a state of uncertainty and thus compounding their fear levels.

Over the last few years awareness and training around domestic violence has improved significantly in many agencies. However, there are still professionals across all agencies who are 'uncertain about appropriate and sensitive practice, impacting on their ability to offer support and protection to women and children' (Mullender, 1996; Humphreys and Thiara, 2002). Discourses of denial and minimisation remain influential in some quarters exacerbated by gender-neutral models which fail to understand the gendered social contexts in which the domestic violence process takes place.

Blaming the victim

Another theme which women mentioned frequently was their perception that agency workers viewed them with suspicion and/or blamed them in some way for the violence; this was especially the case in relation to their children, as Christine points out: *I was under depression again, with postnatal depression and stuff .... and I can remember at one point I even phoned the health visitor, and she came, but she came with some sort of a survey asking me if I ever felt like hitting my children, which I, and I said 'no'!*

Christine had contacted her health visitor seeking support and felt aggrieved that the health visitor's response did not explore her specific situation but rather implied criticism of her ability to treat her children well. Ellen Pence's observations on organisations, their structures and how they can produce victim blaming is useful here. Pence points out that each agency focuses on a particular area of work, and within each agency, there is further job specialisation. Each agency worker, therefore, has a specific, relatively narrow focus and as a result rarely gets a well-rounded view of the lives of women experiencing (or having left) domestic violence. Drawing on their agency's perspective on domestic violence, policy and practice the worker 'deals with' the woman (seen as an informant) having no time to discuss her particular situation, indeed workers are trained *not* to engage in dialogue (Pence, 2005a). Here the health visitor's primary concern was with the safety of the children and in focusing solely on this concern, rather than taking a more holistic approach, she alienated Christine and failed to give her the support she needed.

Mandy was outraged that, since her children had been put on the 'at risk' register by Social Services, she was indirectly being blamed for her ex-partner's violence. She was under surveillance (as the incident over the chicken pox spots below illustrates) whilst her violent ex-partner now lived with another woman (and her children) who were not under surveillance:

> *I mean all the way along, kids are on this 'at risk' register, it's not my fault that they're on it, it's his. I mean like, I've had 'em on me back all time and [social worker] says to me other time, you know, like down on their papers I'm classed as like mothering my children good, do you know what I mean ... After all that, it were [ex-partner], it were him that hit 'em, he's off, he can live with a bird and she don't get nobody on her back, do you know what I mean ... It's like one time [son] he had chicken spots like, so one day I got a knock on door and it were social services, she said, 'we've come to see your little boy', and I said, 'what do you mean?' she said, 'because we've had a report that you've stubbed cigarettes out on your little boy'. I think you what! I were going mental, I phoned my health visitor up down at [area] she went, 'it's me Mandy I didn't forewarn you because I know' she says 'there's nowt to be concerned about'. As luck had it I'd still got, you know, when doctor comes out to see him, I'd still got that letter, and like, because [son's] black, he's had chicken spots and they leave white marks. Do you know what I mean, so yeah. I mean all that!* (Mandy)

The belief that women are to blame for the violence (either wholly or equally responsible) was also found in a number of police responses. Women reported that the police (mainly male) seemed to side with the violent man (Stanko, 1985, p. 53; Hanmer, 1989, p. 101; Hatty, 1989, p. 77; Grace, 1995, p. 39). Some officers, for example, spoke to the man first, listened to and believed him rather than the woman who had called the police:

> *A lot of police **men** were on [ex-partner's] side. I've had ... police women, mostly women obviously. But police **men** some of them have been really cruel. Yeah, I once phoned them up when [youngest son] was six days old, this one incident, and I waited for them at shop, and they'd been to see him first, and he [policeman] come down to me and he says 'He says he's not going to hurt you, you know, why don't you go back love you've got a lovely house there, you know!'* (Sally, her emphases).

It is interesting to note how this police officer almost speaks on behalf of the violent male partner, emphasising that Sally should go back to her 'lovely' home thus (knowingly or unknowingly) reinforcing awareness of women's different attachment to their homes (see Chapter 4). Some women said they felt a lack of sympathy from some officers and this was also found in Humphreys and Thiara (2002, p. 57). They were also made to feel responsible for the violence (see also Grace 1995, p. 39) both for provoking violence and for making sure it stopped; one police officer said to the violent male partner: *'Just go lad, just let her calm down she'll come to her senses'*, as Betty expostulated, *Me, come to my bloody senses!* Stanko points out that 'male solidarity can present another barrier to women complaining about male violence' (1985, p. 111) and in this study some police officers (as above) appeared to side with the ex-husband's point of view. Others, drawing on discourse that holds women responsible for emotional management in the family (see Chapter 2) told women: *You shouldn't provoke your husband, just try and keep him calm.* Again, at times police officers were attempting to be supportive but ultimately gave women contradictory messages:

> *Well I've been dealing with a PC [name] at the moment and he seems really nice and he's got him to get supervised phone calls from prison and things like that, and he says, 'we'll put you an alarm in when he comes out', and all I said were, just in comment, I said, 'well it's not so much when I'm in house it's when I'm at school or walking round', and he says, 'well we can only do so much can't we'. And that, then I just went down again, do you know what I mean, I didn't expect them to do anything but I didn't need him saying that. He said it nasty. You know, as to say well what am I supposed to do, you know* (Sally).

Ellen Pence's observations on organisations, their structures and how they can produce victim blaming, noted previously, are also useful in Sally's case (2005a). Sally was initially pleased with the response of the policeman to her situation; he was competent and helpful in advising her about the possibility of home alarms, but when she attempted to engage him in dialogue about her quite reasonable fears of violence outside her home, this went beyond what he saw as the police policy and/or police responsibility on domestic violence. From what Sally tells us it seems that he took her expression of fear about her safety outside the house as a criticism of the police, rather than an attempt to engage in dialogue, and his impatient response that the police could only do so much, had a huge impact lowering her level of confidence and feelings of safety.

As we have just seen inconsistency was found in agency responses. With reference to the police the experience of the women said they tended to lose patience over time and with repeated calls for help. Mandy expressed it thus: *Your very first time you go, yeah they can't do enough for you, if you're going to press charges and everything they can't do enough. But you know if you go to them a second time they're not particularly interested, a third time forget it. Because well they've done it before do you know what I mean, like you've always gone back so you must like it.* Mandy (as other women) also felt disillusioned with the criminal justice system more broadly. Her abusive partner was convicted for assaulting the children (taking the violence seriously) but in her opinion his sentence was too lenient (not taking the violence seriously enough; see also Humphreys and Thiara, 2002, pp. 50–1):

> *He got, for whipping [older son] he got six months, and for [younger son] he got six months, so then he got locked up. I went to the police ... and I mean the sentence were marvellous, six months for [name of younger son], six months for [name of younger son], three months for me, to run concurrent, he did eight weeks, under a third ... He'd been out a day er because I'd finished with him while he were in prison, he'd been out a day, he broke two of me ribs, perforated me eardrum and blacked me eye (laughs).*

Inconsistency was also revealed due to agencies focusing on different issues and drawing on different explanations for domestic violence, as Betty explains:

> *When first he went to prison I went straight down for a divorce, and then that Chaplain bloke at prison! And they put it in such a way you know and they say, 'Well, you took him for better or worse, do you think you should divorce him?' And I felt ever so guilty and I said, 'oh no, it doesn't matter' and I went down to the solicitor and cancelled it and said, 'No I'll give it another try' (Betty).*

Her position in seeking safety through divorce was validated by the criminal justice system on this occasion, but this was then undermined by the prison chaplain who reminded her of her marriage vows, advising her not to leave her husband. As a result Betty suffered many more years of the most appalling physical, sexual and emotional violence.

Challenging domestic violence

Domestic violence is now accepted as a serious issue in the health (BMA, 1998; Department of Health, 1999, 2000a, 2000b, 2002), as well as the criminal justice field and there are important roles that all agency workers can play in women's efforts to gain safety in the community and to challenge domestic violence. Refuges/shelters, for example, were vital for half of the women in the present study and women said that mostly responses in refuges were very helpful in challenging domestic violence; comments were made about feeling safe and about the support gained by being with others who had been through similar experiences, one woman said: *Yeah I weren't one on me own, it were really good. I mean if I had my life to live again I think I'd live in a refuge full time (laughs)!* The main difficulties encountered were: overcrowding, sharing amenities, poor standards of hygiene, lack of privacy, behaviour of other residents (including children), the lack of provision for women with older male children and the need for staff to be available 24 hours a day (see also Office of the Deputy Prime Minister, 2002, pp. 49–50).

Doctors were also often spoken about in positive terms as regards to response but they were not always proactive in probing about possible causes of injuries, depression, anxiety and/or suicidality (see also Humphreys and Thiara, 2002, p. 67) and medication was frequently prescribed:

> *I can remember that I just had depression for long periods of time and I think the doctors don't know what to do with you really and they just put me on these tranquillisers* (Christine).

> *My doctor showed deep concern, so he knew everything ... he were very supportive, if ever I needed to talk I was there, all I'd got to do was to make an appointment and he was there for me. He were, yeah, he were good and like he said, you know, I was strong enough to come out of it* (Janice).

Health visitors were seen as supportive in this study; providing advice on options for women and accompanying them to other agencies like refuges, taking virtually a befriending role, as Mandy says: *You can ask [name of health visitor] all this, because she used to come round, just even for a chat, I mean she were dead good her, she were really good. Yes, she were more like a friend than a health visitor.* The role of 'befriending' was not one that most professional workers were able to adopt since most agencies respond to crises over the short term and workers simply do not have the time to develop an advocacy or befriending role. It was for this reason that in this research a survivor support group was founded to try and develop this kind of support in a somewhat more formalised way (see below).

A positive response from a social agency, and especially the police, was one perceived as speedy, strong and effective. For example one woman gave a positive report of the speed with which the police recovered her child and took her ex-partner to court:

> *He [ex-partner] was actually in the house then and I daren't go in the house you know because like if I'd have gone in then he'd have like really, really beat me up. And I stopped away while police came and got [baby's name] and got me in and then they took him in. He were in court next day for it!*

A common fear having left the violent relationship was that of children being snatched from school. When Betty finally left her husband to live on her own with her children she found the police extremely helpful to her, particularly as regards the children's safety:

> *Police went and told them [school] that nobody at all could pick kids up except me and if I weren't going to pick them up I'd got to tell them in morning that me mum were going to pick them up, but no-one else could pick them up at all. And they couldn't even come out of class like other kids used to, they had to sit in class and wait for me to get there. And when first they went back to school, after I'd come out of battered wives, police watched school at playtimes and dinner times.*

Three mothers also spoke to school teachers about this and they rated schools' response as generally good; Betty again said: *And teachers watched right careful, watched them right careful and they wouldn't let them out.* Although she had experienced less helpful responses in a previous neighbourhood, Betty had high praise for the police in the neighbourhood where she lived at the time of the interview: *I can't say nowt about police. I mean everybody says police are no good, but they were marvellous with me, they were absolutely marvellous.*

The interrelationship between informal and agency support

I now turn to look at the interrelationship between informal and agency support, which has rarely been explored. Women experiencing and leaving domestic violence need human resources in the form of informal and formal support for themselves and their children, housing resources and financial resources. As we have seen women's access to human resources in their support networks was gradually lessened over time by male coercive and violent practices. Nevertheless, the majority of women retained some contact with a small number of family members and/or friends. One material aspect of support is, therefore, the number of potential supporters available to a woman and how willing and able are they to give support.

I found that where a woman was able to have contact with her mother (or other close female relative or female friend) she provided vital support in many different ways (as seen in Chapter 6) but also in linking women with agency support. They were the ones who encouraged their daughters to go to the police, the doctor, the solicitor or whoever might be appropriate, and frequently accompanied them on such visits: *It were Wednesday or Thursday before I went down to me Mum's. She knew instantly summat had gone off. She made me go to doctors, we went to see doctor, doctor went up wall* (Janice). Female friends and in some cases neighbours (as we saw in Lucy's case) also accompanied women when they had contact with social agencies.

Sometimes the relationship was reversed and it was social agencies who contacted family members. In Betty's case, although her parents suspected there were problems in the relationship they only learned about it officially when Betty went to the police who then brought her back to the parental home:

> *They [mother and father]found out when police took me back to me mum's that night, they picked him up ... policewoman said, me dad were out searching canals and everything for me, looking everywhere for me, thought I'd took an overdose ... and she, policewoman, says to me mother, 'don't ask her any questions or anything just leave her and she'll tell you in her own time'.*

After ending a violent relationship, informal supporters continued to be helpful in mediating between the women and formal support agencies. They encouraged women to go to the police, the doctor, the solicitor or whoever might be appropriate and/or they accompanied them on such visits. In Lucy's case, again, the gendered nature of support is noticeable as her friend is a single woman:

> *She used to like go with me to places, like she advised me to see a solicitor and she like took me, when the time came for me to sign on, she used to*

go with me there, if I had to go to the doctors she used to go with me there, yeah. She was always there for me at that time, and that's when I needed her most … fortunately she were on her own at the time so I think she had more time for me than she perhaps would have done if she'd been married then. Yeah, mm, so she were a good friend.

Contacts between women's supporters and social agencies provide opportunities for the agency to provide information on domestic violence, and services, to members of women's support networks. Currently parents and friends of women experiencing domestic violence are neglected in terms of enhancing their support efforts.

One example of informal and formal support pulling in different directions occurred during the course of the fieldwork which shows how Sally's level of support was enhanced by having access to a survivor support group. Sally's ex-partner unexpectedly arrived at her house, hammering repeatedly on the door, and shouting abuse through her letterbox, petrifying Sally[4] and the two children (aged 5 and 3). She telephoned the police for help telling them he was police-listed as 'dangerous – to be approached with caution' and that she was fearful for their safety, only to be told that there was no-one available to attend to this incident.

In fear and with the ex-partner still outside her house, Sally then rang a female friend from the survivors' support group, who immediately came round with her partner, managing to get into the house whilst the ex-partner was sitting in his car. However, the ex-partner saw them arrive and ran to the front door, proceeding to kick at it and shout abuse at everyone in the house. This time Sally's friend telephoned the police informing them that the violent ex-partner had now been outside the house for $\frac{3}{4}$ hour, to be told a second time that no-one was available to attend; the words reported to me were, 'Do you know how many women I have phoning me every day because their husbands are outside the house? Phone again if he beats the door down'. Eventually, after a third telephone call, the police did arrive but Sally's ex-partner had left by this time. In this case, no physical injuries were incurred but Sally and the children had been terrorised in their own home, causing immediate fear and emotional harm, but also continuing fear and worry that if he turned up again the police would not arrive in time to be of assistance. On the positive side, at least Sally was not alone in the house and this must have been one reason why the ex-partner decided to leave the house. So here we have a good example of informal and formal responses being at odds; the informal response was helpful whilst the formal response was unhelpful.

There were other examples where social agencies undermined positive informal support for the woman's stance in ending the abusive relationship (as we saw in Betty's case above). In Sally's case, for instance, supervised access to the children was ordered by the court and provided her ex-partner with further opportunities to threaten and abuse her outside the visitation centre, as she describes it:

> *He were calling me names, he were swearing and throwing Durex at me, he were chasing me up and down road, speeding with kids in car. Everything! You name it he did it! Coming up to me face saying 'I hope I do go to prison because I can't be responsible for what happens to you if I do'.*

As previous research has found, there are huge safety issues attached to contact with violent ex-partners (see Chapter 3) and access arrangements were frequently abused by them (see for example Hester and Radford, 1992; Hester et al., 1994; Hester, Pearson and Harwin, 2000).

There is a significant minority of women who have no informal supporters (or virtually none) and who become, therefore, totally dependent on social agency support. They have had to flee many miles from their own homes and communities and are re-housed into neighbourhoods where they know no-one. Visiting their former home is out of the question because being seen is too dangerous. These women have high levels of support needs.

Catherine, for example, had an especially problematic support context; no friends in the neighbourhood and living 70 miles away from family and friends, although she was starting to make friends through the survivor support group. She suffered a major setback when her sisters came down to her house to warn her that her ex-partner had been given her new address by Social Services.[5] He had told them that he was eager to make contact with the children again, that he had got a new job and was now regularly attending Alcoholics Anonymous. From this point on she was terrified that he would turn up at her house at any time. In the event he wrote her a letter threatening to take the children away from her if she refused to go back to their hometown to see him (he booked her and the children into bed and breakfast accommodation). Now that he had her new address, fearful of him taking the children and in view of the paucity of support, Catherine returned to her home town where he 'persuaded' her to try again with the relationship. In this case once again formal agency support undermined the efforts which were being put into enhancing Catherine's informal support through the survivor support group.

Conclusion

For women who have ended a violent relationship, feeling safe was partly about factors, such as the safety of the neighbourhood they lived in, the quality of their housing, access to support (formal and informal), access to security equipment, speedy and appropriate action being taken by agencies, and it was also about the manner in which responses were made. Informal and formal responses to women experiencing and leaving domestic violence were varied. Responses which denied, minimised and/or blamed women for domestic violence were in evidence, but, there were also many helpful responses. The majority of women participants were enabled (eventually) to lead violence-free lives.

Chapters 6 and 7 have shown that women turn for support to a wide range of potential supporters; far wider than the criminal justice agencies which have been historically prioritised in the domestic violence field. Support was inconsistent in the wider community setting (as it was from family and friends) however there was also much willingness and desire to help women. It is crucial to maintain pressure on agencies to improve their responses (as some already have). Women need support from as wide a range of sources as possible since this is a social problem (as well as an individual problem). As we have seen, separating informal from formal support is something of a false dichotomy since there is overlap and intersection between the two. Each time a woman makes contact with a friend, family member or agency worker about the abuse she is experiencing, there is the possibility for a helpful or unhelpful response. In this study there were many opportunities where responses could have been far more helpful and these would have enhanced women and children's safety levels. In order to achieve helpful responses, social agencies and those in the wider community need higher levels of funding and resources if we are serious about enhancing multiple support routes for women attempting to construct violence-free lives.

Conclusion

> *[Women] do need somebody, just a friendly face, just to visit now and again, I mean not every day just once or twice a week, or when they've got an hour at night, just somebody to say well at least they've been, at least somebody cares.* (Rachel)

Recent decades have seen reform of western women's social and legal status (at least in some areas) moving women slowly towards a more equitable status with men. The state is now obliged to protect women in their homes from male violence, for example, and violence against women in the 'private' sphere, is now largely recognised as a *social problem* with roots and *solutions* in the social system (Leander and Danielsson, 2001). At the same time, in many western states, we have seen an increasing social divide between the wealthy and those with the least resources, further disadvantaging women in poverty.

Domestic violence goes against the tide of gender reform as it is a context in which men seek to enforce and maintain traditional gender differences, gender dichotomies and male privileges. Women participants in the present study experienced both domestic violence and a severe lack of material resources. Yet, even in these severely constrained circumstances, they maintained agentic stances, actively pursuing safety for themselves and their children. Women drew on internal resources, on drugs and/or medication, as well as turning to a wide range of potential support/ers in the seven social dimensions examined (power, emotion, children, home, economic, informal and community). Taking a contextual approach to women's experiences in domestic violence revealed the many instances (across the board) where the *external structural context*, as well as *individual responses* to women, were less than helpful in the process of gaining safety; indeed, 'the break down of resettlement is often linked to the absence of support' (Kelly and Humphreys, 2001, p. 270). Unhelpful responses shifted responsibility for abuse and violence away from the perpetrator to the woman or to other factors such as alcohol, or stress, or women 'asking for it' and this contributed to the normalisation of such behaviour (Bagshaw and Chung, 2000). These responses tended to deny or minimise the violence, to blame the woman for what she was experiencing during the relationship and the losses endured after ending the relationship.

Loss is an important theme in understanding the complexities and difficulties for women in ending a violent relationship; not only do women lose their relationship they often also lose their home and community. Traditionally, these losses have been seen as reflecting unfavourably on the women who leave. Women have been perceived as to blame and, moreover, have blamed themselves for domestic violence; '... the loss is more than a matter of ceasing to act in a given capacity; it is ultimate proof of an incapacity ... To loss of substance is thereby added loss of face' (Goffman, 1952, p. 455). As we saw, women started out by feeling competent in relation to 'emotional management' but as time went by, with little change in behaviour from their male partners, they felt increasingly humiliated and ashamed for their assumed 'failure' in this gender role. What is needed in relation to domestic violence is a shifting of this burden of stigma, humiliation and blame so that disclosing domestic violence no longer reflects unfavourably on women.

The wider social context, which includes helpful support responses, must be the focus of attempts to shift the discourse of blame away from women. Survivors and workers in the domestic violence field have recognised the need for enhancing support (as Rachel above), and historically elements of outreach and advocacy work have been part of refuge/shelter provision:

> Outreach is a term used to describe domestic violence services extended to women, and sometimes children, based in their homes and communities. Outreach in the UK has two different aspects which can overlap: outreach to women who are currently living in, or moving out of violent relationships but not using a refuge; and re-settlement support for women, and to a lesser extent their children, when they leave a refuge (Kelly and Humphreys, 2001, p. 247)

More recently new forms of outreach and advocacy have been emerging which take safety planning and pro-active approaches to domestic violence. Fundamental to these services is the principle of partnership (working with women in assessing risks), the principle of *not* assuming which is the best or safest option for any woman, and taking a 'rights based focus' (see Kelly and Humphreys, 2001). These developments are crucial and need to be adopted in a far wider and more systematic way than is presently the case.

I argue that there is more that needs to be done, in addition to the vital work with individual women (perpetrators and children), to address wider social contexts. Whilst individual outreach and advocacy are absolutely necessary, the main finding which emerges from this study of domestic violence is that women's agency occurs in contexts where social and material resources are highly constrained and this has two major implications:

- The need to focus on structural failures which systematically disadvantage women in terms of improving their material resources.
- The need to focus on more appropriate support responses from informal support networks and in the wider community.

A third finding arising from this study (although not an initial focus) is the significance of children to women implying:

- The need to join others in emphasising that research with, work with and support for, children in domestic violence is imperative.

Enhancing systems

The question which drives this section is, how can women's material resources be enhanced? Women are already actively pursuing many strategies to combat domestic violence but are often being failed by the prevailing material and structural conditions in key social contexts, predominantly the economic system, the housing system and the community infrastructure.

The economic system

Economic independence for women is an essential plank in an overall strategy to decrease domestic violence (as recognised in projects in 'developing' countries) and to alleviate poverty more widely. The current economic system in the west seems to hold out to women the promise of economic independence and control over their lives. However, in practice, the overall gender order and regimes of gender mitigate against this. The current gender regime in the family continues to be conservative with women tending to take the major part of childcare, domestic work and emotional management. In order to potentially gain financial independence through work in the 'public' sphere, women must reconcile the competing demands of parenting, caring, home maintenance and paid work. Moreover, the gender regime in the labour market disadvantages women in a lower social class and/or with few or no qualifications. Such women face a range of difficult factors: job insecurity, low wages and ghettoisation of 'women's work' (see Chapter 5). The financial rewards are often insufficient for the women to gain economic independence and control over their lives. For this reason, women may choose to prioritise their parenting role and/or because they find greater personal reward in mothering. As we saw in Chapter 3 women's identities are enhanced in culturally normative ways through mothering.

Domestic violence is a context in which men seek to enforce and maintain male privileges. In the present study male partners actively disrupted women's attempts to participate in the labour market. Some women, therefore, became economically dependent on their partners, which in itself contributed to family impoverishment. The minority of women who continued to work risked increased violence to stop them from working, and risked increased violence aimed at the children.

Far more research is needed (especially in the UK) which focuses on the relationship between structural economic factors and domestic violence. Moreover, employers can also play a part in developing and publicising policies on domestic violence against women. These would help to challenge women's sense of shame and self-blame and encourage them to go for assistance to their employers (if employed). On a wider scale, strategies are needed which urgently address the wages gap between those in part-time work (mainly women) and those in full-time work. This would clearly benefit families financially but also it could be a step towards encouraging further equality in sharing roles in the home.

Similarly, research is needed which focuses on poverty in relation to domestic violence. Women in this study experienced severe levels of poverty both during and after ending the abusive relationship, and they experienced high levels of debt and additional expense after ending the relationship. Community care grants are needed to furnish and decorate new homes for women who have to leave their own homes in order to flee violence. Also a new grant of benefit is needed for women without paid employment who have increased transport and communication costs.

To repeat, research is urgently needed into domestic violence and women's employment and into the relationship between domestic violence and poverty. Many efforts to alleviate poverty currently encourage more women into the labour market, and new forms of informal and insecure employment are often targeted at women workers because they are viewed as providing cheap and unskilled labour. It seems equally, if not more, important to address the type of work and the pay and conditions women experience at work. Training and further education would also be vital to encourage women to develop more advanced skills to ultimately gain economic independence.

The housing system

It is important to see women's survival primarily as a process of gaining safety and how best this can be achieved; the 'many routes to safety' idea of Humphreys and Thiara (2002). For the women participants in this study, feelings of safety, security and identity were closely tied to their homes. Women spent more time in the home, had far more involvement in home maintenance, interacted more within the home than their male partners and mediated between the home and the outside world. Consequently they felt a continuing strong sense of attachment to their homes (despite the disruption caused by experiencing abuse). These feelings were connected with positive memories of bringing up their children, of creating a home for the family, and with building small networks of family and friends. As pointed out earlier, leaving home signified major losses for themselves as well as their children and homelessness as a safer option than staying at home was only ever a last resort.

In relation to home and housing, research on domestic violence survivors has tended to focus on their re-settlement housing needs since many women were forced to leave their own homes. This situation is changing, however, and it is problematic to conceptualise women survivors of domestic violence as necessarily having to leave home; in the present study two out of ten women stayed in their own homes and Stalford et al. (2003) reported over half of their sample of 47 women as not leaving. Moreover, the strength of women's attachments to their homes is an argument for strengthening routes out of abusive relationships which enable women and children to stay, to stop the violence or have the abusive male partner leave. Using a civil protection order is one possibility (in the UK these include non-molestation and occupation orders) and more women are now using these, Humphreys and

Thiara (2002, p. 53) found that three-quarters of the women who used protection orders (n=77) had benefited from them; over one-third reported them as having been successful in stopping abuse, a further 40 per cent said they were of some help.

Despite the changing situation on home and housing, not all women use protection orders, and not all women find them helpful, indeed for some women they may open up the risk of further and even increased threat and attack in the home. Many women do have to leave their homes; for example, Humphreys and Thiara report that 64 per cent of their sample of 200 women had contacted their local authority housing department (2002, p. 73). It is essential, therefore, to continue to argue the case for further, better and more stable provision of safe temporary and permanent housing for women who become homeless due to domestic violence. Refuges, temporary move-on housing and outreach services need to be put on a secure funding basis; it is a sobering thought that refuges are often funded on a year-on-year basis and presently only 12 per cent of refuges have a funded outreach project (Humphreys and Thiara, 2002, p. 43).

With reference to permanent housing, local authority housing departments and housing associations need to ensure that offers made to women are of reasonable quality and are located in a safe area. One woman in this study was housed in bed and breakfast accommodation which was completely unsuitable for a woman fleeing domestic violence; this form of accommodation should not be used if at all possible. Women also needed to have homes that were secure and safe internally and so any repairs that are needed should be carried out speedily. If this does not happen it is more likely that women will return to the abuser (as Carol did in this study) and/or become homeless once more. Repeat homelessness is not uncommon amongst women ending violent relationships and this is clearly costly emotionally to women and children, and costly to the public purse. Finally, gender-neutral housing policies which disadvantage women fleeing violence making them liable for rent arrears and other debts must be seriously questioned.

To summarise, women develop social bonds and feelings of safety and security in their homes, despite the disruption of domestic violence. Hopefully, more women will be enabled to remain in their own homes with improved protection orders to protect against domestic violence. However, if they do have to leave their homes and communities, as a last resort in search of safety, then everything possible should be done to provide support in the short and long term. Temporary and permanent housing is crucial in this respect and there needs to be longer term re-settlement and/or outreach support to guard against re-victimisation (Home Office, 1999, 2000). The stable funding of refuges and outreach services needs to be a government priority. Whether home is perceived by women as associated with a friendly neighbourhood clearly depends on responses from those in the wider community and so I turn to look at this in the next section.

The community infrastructure

Moving away from violence into an unsafe area had a negative impact on the initial sense of belonging in that area (compounding the lack of security already felt by women) and they were also less likely to experience supportive neighbours. Lack of support from neighbours made it more difficult for women to settle into their new neighbourhoods and become part of the community. Women with supportive neighbours felt a sense of belonging in the area, they felt increased levels of safety in knowing that someone would be there to help out if needed and they gained immeasurably in terms of small loans or gifts and reciprocal help. Some responses from neighbours tended to draw on a traditional discourse which denied, minimised or blamed women for their predicament. Myths surrounding domestic violence continue to be perpetuated in some quarters.

The lack of an adequate social infrastructure in the community designed to meet women's needs for support and for making contact with other women was a major contributor to their difficulties. The evidence from this study shows that women leaving violent relationships were living in a community environment which tended to hinder rather than help them to become more self-confident and build violence free lives for themselves and their children. The infrastructure women need to lead enriched and independent lives needs further research and development.

To summarise, the findings indicate that neighbourhoods can make important contributions to women seeking safety. In the short term, public awareness campaigns are needed which highlight that domestic violence is not such an exceptional experience and which counteract the myths about domestic violence which continue to circulate. The Women's National Commission (2004) in the UK produced a useful briefing in relation to domestic violence and child contact, which demonstrates one way in which such publicity could be produced, as this extract:

> **MYTH:** Domestic violence is not widespread, as many men are victims as women.
>
> **FACT:** Domestic violence is one of the greatest criminal problems facing the UK, accounting for a quarter of all violent crime[1] ... Crime statistics and research both show that domestic violence is gender specific – i.e. predominantly experienced by women and perpetrated by men[2] ...
>
> **MYTH:** Domestic violence does not feature in most relationship breakdown or divorce cases.
>
> **FACT:** Of 2,500 families entering mediation, approximately 75 per cent of parents indicated that domestic violence had occurred during the relationship.[3]

In the longer term, strategic decisions are needed on providing a range of spaces, locations and levels in the community where survivors can get involved on a social basis to enhance the networking of female friendships. It is also likely that some survivors may be interested in becoming involved in working against domestic violence (as many already have) in a variety of different ways and at different levels. This, too, would call for careful research and development.

Enhancing informal support

There remains a tendency, both in mainstream and feminist work on domestic violence, to reproduce the modernist dichotomy of public and private. One example of this is in posing possible solutions to domestic violence as *either* involving work with the state/criminal justice system (public sector) *or* working with the community and informal supporters (private sector). Although the reasons for prioritising agency support (and especially the criminal justice system) are historical and dictated largely by the necessity of responding to crises, this has perpetuated a false dichotomy between private and public. Women's insecurity results from the impact of all forms of violence on the continuum of male violence. Violence in the home often spills out into public spaces and violence may continue and indeed worsen when a woman ends the relationship. At the same time a woman who is abused in her home does not necessarily feel safer on the street or in public spaces. Separating private from public violence, and private from public support, is a false dichotomy from a feminist perspective which would want to address all forms of male violence which impact on women's freedom of movement and feelings of safety.

Posing the question in responding to domestic violence as either working with the state or working with/in the community limits feminist activism. Women need access to crisis *and* long-term support, both are essential factors in women moving from victim status to survivor status.[4] The problematic nature of working with the state to change attitudes/discourse towards male violence was recognised from the start as the institutional systems to which women turned for help could so easily reproduce their dependence and reinforce their abuse (Schecter, 1978 cited in Stark, 2004; Dobash and Dobash, 1979; Stark, Flitcraft and Frazier, 1979; Stark and Flitcraft, 1996 cited in Stark, 2004). Inter-agency work poses its own problems (Abrar, 1996; Harwin, Hague and Malos, 1999), particularly in relation to differential power relationships between statutory agency workers, support groups and individual women in the community. There is an ever-present danger of reproducing the coercive power relations experienced in the violent relationship, as Mandy says:

> *I mean my battle at the moment is with the council, and social workers, and police. You know like, they're like telling me, like pushing me, it's like they've got me in the same position as my ex-partner, saying 'do this' and 'do that'. Like pushing me, and I'm having to say 'well no'. Do you know what I mean? He's told me what to do, he's like directed my life, you're not going to do it. I were a victim to him, but I'm not going to be your victim.*

It is clear that working with the community raises the same or similar issues of power as working with the state and its agencies (see Jones 2004 on the difficulties faced by the Rape Crisis movement in working with the state). Both spheres pose difficulties for feminist activists and researchers, but at the same time, both spheres are potential sites of action (see Gupta 2004 on debates within SBS and this issue within Muslim communities). The community and the state are culturally intertwined and in working with either/both Gupta makes the important point that feminists have to keep on asking: 'how do we work together with those who perpetrate, sanction or condone domestic violence?'

The findings of this study reveal the central role of informal support networks in relation to domestic violence. Women disclosed domestic violence to their family and friends before turning elsewhere for support. Women did receive many different forms of support from family and friends. However, overall the responses women received from their family and friends were inconsistent in their helpfulness. There was also a lack of knowledge about what actions women could take and who they could turn to for support. Women's potential supporters were themselves in relative poverty and often did not have access to the resources their daughters/sisters/friends needed, such as money and alternative housing. At the same time the men in women's informal networks tended to be reluctant to challenge violence. However, it is important to stress that despite all these constraints most people in women's social networks did want to help and tried to help in some way. So, although relationships with families were strained during the violence, women's mothers proved vital in giving support (half of the women had maternal support) and it was mainly female relatives and female friends who supported women without maternal support. In a minority of cases brothers were also very helpful in providing company and practical support.

In summary, for people from whom women sought help, requests needed to be taken very seriously; careful listening was essential and it was important not to put responsibility for the abuse back onto the woman. Further research is needed on how parents, other family members and friends can access information and awareness about domestic violence and which groups can provide women with support. Moreover, the points of intersection between informal support/ers and formal support are potential sites for increasing and improving helpful support responses for women and children.

Tackling domestic violence is an international and national policy matter but domestic violence impacts locally in the community. We need more creative thinking on ways of enhancing informal support not only to maximise the effectiveness of crisis intervention but to respond to the ongoing abuse of power and control over women and children's lives. If we want to achieve lasting social change then projects in the community are needed which engage with domestic violence in ways that are specifically targeted to a particular community.

Enhancing support for children

Whilst the roles and attitudes of women in society *are* changing, gendered patterns of domestic work and caring in the family remain relatively static with children primarily cared for by mothers, and fathers primarily seen as economic providers. In this study mother-child dynamics were described by women participants as quite different from father-child dynamics. Women's interactions with their children brought many rewarding and life-enhancing experiences, despite abuse and violence from male partners. Children often provided women with support, verbally and in practice, both in general and in connection with the abuse. Women's decision making processes and ability to act to stop the violence were both significantly influenced by consideration of and for their children.

In relation to domestic violence during pregnancy, it remains difficult to state conclusively that pregnant women are more at risk from domestic violence than women who are not pregnant, due to differences in research designs. Nevertheless, there is now a growing body of research which shows that violence during pregnancy is damaging to both the mother and the unborn child. The present study supports this and supports the steps that are now being taken to train health professionals on this topic and to screen all women for domestic violence.

Women tried to protect their children from being involved in the abuse and violence. Indeed the actions they took to stop the violence were for the children as well as for themselves. They tried to protect them by ensuring, as far as they could, that children did not witness or overhear any abuse or violence. However, as we saw, the key message from research on children and domestic violence is that this model of protection is almost always incorrect. The majority of children report knowing about the violence and many children are able to describe abusive and violent attacks in detail.

The outcome of the model women drew on, of protecting their children from hearing or seeing violence, resulted in delayed help-seeking. However, women who believed their children *were* being harmed by the violence were more likely to end the relationship. This tells us how important research on the impact of domestic violence on children is and that it needs to be far more widely disseminated. Mothers (and fathers) need to be absolutely clear about the adverse effects of domestic violence on children and be encouraged, if at all worried, to seek advice as soon as possible. This does not necessarily mean ending or leaving the relationship, but it does mean women going outside the family, breaking their silence, and speaking to others about domestic violence.

We need to listen more to what children have to say about the impacts of being involved in domestic violence, and we need further research on the gendering of abuse against children. In the last five years some schools have started to deliver educational programmes for children and young people addressing issues of violence against women and girls,[5] which is a positive development, however, Ellis (2004) found that most funding for such work was short-term, making programmes potentially unsustainable. Schools need to be more proactive in tackling children's problematic behaviours and attitudes around violence, particularly in relation to gender and heterosexuality, homophobic abuse and bullying, and make links with appropriate support services when children disclose domestic violence. Another important area, based on the findings of this study, would be work on emotional literacy, to address extremes of gender polarisation around expressing and managing feelings. To repeat, this work is already starting to happen in schools, but it needs to be integrated into the core curriculum of all schools.

Concluding remarks

The combination of domestic violence and poverty created particularly constraining contexts for women trying to achieve a violence-free existence. However, this research revealed the resilience and resourcefulness of the women participants who, with appropriate support, eventually achieved independent lives for themselves. In the longer term, to achieve lasting social change, messages against domestic violence need strengthening and there need to be specific awareness campaigns which raise women's awareness of abusive and violent behaviours from men as not being 'normal' or what you do in heterosexual relationships. Gender-neutral approaches fail to tackle the problems women frequently have in defining certain practices as abusive.

Women are still seen as skilled in emotion work (more skilled than men are) and as the carers of children and others. This is problematic in the sense that an identity which is caring can be manipulated by abusive men to their own ends. Furthermore, because women themselves believe in their ability to negotiate change and deal with emotional issues, it encourages women to stay in an abusive relationship without seeking support elsewhere. Continued acceptance of gendered discourse and practice on emotion work and caring is perpetuated in the print and visual media. One example would be the ubiquitous book, *Men are from Mars, Women are from Venus* which reinforces assumptions about polarised gender differences and teaches women and men to accept the status quo. Another recent controversial example is *Bring Your Man to Heel* (BBC2 series, August 2005). This programme is based on the theory that if you can train a dog to behave, then women can use the same techniques on men. There has been much justified criticism about this series in terms of the programme makers' contempt for men. However, what has not been noted is that at the same time it puts responsibility onto women for changing men's behaviour, rather than men looking at and changing their own behaviour. The assumption of women's (wives or partners) responsibility for men's behaviour in the home is commonplace and is often applied to relationships where domestic violence occurs which results in women's experiences of shame and self-blame. Addressing the emotions of shame and blame experienced by women is crucial. We must continue the ongoing work to de-stigmatise domestic violence by talking about it far more widely and challenging any responses which would deny or minimise violence and blame women.

In the public sphere and the home, structured gendered divisions remain a powerful force in women's lives. It is women who are expected to bear the brunt of providing support to children and relatives. Women are often expected to sacrifice themselves within households for the benefit of others; for example by having less food, or by going without other things. As Land and Rose say social policy has failed to take account of the gendered nature of such altruism, 'social policy, because of the significance of altruism in maintaining social solidarity, has a long history of lovingly detailing the self-sacrifice of women, above all poor women, and yet it does not see the engendered character of the act nor does it feel it necessary to determine its social origins' (1985, p. 79). From the evidence of my research it appears that there is still truth in this, for women who experience domestic violence, as well as for those who do not.

Many more people are needed to challenge male violence against women and solutions to this widespread problem must come from the local as well as national and international levels. Focusing on either agency support or informal support networks does not do justice to the scale of the problem; both domains of support are needed and indeed interact with each other. Let us return to the original meaning of the term 'zero tolerance' which was used in the early campaigns to denounce violence against women (Foley, 1993) continuing to work on creating such a climate towards domestic violence.

Notes

Introduction

1 There were many linguistic struggles to be engaged with in writing this book. Deciding which term best described the experiences women related to me was especially problematic. There are a range of gender-neutral terms currently in use, such as, intimate partner violence, common couple violence, family violence, family conflict, domestic violence and coercive control. And there are specifically gendered terms such as, male violence against women, violence against women, violence against women by known men and male coercive control. I decided to use the term domestic violence, since it is the term most commonly recognised worldwide, despite reservations, in particular the way it obscures the gendered dynamics involved and implies such violence only takes place 'in the home'. See Radford (2003) for an insightful discussion on definitional debates in relation to domestic violence in the UK.

2 All the names referred to in this book are pseudonyms to protect women's anonymity.

3 ESRC/Joseph Rowntree, 'Violence, abuse and the stress coping process' 1991–1992; 'Rotherham domestic violence repeat victimization project' 1995 –1996.

4 Patriarchy is a much contested term, in this book I use it in a limited sense as a short-hand to describe male dominance in a particular historical gender order.

5 The malmaritata was either a wife who had fled her abusive husband or a wife whose husband instituted her in an asylum for correction (Cohen, 1992, p. 161).

6 This is not to say that social agencies have achieved high standards of service to women experiencing abuse/violence, there is still a considerable way to go; Amina Mama (2000) for instance identifies the many ways in which agency responses to black women often exacerbate the negative consequences of domestic violence.

7 The 'battered woman' is linked in the public imaginary with visible injuries, and women experiencing domestic violence where there are no visible injuries may not see themselves as experiencing domestic violence.

8 I owe this to Liz Kelly in a private communication 2005.

9 For the reader new to this field good overviews are to be found in: Dobash and Dobash 1979, 1992; Kelly, 1988; Yllo and Bograd, 1988 and Stanko, 1990.

10 The British Crime Surveys of 1996 and 2001 included self-completion modules on 'domestic violence and these are viewed as providing a far more complete measure of domestic violence' (Mirrlees-Black, 1999; Walby and Allen, 2004). Prevalence rates derived from the 2001 self-completion

module, for instance, were around five times higher for all adults than those obtained from the face-to-face interviews (Dodd et al., 2004, p. 74).

Chapter 1   Coercion and 'Consensus'

1 'Patriarchy' is a much contested term and here I use it in a limited sense as a short-hand to describe male dominance in a particular historical gender order.
2 Lundgren (1998) has interviewed couples in four different groups, however, her analysis in this article is based on a series of interviews with one couple who were part of a fundamentalist Christian group that was particularly close-knit and restrictive.
3 Susan Griffin argued that a 'male protection racket' exists in which male partners supposedly protect women from other men, women become more dependent on them and hence become more vulnerable to abuse by them (1971 cited in Kelly, 1988, p. 23); Hanmer and Stanko (1985) also deconstruct the discourse of 'male protection' exposing it as rhetoric.
4 There is a lot of debate about the existence and significance of this concept (Frosh, Phoenix and Pattman, 2002, p. 11) however interviews with women revealed that attributes like the ability to fight can be attractive to heterosexual women. The concept comes from R.W. Connell (1987, 1995) and refers to a dominant form of masculinity which is constructed in relation to subordinated masculinities and in relation to women (Connell, 1987, p. 183); 'hegemonic' masculinity is not a fixed character type but as a position in a given pattern of gender relations is always contestable. (Connell, 1995, p. 76).
5 This approach to gender has been influential especially in the field of 'masculinities and crime' in criminology (see for example Collier, 1998; Jefferson and Collier, 1997; Newburn and Stanko, 1994).
6 Dobash et al. (1996) found a correlation between a reduction of patriarchal attitudes and a reduction in the extent to which men used violence against their partner.
7 Moreover, research has also revealed that work site settings, which take women out of the home, often tend to reinforce hegemonic masculinity and femininity (see e.g. Hochschild, 1983; Adkins, 1995), and hence heterosexuality.
8 Chapter 2 details men's use of this strategy.

Chapter 2   Love and Shame

1 Here I refer to self-blame and blame imputed by others, however I look at the latter aspect in Chapter 6.
2 This is not to imply fixity but gendered emotional dynamics can at times seem to interlock in this way.
3 The ideal of beauty is not simply re-enforced by individual men but through patriarchal institutions in western societies, see Naomi Wolf, 1991, *The Beauty Myth*, which examines the cosmetics industry and the marketing of unrealistic standards of beauty.

4 The ways in which this message is reinforced in the media are legion; see for example 'Ten Years Younger' on Channel 4.

Chapter 3   Mothers and Children

1 See Department of Trade and Industry 2005 Work and Families: choice and flexibility, a consultation document.
2 Mandy's partner insisted in accompanying her to every ante-natal appointment. She was unsure whether this was because he didn't like her to be examined by the doctors. Whilst she was undressing in the toilet he had read her diary which had a few snippets in it saying, 'you know I hate him blah blah' which started an argument. The nurse asked whether he was staying for the birth and Mandy replied, 'I don't know, you better ask him'. So when the nurse walked out he said, 'what do you mean better ask him', punched Mandy in her face and then stormed out.
3 The study sample comprised only women who had left their violent relationships and so women who don't leave may continue to believe that keeping the family together is better for their children (see Hague and Wilson, 1996; Mullender, 1996).
4 Helen Baker argues that even at the limits of our existence as, for example, in domestic violence contexts, discourses of strengths and weaknesses act upon women at this time. Women are constructed in certain terms, essentially as weak, and often refuse to see themselves as 'strong', since certainty of strength would indicate a lack in femininity. Women do have the potential to be strong, but strength comes into existence at 'bare life' levels when women hit 'rock bottom' (2004).
5 The abuse of animals has now been recognised as one aspect of domestic violence and this can particularly affect children and young people (Stalford, Baker and Beveridge, 2003, p. 27). There is now a charity called Paws for Kids which fosters the pet animals of women and children escaping domestic violence see www.pawsforkids.org.uk.

Chapter 4   Home and Security

1 This was a hostel and not a Women's Aid refuge.

Chapter 5   Work and Money

1 For further information see the Mifumi Project web site at http://www.mifumi.org/.
2 There has also been recent important work on the financial costs of domestic violence to the public sector, the measurement of which poses difficulties, but this is not an area of work I address here due to my focus on women's perspectives; See Crisp and Stanko (2001) and Walby (2004) for helpful reviews of studies on the public costs of domestic violence.
3 They also found that two-thirds, 67 per cent, said they were physically, sexually and/or emotionally abused during childhood.

4 Tolman and Raphael (2000) found that few TANF participants disclose domestic violence to welfare caseworkers; most States do not track these numbers but where data exist rates are between 5 and 10 per cent of case-load (Raphael and Haennicke, 1999 cited in Tolman and Raphael, 2000, p. 676). These statistics are lower than the prevalence of domestic violence identified by research and overall the number of FVO waivers is low, so women find it difficult to disclose abuse and will therefore fail to access agency support.

5 Individual incomes of men and women 1996/97 to 2001/02, Median total weekly income where all sources of income are included.

6 *Source*: Ofsted, 2003, Registered childcare providers and places in England 30 September 2003; ONS, 2003, mid-2002 population estimates.

7 Research reveals that poor women experience more physical and mental health problems than women in general (Tolman and Rosen, 2001).

8 One study found that 12 per cent of the women who had experienced severe abuse in the past 12 months were also either drug or alcohol 'dependent' compared to 6 per cent of those whose abuse was less recent, and 2 per cent of those who reported no severe abuse (Tolman and Rosen, 2001)

9 Note the problematic nature of a risk assessment approach taking the perspective of professional workers rather than the women themselves.

10 A nationally representative sample of 22,463 women and men aged 16–59 were asked, via a computerised self-completion questionnaire, whether they had been subject to domestic violence, sexual assault or stalking during their lifetime and during the preceding year. Those who had been subject to such incidents were asked details about their experiences.

11 Eight of the women had a gross income of between £61 and £80 per week. One woman was in the £45 per week income bracket because her only son was old enough to be working and so she was on a single person's benefit. Only Mandy was receiving in excess of £125 a week, and this was because she had a disabled son to care for and so was entitled to Disability Living Allowance and Invalid Carer's Allowance in addition to Income Support. Mandy has a disabled son and therefore received Disability Living Allowance and Invalid Carer's Allowance. Lucy, with five children, was entitled to £100 per week but had gas and electricity arrears (from her time in the relationship) taken from her benefit at source taking her income down to £75 per week.

12 Problems remain for women trying to obtain legal protection from violence and the Protection from Harassment Act 1997 is being under used to protect women in situations of post-separation violence (Humphreys and Thiara, 2002, p. 54).

Chapter 6   Family and Friends

1 Signs of physical abuse may not be evident as violent men often learn to target hidden areas of women's bodies for violence, however signs of emotional abuse include: nervousness, depression or withdrawal, being overly anxious about her partner and his moods, stopping seeing her family and friends.

2 At the present time it tends to be women who seek help in stopping the violence but in future it is to be hoped that increasingly men will also seek help with their violence; in this work, however, I focus solely on support for women and children.

Chapter 7   Community and Safety

1 Two women were in temporary accommodation on interview.
2 There has been a range of new guidance around domestic violence since this study was carried out, but the need for police officers to take strong action with domestic violence perpetrators was in place with the earlier guidance in Home Office Circular 19/2000.
3 Humphreys and Thiara (2002, p. 49) found that when rating their experience of first contact almost equal numbers of women found the police very helpful (36.7 per cent), fairly helpful (32.8 per cent) and unhelpful (30.5 per cent).
4 In Sally's case her ex-partner was finally arrested whilst attacking her outside the house; he was charged with two offences, this assault and a previous unconnected offence; when the case came to court he was sentenced to three months imprisonment, not for the assault on her but for the prior offence.
5 I have no way of checking the accuracy of this information but this was what I was told by Catherine and I have no reason to doubt her word, and whatever the case was, someone had given him her new address.

Conclusion

1 Advisory Board on Family Law: Children Act Sub Committee (1999) 'Report to the Lord Chancellor on the Question of Parental Contact in cases where there is Domestic Violence'.
2 Hunt and Roberts (2004) 'Child contact with non-resident parents' Family Policy Briefing.
3 A v N (Committal: Refusal of Contact) [1996].
4 In relation to rape, for example, the government is prioritising Sexual Assault Referral Centres (SARCs) which provide crisis services but in many places this has resulted in the marginalisation of Rape Crisis Centres which provide long-term support (Jones, 2004).
5 'In England there were five key programmes. The Sandwell pack "Violence free relationships"; the Westminster programme; work based on Protective Behaviours – a personal safety programme; Islington's STOP pack ... and five current or past programmes developed by Leeds Inter-Agency Project (LIAP) ...' (Ellis, 2004, p. 3); see also Womankind 'Challenging violence: changing lives', PSHE and the Welsh PSE Framework.

References

Abrahams, C. 1994 *The hidden victims: children and domestic violence*, London: NCH Action for Children.

Abrar, S. 1996 Feminist intervention and local domestic violence policy, *Parliamentary Affairs*, Vol. 49(1), 191–205.

Adkins, L. 1995 *Gendered work, sexuality, family and the labour market*, Buckingham: Open University Press.

American Psychological Association 1996 *Violence and the family*, Report of the American Psychological Association Presidential Task Force on Violence and the Family, http://www.apa.org/pi/wpo/maleviol.html accessed 3 September.

Archer, J. 2000 'Sex differences in aggression between heterosexual partners: a meta-analytic review', *Psychological Bulletin*, 126, 651–80.

Aris, R., Harrison, C. and Humphreys, C. 2002 *Safety and child contact: an analysis of the role of child contact centres in the context of domestic violence and child welfare concerns*, London: Lord Chancellor's Department, Executive Summary; http://www.dca.gov.uk/research/2002/10-02es.htm accessed 3 September 2005.

Backett, K. 1982 *Mothers and fathers: a study of the development and negotiation of parental behaviour*, London: Macmillan.

Backett, K. 1987 'The negotiation of fatherhood' in C. Lewis and M. O'Brien, *Reassessing fatherhood*, London: Sage.

Bagshaw, D. and Chung, D. 2000 'Gender politics and research: male and female violence in intimate relationships', *Violence Against Women*, 8, 4–24.

Baker, H. 2004 *Law, domestic violence and the limits of existence*, Unpublished paper given at the British Society of Criminology Annual Conference, University of Portsmouth.

Ball, C. and Ball, M. 1982 *What the neighbours say: a report on a study of neighbours*, Berkhampsted, Herts: The Volunteer Centre.

Barbalet, J. 2002 'Introduction: why emotions are crucial', in J. Barbalet (ed.) *Emotions and sociology*, Oxford: Blackwell Publishing/The Sociological Review.

Batsleer, J., Burman, E., Chantler, K., McIntoch, H.S., Pantling, K., Smailes, S. and Warner, S. 2002 *Domestic violence and minoritisation – supporting women to independence*, Manchester: Women's Studies Research Centre, Manchester Metropolitan University.

BBC 2005 *Bring your man to heel*, series of six TV programmes, BBC2, from Monday 22 August.

Bean, C. 1992 *Women murdered by the men they loved*, New York: Haworth.

Bell, A., Finch, N., La Valle, I., Sainsbury, R. and Skinner, C. 2005 *A question of balance: lone parents, childcare and work*, Department for Work and Pensions, Research Report No. 230, www.dwp.gov.uk/ accessed 3 September 2005.

Belle, D. 1983 'The impact of poverty on social networks and supports', *Marriage and Family Review*, 5, 89–103.

Bendelow, G. and Williams, S.J. (eds) 1998 *Emotions in social life: critical themes and contemporary issues*, London and New York: Routledge.

Benjamin, J. 1990 *The bonds of love: psychoanalysis, feminism, and the problem of domination*, London: Virago.

Benjamin, O. 1999 'Therapeutic discourse, power and change: emotion and negotiation in marital conversations', *Sociology* 32, 771–93.

Binney, V., Harkell, G. and Nixon, J. 1981 *Leaving violent men: a study of refuges and housing for battered women*, London: WAFE.

Bordo, S. 1993 *Unbearable weight: feminism, Western culture and the body*, Berkeley: University of California Press.

Borkowski, M., Murch, M. and Walker, V. 1983 *Marital violence: the community response*, London: Tavistock.

Bourdieu, P. 1996 'On the family as a realised category', *Theory, Culture and Society* 13, 19–26.

Bradshaw, J. and Millar, J. 1991 *Lone parent families in the U.K.*, London: H.M.S.O.

Braidotti, R. 2005 'A critical cartography of feminist post-postmodernism', *Australian Feminist Studies*, 20(47), 169–80.

Briggs, C.L. 1986 *Learning how to ask: a socio-linguistic appraisal of the role of the interview in social science research*, Cambridge: Cambridge University Press.

British Medical Association (BMA) 1998 *Domestic violence: a health care issue*, D. Morgan (ed.), London: BMA.

Brody, L. 1999 *Gender, emotion and the family*, Cambridge, Mass.: Harvard University Press.

Brownmiller, S. 1975 *Against our will: men, women and rape*, London: Secker and Warburg.

Bryson, V. 1992 *Feminist political theory: an introduction*, Basingstoke, Macmillan.

Bull, J. 1993 *Housing consequences of relationship breakdown*, Department of Environment, London: H.M.S.O.

Bulmer, M. 1979 Concepts in the analysis of qualitative data, *Sociological Review*, 27(4), 651–79.

Burman, M., Brown, J. and Batchelor, S. 2003 'Taking it to Heart': Girls and the meanings of Violence' in Stanko, E.A. (ed.) *The Meaning of Violence*, London: Routledge.

Butler, J. 1990 *Gender trouble*, New York, London: Routledge.

Campbell, B. 1993 *Goliath: Britain's dangerous places*, London: Methuen.

Campbell, J.C. 1992 'If I can't have you, no one can: power and control in homicide of female partners' in J. Radford and D.E.H. Russell (eds), *Femicide*, Toronto: Maxwell Macmillan.

Carby, H. 1982 'White woman listen! Black feminism and the boundaries of sisterhood' in Centre for Contemporary Studies, *The empire strikes back: race and racism in 70's Britain*, London: Hutchinson.

Carrington, K. and Phillips, J. 2003 *Domestic violence in Australia – an overview of the issues*, http://www.aph.gov.au/library/intguide/SP/Dom_violence.htm accessed 9 November 2004.

Cavanagh, C. 1978 *Battered women and social control: a study of the help-seeking behaviour of battered women and the help-giving behaviour of those from whom they seek help*, Thesis for M.Sc. Department of Sociology, University of Sterling.

Chapman, T. 1999 'Spoiled home identities: the experience of burglary', in T. Chapman and J. Hockey (eds), *Ideal homes? Social change and domestic life*, London and New York: Routledge.

Charles, N. 1994 'The housing needs of women and children escaping domestic violence', *Journal of Social Policy*, 23(4), 465–87.

Chodorow, N. 1978 *The reproduction of mothering*, Berkeley: University of California Press.

City Council 1995 *Areas of poverty 1994*, City Council.

Clifton, J. 1985 'Refuges and self-help', in N. Johnson (ed.) *Marital violence*, London: Routledge Kegan and Paul.

Cohen, S. 1992 *The evolution of women's asylums since 1500: from refuges for ex-prostitutes to shelters for battered women*, New York and Oxford: Oxford University Press.

Cockburn, C. 1983 *Brothers: Male dominance and technological change*, London: Pluto Press.

Cockburn, C. 1991 *In the way of women: men's resistance to sex equality in organizations*, London: Macmillan.

Cockburn, C. 2004 *The line: women, partition and the gender order in Cyprus*, London and New York: Zed Books.

Collier, R. 1998 *Masculinities, crime and criminology: men, heterosexuality and the criminal(ized) other*, London: Sage.

Connell, R.W. 1987 *Gender and power*, London: Allen and Unwin.

Connell, R.W. 1995 *Masculinities: knowledge, power and social change*, Cambridge: Polity Press.

Connell, R.W. 2002 *Gender*, Cambridge: Polity.

Coveney, L., Jackson, M., Jeffreys, S., Kaye, L. and Mahony, P. 1984 *The sexuality papers: male sexuality and the social control of women*, London; Dover, NH: Hutchinson in association with the Explorations in Feminism Collective.

Crisp, D. and Stanko, B. 2001 Monitoring costs and evaluating needs, in J. Taylor-Browne (ed.) *What works in reducing domestic violence? A comprehensive guide for professionals*, London: Whiting and Birch, pp. 335–58.

Crossley, N. 2005 *Key concepts in critical social theory*, London and Thousand Oaks, CA: Sage.

Daly, M. and Saraceno, C. 2002 'Social exclusion and gender relations', In B. Hobson, J. Lewis and B. Siim (eds) *Contested concepts in gender and social politics*, Cheltenham: Edward Elgar, pp. 84–104.

Daly, M. and Rake, K. 2003 *Gender and the welfare state: care, work and welfare in Europe and the USA*, Cambridge, UK; Malden, MA: Polity Press.

Darke, J. 1994 'Women and the meaning of home', in R. Gilroy and R. Woods (eds) *Housing women*, London: Routledge.

Davis, C. 2003 *Housing associations – rehousing women leaving domestic violence: new challenges and good practice*, Bristol: Policy Press.

De Beauvoir, S. 1997 [1949] *The second sex*, London: Vintage.

Deem, R. 1986 *All work and no play?: a study of women and leisure*, Milton Keynes: Open University Press.

Denzin, N.K. 1984 *On understanding emotion*, San Francisco; London: Jossey-Bass.

Department of Health 1999 *Working together to safeguard children: a guide to inter-agency working to safeguard and promote the welfare of children*, London: The Stationery Office.

Department of Health 2000a *Domestic violence: a resource manual for health care professionals*, London: The Stationery Office.

Department of Health 2000b *Framework for the assessment of children in need and their families*, London: The Stationery Office.

Department of Health 2002 *Women's mental health: into the mainstream, strategic development of mental health care for women*; www.doh.gov.uk accessed 2 February 2004.

Department of Trade and Industry 2005 *Work and Families: choice and flexibility, a consultation document*, www.dti.gov.uk/er/choice_flexibility_consultation.doc accessed 4 August 2005.

Derr, M.K. and Taylor, M.J. 2004 The link between childhood and adult abuse among long-term welfare recipients, *Children and Youth Services Review*, 26(2), pp. 173–84.

Dispatches 1994 'Getting away with rape', *Channel 4*, 6 February.

Dobash, R.E. and Dobash, R.P. 1979 *Violence against wives: a case against the patriarchy*, London: Open Books.

Dobash, R.E. and Dobash, R.P. 1992 *Women, violence and social change*, London and New York: Routledge.

Dobash, R.P., et al. 1996 *Re-education programmes for violent men: an evaluation*, London: Home Office Research and Statistics Directorate.

Dobash, R.E. and Dobash, R.P. 2000 'The politics and policies of responding to violence against women' in *Home truths about domestic violence: feminist influences on policy and practice – a reader*, London and New York: Routledge, pp. 187–204.

Dodd, T., Nicholas, S., Povey, D. and Walker, A. 2004 *Crime in England and Wales 2003/2004*, Home Office Statistical Bulletin 10/04, London: Stationery Office.

Dominy, N. and Radford, L. 1996 *'Domestic' violence in Surrey: Developing an effective inter-agency response*, London: Roehampton Institute.

Douglas, M. 1991 'The idea of a home: a kind of space', *Social Research* 58(1), 287–307.

Dovey, K. 1985 'Home and homelessness' in I. Altman and C. Werner (eds) *Home environments*, New York: Plenum.

Duncombe, J. and Marsden, D. 1993 'Love and intimacy: the gender division of emotion and "emotion work"', *Sociology*, 27(2), 221–41.

Duncombe, J. and Marsden, D. 1996 'Extending the social: a response to Ian Craib', *Sociology*, 30(1), 155–8.

Duncombe, J. and Marsden, D. 1998 '"Stepford wives" and "hollow men"? Doing emotion work, doing gender and "authenticity" in intimate heterosexual relationships', in G. Bendelow and S.J. Williams (eds) 1998 *Emotions in social life: critical themes and contemporary issues*, London and New York: Routledge.

Edleson, J.L. 1999 'The overlap between child maltreatment and woman battering', *Violence Against Women*, 5, February 134–54.

Ellis, J. 2004 *Preventing violence against women and girls: a study of educational programmes for children and young people*, Coventry: Womankind/University of Warwick.

Fagan, C. 2000 *Who works long hours and why?* Paper presented at the 2000 BSA Annual Conference, Manchester: Department of Sociology, University of Manchester.

Ferguson, T.J. and Eyre, H.L. 2000 'Engendering gender differences in shame and guilt: sterotypes, socialization, and situational pressures' in A.H. Fischer (ed.) *Gender and emotion: social psychological perspectives*, Cambridge: Cambridge University Press.

Ferraro, K. 1989 'The legal response to woman battering in the United States' in J. Hanmer, L. Radford and E.A. Stanko (eds) *Women, policing and male violence: international perspectives*, Routledge: London and New York.

Fiebert, M. 1997 Annotated bibliography: references examining assaults by women on their spouses/partners, *Sexuality and Culture* 1, 273–86.

Finch, J. and Mason, J. 1993 *Negotiating family responsibilities*, London: Routledge.

Fine, M. and Weis, L. 2000 Disappearing acts: the state and violence against women in the twentieth century, *Signs: Journal of Women in Culture and Society*, 25(41), 1139–45.

Finkelhor, D. and Yllo, K. 1983 *The dark side of families*, London: Sage.

Firestone, S. 1972 *The dialectic of sex: the case for feminist revolution*, London: The Women's Press.

Fischer, A.H. (ed.) 2000 *Gender and emotion: social psychological perspectives*, Cambridge: Cambridge University Press.

Florida Governor's Task Force on Domestic and Sexual Violence 1997 *Florida Mortality Review Project*.

Foley, R. 1993 Zero Tolerance, *Trouble and Strife*, 27, 16–20.

Ford, R., Marsh, A. and McKay, S. 1995 *Changes in lone parenthood 1989 to 1993*, a study carried out on behalf of the Department of Social Security by the Policy Studies Institute, DSS Research Report No. 40, London: H.M.S.O.

Forman, J. 1995 *Is there a correlation between child sexual abuse and domestic violence? An exploratory study of the links between child sexual abuse and domestic violence in a sample of intrafamilial child sexual abuse cases*, Glasgow: Women's Support Project.

Frosh, S., Phoenix, A. and Pattman, R. 2002 *Young masculinities: Understanding boys in contemporary society*, Basingstoke: Palgrave.

Foucault, M. 1980 *Power/knowledge: selected interviews and other writings, 1972–1977*, edited by C. Gordon, New York: Pantheon Books.

Foucault, M. 1983 'Afterword: the subject of power', In H. Dreyfus and P. Rabinow (eds), *Michel Foucault: Beyond structuralism and hermeneutics*, Chicago: University of Chicago Press, pp. 208–26.

Galtung, J. 1975 *Essays in peace research*, Copenhagen: Christian Ejlers.

Giddens, A. 1984 *The constitution of society: outline of the theory of structuration*, Cambridge: Polity Press.

Giddens, A. 1990 *The consequences of modernity*, Cambridge: Polity.

Giddens, A. 1991 *Modernity and self identity*, Cambridge: Polity.

Gilligan, C. 1982 *In a different voice: psychological theory and women's development*, Cambridge, Mass: Harvard University Press.

Glaser, B.G. and Strauss, A.L. 1967 *The discovery of grounded theory: strategies for qualitative research*, New York: Aldine de Gruyter.

Goffman, E. 1952 'On cooling the mark out: some aspects of adaptation to failure', Indianapolis: Bobbs-Merrill.

Goffman, E. 1959 *The Presentation of Self in Everyday Life*, New York: Doubleday Anchor.

Goldsack, L. 1999 'A haven in a heartless world? Women and domestic violence', in T. Chapman and J. Hockey (eds), *Ideal homes? Social change and domestic life*, London and New York: Routledge, pp. 121–32.

Gorin, S. 2004 *Understanding what children say: children's experiences of domestic violence, parental substance misuse and parental health problems*, London: National Children's Bureau.

Grace, S. 1995 *Policing domestic violence in the 1990s*, Home Office Research Study 139, Home Office Research and Planning Unit, London: H.M.S.O.

Gramsci, A. 1971 *Selections from the prison notebooks of Antonio Gramsci*, edited and translated by Q. Hoare and G. Nowell Smith, New York and London: Lawrence and Wishart.

Gregory, J. and Lees, S. 1999 *Policing sexual assault*, London: Routledge.

Griffiths, S. 2000 'Women, anger and domestic violence: the implications for legal defences to murder', in J. Hanmer and C. Itzin (eds) *Home truths about domestic violence: feminist influences on policy and practice – a reader*, London and New York: Routledge.

Gupta, R. (ed.) 2003 *From homebreakers to jailbreakers: Southall Black Sisters*, London: Zed Books.

Gupta, R. 2004 'Wake up, activists are pounding on doors of ivory towers', The *Times Higher Education Supplement*, 28 May, pp. 20–1.

Hague, G. and Malos, E. 1994 'Children, domestic violence and housing: the impact of homelessness' in A. Mullender, and R. Morley (eds) *Children living with domestic violence: putting men's abuse of women on the child care agenda*, London: Whiting & Birch.

Hague, G. and Wilson, C. 1996 *The silenced pain: domestic violence, 1945–1970*, Bristol: Policy Press.

Hanmer, J. 1978 'Violence and the social control of women' in G. Littlejohn, B. Smart, J. Wakeford and N. Yuval-Davis (eds) *Power and the state*, London: Croom Helm, pp. 217–38.

Hanmer, J. 1989 'Women and policing in Britain', in J. Hanmer, J. Radford and E.A. Stanko (eds) *Women, policing and male violence: international perspectives*, London and New York: Routledge.

Hanmer, J. 1995 *Sexual violence and social support: the experience of English and Asian women*, Paper given at the Sexual Abuse of Women and Girls Conference, Stockholm, Sweden: ROKS (Swedish Organisation of Emergency Shelters) January.

Hanmer, J. 1996 'Women and violence: commonalities and diversities' in B. Fawcett, B. Featherstone, J. Hearn and C. Toft (eds) *Violence and gender relations: theories and interventions*, London: Sage.

Hanmer, J. 2000 'Domestic violence and gender relations: contexts and connections' in J. Hanmer and C. Itzin (eds), *Home truths about domestic violence: feminist influences on policy and practice, a reader*, London: Routledge.

Hanmer, J. and Maynard, M. (eds) 1987 *Women, violence and social control*, London: Macmillan.

Hanmer, J. and Saunders, S. 1984 *Well founded fear: a community study of violence to women*, London: Hutchinson.

Hanmer, J. and Stanko, E. 1985 Stripping away the rhetoric of protection: violence to women, law and the state in Britain and the USA, *International Journal of the Sociology of Law*, 13(4), 357–74

Hanmer, J. and Itzin, C. (eds) 2000 *Home truths about domestic violence: feminist influences on policy and practice – a reader*, London and New York: Routledge.

Hannah-Moffat, K. 2004 'Gendering risk at what cost? Negotiations of gender and risk in Canadian women's prisons', *Feminism and Psychology*, 14(2), 241–7.

Harwin, N., Hague, G. and Malos, E. 1999 *The multi-agency approach to domestic violence: new opportunities, old challenges?* London: Whiting and Birch.

Hatty, S. 1989 'Policing and male violence in Australia' in J. Hanmer, J. Radford and E.A. Stanko (eds) *Women, policing and male violence: international perspectives*, London and New York: Routledge.

Hearn, J. 1996 'The organization(s) of violence: men, gender relations, organizations and violences' in B. Fawcett, B. Featherstone, J. Hearn and C. Toft (eds) *Violence and gender relations: theories and interventions*, London: Sage.

Hearn, J. 1998 *The violences of men: how men talk about and how agencies respond to men's violence to women*, London: Sage.

Hearn, J. and Parkin, W. 1983 Gender and organisations: a selective review and a critique of a neglected area, *Organisation Studies*, 4, 219–42.

Hearn, J. and Parkin, W. 1987 *'Sex' at work: the power and paradox of organisation sexuality*, Brighton: Wheatsheaf.

Heise, L.L. 1996 'Violence against women: global organizing for change' in J.L. Edleson and Z.C. Edleson (eds) *Future intervention with battered women and their families*, Thousand Oaks, CA, London, New Delhi: Sage.

Henderson, A.D. 1990 'Children of abused wives: their influence on their mothers' decisions', *Canada's Mental Health*, 88, 10–13.

Henriques, J., Hollway, W., Urwin, C., Venn, C. and Walkerdine, V. 1984 *Changing the subject: psychology, social regulation and subjectivity*, London and New York: Methuen.

Hester, M. and Radford, L. 1992 'Domestic violence and access arrangements for children in Denmark and Britain', *Journal of Social Welfare and Family Law*, Vol. 1, 57–70.

Hester, M., Humphries, J., Pearson, C., Qaiser, Radford, L. and Woodfield, K. 1994 'Separation, divorce, child contact and domestic violence' in A. Mullender and R. Morley (eds) *Children living with domestic violence: putting men's abuse of women on the child care agenda*, London: Whiting & Birch.

Hester, M. and Radford, L. 1996 *Domestic violence and child contact arrangements in England and Denmark*, Bristol: Policy Press.

Hester, M., Kelly, L. and Radford, J. (eds) 1996 *Women, violence and male power: feminist activism, research and practice*, Buckingham: Open University Press.

Hester, M., Pearson, C. and Harwin, N. 2000 *Making an impact: children and domestic violence – a reader*, London: Jessica Kingsley.

Hilton, N.Z. 1992 Battered women's concerns about their children witnessing wife assault, *Journal of Interpersonal Violence*, 7(1), 77–86.

Hoare, Q. and Nowell Smith, G. (eds) 1971 *Selections from the prison notebooks of Antonio Gramsci*, New York: International Publishers.

Hochschild, A.R. 1983 *The managed heart: the commercialization of human feeling*, Berkeley: University of California Press.

Hoff, L.A. 1990 *Battered women as survivors*, London and New York: Routledge.

Holland, J., Ramazanoglu, C., Sharpe, S. and Thomson, R. 2004 [1998] *The male in the head: young people, heterosexuality and power*, 2nd edn. London: The Tufnell Press.

Hollway, W. 1996 'Gender and power in organizations' In B. Fawcett, B. Featherstone, J. Hearn and C. Toft (eds) *Violence and gender relations: theories and interventions*, London and Thousand Oaks, CA: Sage.

Home Office 1998 *Supporting families: a consultation document*, http://www.homeoffice.gov.uk/docs/suppfam.html accessed 6 August 2005.

Home Office 2005 *Domestic violence: a national report* 2005 www.crimereduction.gov.uk accessed 3 September, 2005.

Holter, H. (ed.) 1984 *Patriarchy in a welfare society*, Bergen: University of Bergen Press.

Home Office/Cabinet Office 1999 *Living without fear: an integrated approach to tackling violence against women*, London: Cabinet Office Women's Unit.

Home Office 2000 *Living without fear: multi-agency guidance for addressing domestic violence*, London: Cabinet Office Women's Unit.

Home Office 2003 *Safety and justice: the government's proposals on domestic violence*, CM 5847, London: HMSO.

Home Office Web Site 2004 http://www.homeoffice.gov.uk/crime/domesticviolence/ accessed 27 October 2004.

Homer, M., Leonard, A.E. and Taylor, M.P. 1984 *Private violence: public shame*, Cleveland and Bristol: Cleveland Refuge Aid for Women and Children/ Women's Aid Federation England.

hooks, bell 1982 *Ain't I a woman, black women and feminism*, London: Pluto.

Horley, S. 2002 *Power and control: why charming men can make dangerous lovers*, London: Vermilion.

Hotaling, G. and Sugarman, D. 1990 'A risk marker analysis of assaulted wives', *Journal of Family Violence*, 5(1), 1–13.

Humphreys, C. 2000 *Social work, domestic violence and child protection: challenging practice*, Bristol: The Policy Press.

Humphreys, C. 2003 Focusing on safety – domestic violence and the role of child contact centres, *Children and Family Law Quarterly*, 15(3), 237–53.

Humphreys, C. and Thiara, R. 2002 *Routes to safety*, Bristol: WAFE.

Humphreys, C. and Thiara, R.K. 2003 'Neither justice nor protection: women's experiences of post-separation violence', *Journal of Social Welfare and Family Law*, 25(3), 195–214.

Hunt, J. and Roberts, C. 2004 *Child contact with non-resident parents*, Family Policy Briefing 3, Department of Social Policy and Social Work, Oxford: University of Oxford, http://www.apsoc.ox.ac.uk/Docs/Childcontact.pdf accessed 3 September 2005.

Immigrant Women's Speakout Association 2000 *Trapped in violence*, New South Wales, Australia.

Itzin, C. 2000a 'Gendering domestic violence: the influence of feminism on policy and practice' in J. Hanmer and C. Itzin (eds) *Home truths about domestic violence: feminist influences on policy and practice – a reader*, London and New York: Routledge.

Jackson, S. 1993 Even sociologists fall in love: an exploration in the sociology of emotions, Sociology, 27(2), 201–20.

Jackson, R. 1994 *Mothers who leave: behind the myth of women without their children*, London: HarperCollins.

Jaffe, P., Wolfe, D., Wilson, S.K. and Zak, L. 1986 'Family violence and child adjustment: a comparative analysis of girls' and boys' behavioural symptoms', *American Journal of Psychiatry*, 143, 74–7.

Jaffe, P.G., Wolfe, D.A. and Wilson, S.K. (eds) 1990 *Children of battered women*, Newbury Park, CA: Sage.

Jaffe, P.G., Lemon, N.K.D., Poisson, S.E. 2003 *Child custody and domestic violence: a call for safety and accountability*, Thousand Oaks, CA and London: Sage.

Jaggar, A.M. 1989 'Love and knowledge: emotion in feminist epistemology' in A.M. Jaggar and S.R. Bordo (eds) *Gender/Body/Knowledge: feminist reconstructions of being and knowing*, New Brunswich, NJ: Rutgers University Press.

Jamieson, L. 1998 *Intimacy, personal relationships in modern societies*, Cambridge: Polity Press.

Jaskinski, J.L. 2004 'Pregnancy and domestic violence: a review of the literature', *Trauma, Violence and Abuse*, Vol. 5(1), 47–64.

Jefferson, T. and Collier, R. 1997 'Masculinities and crime', in M. Maguire, R. Morgan and R. Reiner (eds) *The Oxford handbook of criminology*, Oxford: Clarendon.

Johnson, H. 1995 'Risk factors associated with non-lethal violence against women by married partners' in C.R. Block and R. Block (eds) *'Trends, risks and interventions in lethal violence'*, Vol. 3. National Institute of Justice, Washington D.C.

Jones, H. 2004 'Opportunities and obstacles: the Rape Crisis Federation in the UK', *Journal of International Gender Studies*, Vol. 8.

Kahn, J. 2003 *Missing out on education: children and young people speak out*, London: Save the Children.

Kallstrom Cater, A. 2004 *Negotiating normality and deviation – father's violence against mother from children's perspectives*, Doctoral Dissertation, Orebro, Sweden: Orebro University.

Kelly, L. 1988 *Surviving sexual violence*, Cambridge: Polity Press.

Kelly, L. 1994 'The interconnectedness of domestic violence and child abuse: challenges for research, policy and practice' in A. Mullender and R. Morley (eds) *Children living with domestic violence*, London: Whiting & Birch.

Kelly, L. 1996 'Tensions and possibilities: enhancing informal responses to domestic violence' in J.L. Edleson and Z.C. Eisikovits (eds) *Future interventions with battered women and their families*, Thousand Oaks, CA, London and New Delhi: Sage.

Kelly, L. 1999 *Domestic violence matters: an evaluation of a development project*, Home Office Research Study 193, London: Home Office.

Kelly, L. and Humphreys, C. 2001 'Supporting women and children in their communities: Outreach and advocacy approaches to domestic violence', in J. Taylor-Browne (ed.) *What works in reducing domestic violence? A comprehensive guide for professionals*, London: Whiting and Birch.

Kelly, L. and Radford, J. 1996 '"Nothing really happened": the invalidation of women's experiences of sexual violence' in M. Hester, L. Kelly and J. Radford (eds) *Women, violence and male power: feminist activism, research and practice*, Buckingham: Open University Press.

Kenyon, L. 1999 'A home from home: students' transitional experience of home' in T. Chapman and J. Hockey (eds) *Ideal homes? Social change and domestic life*, London and New York: Routledge.

Kimmel, M.S. 2002 'Gender symmetry in domestic violence: A substantive and methodological research review', *Violence against Women*, 8(11), 1332–63.

Kingsmill, D. 2003 *Women's employment and pay*, www.kingsmillreview.gov.uk accessed 3 September 2005.

Kirkwood, C. 1993 *Leaving abusive partners: from the scars of survival to the wisdom for change*, London: Sage.

Koepping, E. 2003 'A game of three monkeys: Kadazan–Dusun villagers and violence against women', *Sojourn*, 18(2), 279–98.

Kolbo, J., Blakely, E.H. and Engleman, D. 1996 'Children who witness domestic violence: a review of empirical literature', *Journal of Interpersonal Violence*, 11(2), 281–93.

Kovalainen, A. 2004 'Rethinking the revival of social capital and trust in social theory: possibilities for feminist analysis' in B.L. Marshall and A. Witz (eds) *Engendering the social: feminist encounters with sociological theory*, Maidenhead: Open University Press.

Kring, A. 2000 'Gender and anger' in A.H. Fischer (ed.) *Gender and emotion: social psychological perspectives*, Cambridge: Cambridge University Press.

Kurz, D. 1996 Separation, divorce and wife abuse, *Violence Against Women*, 2, 63–81.

Land, H. and Rose, H. 1985 Compulsory altruism for some or an altruistic society for all? in P. Bean, J. Ferris and D. Whynes (eds) *In defence of welfare*, London: Tavistock.

Lawrence, S. 2002 *Domestic violence and welfare policy: research findings that can inform policies on marriage and child well-being*, Research Forum on Children, Families and New Federalism, National Center for Children in poverty, Issue Brief.

Leander, K. and Danielsson, M. 2001 (1996) 'Violence against women: A social, criminal justice, medical or public health problem?' in P. Östlin, M. Danielsson, F. Diderichsen, A. Häremstan, G. Lindberg (eds) (transl. by D. Duncan) *Gender inequalities in health: a Swedish perspective*, Boston: Harvard School of Public Health.

Lee, N. 2001 *Childhood and society: growing up in an age of uncertainty*, Buckingham: Open University Press.

Lees, S. 1993 *Sugar and spice: sexuality and adolescent girls*, London: Penguin.

Levison, D. and Harwin, N. 2001 *Reducing domestic violence ... What works? Accommodation provision*, London: Home Office, Policing and Reducing Crime Briefing Note.

Lewis, C. 2000 *A man's place in the home: fathers and families in the UK*, http://www.jrf.org.uk/knowledge/findings/foundations/440.asp accessed 6 August 2005.

Lloyd, S. 1997 'The effects of domestic violence on female employment', *Law and Policy*, 19, 139–67.

Lundgren, E. 1995 *Feminist theory and violent empiricism*, Brookfield USA: Avebury.

Lundgren, E. 1998 'The hand that strikes and comforts: gender construction and the tension between body and symbol' in R.E. Dobash and R.P. Dobash (eds) *Rethinking violence against women*, California: Sage, pp. 169–98.

Lyon, E. 2002 Welfare and domestic violence against women: lessons from research, Violence Against Women Net, www.vawnet.org accessed 3 September 2005.

Mahony, C. 1997 'Babies, bruises and black eyes', *Nursing Times*, 93(51), 17 December, 14–15.

Malos, E. and Hague, G. 1993 *Domestic violence and housing: local authority responses to women and children escaping domestic violence in the home*, Bristol: WAFE and University of Bristol.

Malos, E. and Hague, G. 1997 'Women, housing, homelessness and domestic violence', *Women's Studies International Forum* 20(3), 397–409.

Mama, A. 1989 *The hidden struggle: statutory and voluntary sector responses to violence against Black women in the home*, London: The London Race and Housing Research Unit.

Mama, A. 2000 'Violence against black women in the home' in J. Hanmer and C. Itzin (eds) *Home truths about domestic violence: feminist influences on policy and practice, a reader*, London: Routledge.

Marsh, A. 2001 'Helping British lone parents get and keep paid work' in J. Millar and K. Rowlingson (eds) *Lone parents, employment and social policy: cross-national comparisons*, Bristol: The Policy Press, pp. 11–36.

Marshall, B. and Witz, A. 2002 *Modernity, masculinity and the social: Interrogating classical sociology*, unpublished paper presented to the American Sociological Association.

Massey, D. 1994 *Space, place and gender*, Cambridge: Polity Press.

Massey, D. 1992 'A place called home' in The question of 'home', *New Formations*, 17, 3–15, Summer.

Mason, G. 2002 *The spectacle of violence: homophobia, gender and knowledge*, London and New York: Routledge.

Matthews, J. 1984 *Good and mad women: the historical construction of femininity in Twentieth Century Australia*, Sydney: Allen and Unwin.

Maynard, M. 1985 'The response of social workers to domestic violence' in J. Pahl (ed.) *Private violence and public policy*, London: Routledge and Kegan Paul.

McGee, C. 2000 *Childhood experiences of domestic violence*, London: Jessica Kingsley.

McGibbon, A., Cooper, L. and Kelly, L. 1989 *What support? An exploratory study of council policy and practice, and local support services in the area of 'domestic' violence within Hammersmith and Fulham*. London: Hammersmith and Fulham Council Community Police Committee Domestic Violence Project.

McMahon, M. 1995 *Engendering motherhood: identity and self transformation in women's lives*, New York: The Guildford Press.

McWilliams, M. and McKiernan, J. 1993 *Bringing it out in the open: domestic violence in Northern Ireland*, Belfast: HMSO.

Meisel, J., Chandler, D. and Menees Rienzi, B. 2003 *Domestic violence prevalence and effects on employment in two California TANF populations*, California Institute of Mental Health.

Mirrlees-Black, C. 1999 *Domestic violence: findings from a new British Crime Survey self completion questionnaire*, Home Office Research Studies 191, London: Home Office.

Mohanty, C.T., Russo, A. and Torres, L. (eds) 1991 *Third world women and the politics of feminism*, Indiana: Indiana University Press.

Mooney, J. 1994 *The hidden figure: Domestic violence in North London*, London: Islington Council and Islington Police Crime Prevention Unit.

Mooney, J. 2000 *Gender, violence and the social order*, Basingstoke and New York: Macmillan/St Martins.

Morley, B. 2000 'Domestic violence and housing' in J. Hanmer and C. Itzin (eds) *Home truths about domestic violence: feminist influences on policy and practice: a reader*, London: Routledge.

Mullender, A. 1996 *Rethinking domestic violence: the social work and probation response*, London: Routledge.

Mullender, A. 2003 Stop hitting mum!: children talk about domestic violence, East Molesey: Young Voice.

Mullender, A. and Morley, R. (eds) 1994 *Children living with domestic violence: putting men's abuse of women on the child care agenda*, London: Whiting & Birch.

Mullender, A., Hague, G., Imam, U., Kelly, L., Malos, E. and Regan, L. 2002 *Children's perspectives on domestic violence*, London: Sage.

Murphy, P. 1993 *Making the Connections: Women, Work, and Abuse*, Orlando, FL: Deutsch.

National Resource Center on Domestic Violence (NRCDV) 2005 *Categorized annotated resource guide on housing and domestic violence*, NRCDV, www.vawnet.org/ DomesticViolence/PublicPolicy/Housing/HousingResources.pdf accessed 3 September 2005.

Newburn, T. and Stanko, E.A. (eds) 1994 *Just boys doing business? Men, masculinities and crime*, London and New York: Routledge.

NiCarthy, G. 1986 *Getting free: a handbook for women in abusive situations*, 2nd edn., Seattle WA: Seal.

Nursing Standard 2004 News in brief, 2 June, Vol. 18(38), 4.

Oakley, A. 1974a *Housewife*, London: Allen Lane.

Oakley, A. 1974b *The sociology of housework*, London: Martin Robertson.

Office of the Deputy Prime Minister (ODPM) 2002 *The provision of accommodation and support for households experiencing domestic violence in England*, London:/H.M.S.O. [Research carried out by D. Levison and D. Kenny of the London Research Centre].

Office for National Statistics 1999 *Omnibus Survey*, Table 6.1 Time use by gender, London: Stationery Office.

Office for National Statistics 2003 Labour Force Survey, London: Stationery Office.

Office for National Statistics 2004 Labour Force Survey, London: Stationery Office.

Office for Standards in Education 2003 *Registered childcare providers and places in England*, 30 September 2003, http://www.ofsted.gov.uk/publications/ index.cfm?fuseaction=pubs.summary&id=3446 accessed 3 September 2005.

Okun, L. 1986 *Woman abuse: facts replacing myths*, State University of New York Press, Albany.

Pahl, J. 1985 'Refuges for battered women: ideology and action', *Feminist review*, 19, 25–43.

Palusci, V.J., Paneth, N. and Smith, E.G. 2005 'Predicting and responding to physical abuse in young children using NCANDS', *Children and Youth Services Review*, 27(6), June, 667–82.

Parsons, T., Bales, R.F. and Shils, E. 1953 *Working papers in the theory of action*, Glencoe, Ill.: The Free Press.

Patel, P. 2000 'Southall Black Sisters: domestic violence campaigns and alliances across the divisions of race, gender and class' in J. Hanmer and C. Itzin (eds) *Home truths about domestic violence: feminist influences on policy and practice – a reader*, London and New York: Routledge.

Peled, E., Jaffe, P.G. and Edelson, J.L. (eds) 1995 *Ending the cycle of violence: community responses to children of battered women*, Thousand Oaks, CA, London and New Delhi: Sage.

Pence, E. and Paymar, M. 1990 *Power and control tactics of men who batter*, (rev. edn.), Duluth: Minnesota Development Programme Inc.

Pence, E. 2005a *The Duluth Model and some of the many lessons we can learn from it*, unpublished paper given at 'Violence against women: coordinating activism, research and service provision', ESRC Seminar on Gender Violence, 15 and 16 March 2005 at the University of Bristol.

Pence, E. 2005b *Praxis and Duluth Domestic Abuse Intervention Project*, unpublished paper given at 'Violence against women: coordinating activism, research and service provision' ESRC Seminar on Gender Violence, 15 and 16 March 2005 at the University of Bristol.

Phoenix, A. 1991 *Young mothers?* Cambridge: Polity Press.

Pilcher, J. and Whelehan, I. 2004 *Fifty key concepts in gender studies*, London and Thousand Oaks, CA: Sage.

Pleck, E. 1987 *Domestic tyranny: The making of American social policy against family violence from colonial times to the present*, New York: Oxford University Press.

Quaid, S. and Itzin, C. 2000 'The criminal justice response to women who kill: an interview with Helena Kennedy' in J. Hanmer and C. Itzin (eds) *Home truths about domestic violence: feminist influences on policy and practice, a reader*, London: Routledge.

Radford, L. 1993 'Pleading for time: justice for battered women who kill' in H. Birch (ed.) *Moving targets*, London: Virago.

Radford, J. 2003 'Professionalising responses to domestic violence in the UK: definitional difficulties', *Community Safety Journal*, 2(1), 32–9.

Radford, L. and Hester, M. 2001 'Overcoming mother blaming? Future directions for research on mothering and domestic violence' in S.A. Graham-Bermann and J.L. Edleson (eds) *Future directions for research on mothering and domestic violence*, Washington, DC: American Psychological Association, pp. 135–55.

Radford, L. and Sayer, S. 2002 *Unreasonable fears? Child contact in the context of domestic violence: a survey of mothers' perception of harm*, Bristol: Women's Aid Federation.

Radford, L., Hester, M., Humphries, J. and Woodfield, K.S. 1997 'For the sake of the children: the law, domestic violence and child contact in England', *Women's Studies International Forum*, 20(4), 471–82.

Rai, D.K. and Thiara, R.K. 1997 *Re-defining spaces: the needs of black women and children in refuge support services and black workers in Women's Aid*, Bristol: Women's Aid Federation England.

Ramazanoglu, C. (ed.) 1993 *Up against Foucault: explorations of some tensions between Foucault and feminism*, London and New York: Routledge.

Ramazanoglu, C. and Holland, J. 1993 'Women's sexuality and men's appropriation of desire' in C. Ramazanoglu (ed.) 1993 *Up against Foucault: explorations of some tensions between Foucault and feminism*, London and New York: Routledge.

Ramazanoglu, C. with J. Holland 2002 *Feminist methodology: challenges and choices*, London and Thousand Oaks: Sage.

Raphael, J.M. and Tolman, R. 1997 *Trapped by poverty, trapped by abuse: new evidence documenting the relationship between domestic violence and welfare* [Report], available on http://www.ssw.umich.edu/trapped/pubs_trapped.pdf accessed 22 June 2005.

Redstockings Manifesto, 7 July 1969, http://shs.westport.k12.ct.us/jwb/Women/ Power/Redstockings.htm accessed 29 August 2005.

Ribbens, J. 1994 *Mothers and their children: a feminist sociology of childrearing*, London: Sage.

Ribbens McCarthy, J. and Edwards, R. 2001 'Illuminating meanings of "the Private" in sociological thought: a response to Joe Bailey', *Sociology* 35(3), 765–77.

Rich, A. 1980 Compulsory heterosexuality and lesbian existence in C.R. Stimpson and E.S. Person (eds) *Women, sex and sexuality*, Chicago: Chicago University Press.

Richie, B.E. 1996 *Compelled to crime: the gender entrapment of battered black women*, New York and London: Routledge.

Roberts, M. 1991 *Living in a man-made world: Gender assumptions in modern housing design*, London and New York: Routledge.

Rodgers, K. 1994 *Wife assault in Canada*, (Canadian Social Trends), Ministry of Supply and Services, Ottawa.

Rose, H. 1978 'The development of Women's Aid', in *Up against the welfare state, social work, community work and society*, Milton Keynes: Open University Press.

Russell, D.E.H. 1995 *Incestuous abuse: its long-term effects: an exploratory study*, Pretoria: HSRC.

Sainsbury, D. (ed.) 1999 *Gender and welfare state regimes*, Oxford: Oxford University Press.

Salazar, L.F., Baker, C.K., Price, A.W. and Carlin, K. 2003 'Moving beyond the individual: examining the effects of domestic violence policies on social norms', *American Journal of Community Psychology*, 32(3–4), 253–65.

Saunders, D.G. 2002 'Are physical assaults by wives and girlfriends a major social problem? A review of the literature', *Violence against Women*, 8(12), 1424–48.

Schechter, S. 1982 *Women and male violence: the visions and struggles of the battered women's movement*, Boston: South End Press.

Scheff, T. 1990 *Microsociology*, Chicago: Chicago University Press.

Seidler, V.J. 1987 'Reason, desire and male sexuality' in P. Caplan (ed.) *The cultural construction of sexuality*, London: Routledge.

Seidler, V.J. 1998 'Masculinity, violence and emotional life' in G. Bendelow and S.J. Williams (eds) 1998 *Emotions in social life: critical themes and contemporary issues*, London and New York: Routledge.

Shepard, M. and Pence, E. 1988 'The effect of battering on the employment status of women', *Affilia*, 3(2), 55–61.

Shepard, M.F. and Pence, E.L. (eds) 1999 *Coordinating community responses to domestic violence: lessons from Duluth and beyond*, Thousand Oaks, CA: Sage.

Shields, S.A. 2002 *Speaking from the heart: gender and the social meaning of emotion*, Cambridge: Cambridge University Press.

Silva, E.G. and Smart, C. (eds) 1999 *The new family?* London: Sage.

Smart, C. 1976 *Women, crime and criminology: a feminist critique*, London: Routledge and Kegan Paul.

Smith, M.D. 1990 'Socio-demographic risk factors in wife abuse, results from a survey of Toronto women', *Canadian Journal of Sociology*, Vol. 15, 39–58.

Smither, S.J. 2001 'Theoretical basis for an intervention with a mother-infant dyad at a shelter for battered women: a brief developmental approach', *Smith College Studies in Social Work*, 72(1), November, 35–51.

Somerville, P. 1990 'Homelessness and the meaning of home: rooflessness or rootlessness?', *International Journal of Urban and Regional Research*, 16(4), 529–39.

Stack, C.B. 1974 *All our kin: strategies for survival in a black community*, New York: Harper and Row.

Stagg, V., Wills, G.D. and Howell, M. 1989 'Psychopathy in early child witnesses of family violence', *Topics in Early Childhood Special Education*, 9, 73–87.

Stalford, H., Baker, H. and Beveridge, F. 2003 *Children and domestic violence in rural areas: a child-focused assessment of service provision*, London: Save the Children.

Stanko, E.A. 1985 *Intimate intrusions: women's experience of male violence*, London: Routledge and Kegan Paul.

Stanko, E.A. 1988 'Fear of crime and the myth of the safe home: a feminist critique of criminology' in K. Yllo and M. Bograd (eds) *Feminist perspectives on wife abuse*, London: Sage.

Stanko, E.A. 1990 *Everyday violence: how women and men experience sexual and physical danger*, London: Pandora.

Stanko, E.A. 1995 'Women, crime and fear', *Annals of American Academy of Political and Social Science*, 539, 46–58.

Stanko, E.A. 1998 'Warnings to women: Police advice and women's safety in Britain', *Violence against women* 2(1), 5–24.

Stanko, E.A., Crisp, D., Hale, C., Lucraft, H. 1998 '*Counting the costs: estimating the impact of domestic violence in the London Borough of Hackney*', Crime Concern, London.

Stark, E. 2004 *Making the personal political: Looking beyond violence*, Paper delivered at Conference, 'Criminalising gendered violence? Local, national and international perspectives', 14–15 September 2004, University of Bristol.

Stark, E. and Flitcraft, A. 1985 'Woman battering, child abuse and social heredity: what is the relationship?' in N. Johnson (ed.) *Marital violence*, London: Routledge and Kegan Paul.

Stark, E. and Flitcraft, A. 1991 'Spouse Abuse' in M.L. Rosenberg and M.A. Fenley (eds) *Violence in America: a public health approach*, New York: Oxford University Press.

Stark, E. and Flitcraft, A. 1996 *Women at Risk: Domestic Violence and Women's Health*, Sage.

Stark, E., Flitcraft, A. and Frazier, W. 1979 Medicine and patriarchal violence. The social construction of a 'private' event, *International Journal of Health Services* 9(3), 461–93.

Steinmetz, S.K. 1977/78 'The battered husband syndrome', *Victimology*, 2, 499–509.

Sullivan, O. 2000 'The division of domestic labour: twenty years of change?' *Sociology*, 34(3), 437–56.

Syers-McNairy, M. 1990 *Women who leave violent relationships: getting on with life*, unpublished doctoral dissertation, University of Minnesota, Minneapolis.

Thornton Dill, B. 1988 'Our mothers' grief: racial ethnic women and the maintenance of families', *Journal of Family History*, 13(4), 428.

Tjaden, P. and Thoennes, N. 1998 *Prevalence, incidence, and consequences of violence against women: findings from the national violence against women study*, National Institute of Justice and the Centers for Disease Control and Prevention, Research in Brief, http://www.ncjrs.org/txtfiles1/nij/183781.txt accessed 3 September 2005.

Tolman, R. 1999 'Guest editor's introduction', *Violence Against Women*, Vol. 5(4), 355–68.

Tolman, R.M. and Raphael, J. 2000 'A review of research on welfare and domestic violence', *Journal of Social Issues*, 56(4), 655–82.

Tolman, R.M. and Rosen, D. 2001 'Domestic violence in the lives of women receiving welfare: mental health, substance dependence and economic well-being', *Violence Against Women*, 7(2), 141–58.

Tombs, S. and Whyte, D. 2002 'Unmasking the crimes of the powerful', *Critical Criminology*, 11, 217–36.

UK 2000 *Time Use Survey, http://www.statistics.gov.uk/timeuse/default.asp* accessed 2 August 2005.

United Nations 1995 UN Beijing Declaration and Platform of Action, D. Violence against women, paragraph 113, http://www.un.org/womenwatch/daw/beijing/platform/declar.htm accessed 28 August 2005.

Unison 2005 *Response to the government consultation document: work and families: choice and flexibility*, http:www.unison.org.uk/ accessed 6 August 2005.

US Department of Justice 2002 *Intimate Partner Violence 1993–2001*, Bureau of Justice Statistics, www.ojp.usdoj.gov/bjs/ accessed 9 November 2004.

Wallbank, J.A. 2001 *Challenging motherhood(s)*, Harlow: Prentice Hall.

Walby, S. 2002 'Reducing gendered violence: defining, measuring and interpreting inter-personal violence and responses to it' in M. Eriksson, A. Nenola and M.M. Nilsen (eds) *Gender and Violence in the Nordic Countries: Report from a conference in Køge, Denmark*, 23–24 November 2001, http://www.nordforsk.org/meny.cfm?m=147,235 accessed 2 August 2005.

Walby, S. and Myhill, A. 2000 *Reducing domestic violence: ...what works? Assessing and managing the risk of domestic violence*, Briefing Note, London: Home Office.

Walby, S. and Myhill, A. 2001 'Assessing and managing risk' in J. Taylor-Browne (ed.) *What works in reducing domestic violence? A comprehensive guide for professionals*, London: Whiting and Birch Ltd.

Walby, S. 2004 *The cost of domestic violence*, London: Women and Equality Unit/DTI, http://www.womenandequalityunit.gov.uk/research/ accessed 28 June 2005.

Walby, S. and Allen, J. 2004 *Domestic violence, sexual assault and stalking: findings from the British Crime Survey*, Home Office Research Study 276, London: Home Office Research, Development and Statistics Directorate, March.

Walker, L. 1984 *The battered woman syndrome*, New York: Springer.

Walklate, S. 2002 'Gendering crime prevention: exploring the tensions between policy and process' in G. Hughes, E. McLaughlin and J. Muncie (eds) *Crime prevention and community safety: new directions*, London, Thousand Oaks, CA and New Delhi: Sage, pp. 58–76.

Wardhaugh, J. 1999 'The unaccommodated woman: home, homelessness and identity', *The Sociological Review*, 47(1), 91–109.

Warner, S. and Pantling, K. 2002 'Minoritisation and motherhood: women, children and domestic violence' in J. Batsleer, E. Burman, K. Chantler, H.S. McIntosh, K. Pantling, S. Smailes and S. Warner (eds) *Domestic violence and minoritisation – supporting women to independence*, Manchester: Women's Studies Research Centre, Manchester Metropolitan University.

Weiss, E. 2000 *Surviving domestic violence: voices of women who broke free*, Utah: Agreka Books.

White, M. and Perkins, A. 1998 More women shun baffling CSA, *The Guardian*, 21 April 1998.

Wilcox, P.S. 1996 *Social support and women leaving violent relationships*, Unpublished doctoral thesis, University of Bradford.

Wilcox, P.S. 2000a 'Me mother's bank and me nanan's, you know, support': Women who left domestic violence in England and issues of informal support, *Women's Studies International Forum*, 23(1), 1–13.

Wilcox, P.S. 2000b 'Lone motherhood: the impact on living standards of leaving a violent relationship', *Social Policy and Administration*, 34(2), 176–90.

Williams, F. 1993 'Women and community' in J. Bornat, C. Pereira, D. Pilgrim and F. Williams (eds) *Community care: a reader*, Basingstoke: Macmillan.

Williams, G. 2004 'Hidden dangers', *Community Care*, 21 October 2004, 44–5.

Williams, R. 1976 *Keywords*, London: Fontana.

Williams, S.J. and Bendelow, G.A. 1996 'Emotions and "sociological" imperialism: a rejoinder to Craib', *Sociology*, 30(1), 145–53.

Wilson, M., Daly, M. and Wright, C. 1993 'Uxoricide in Canada: demographic risk patterns', *Violence and Victims*, 8(1), 3–60.

Witz, A. and Marshall, B.L. 2004 *Engendering the social: feminist encounters with sociological theory*, Maidenhead: Open University Press.

Wolf, N. 1991 *The beauty myth: how images of beauty are used against women*, New York and London: Anchor Books, Doubleday.

Wolfe, D., Jaffe, P., Wilson, S. and Zak, L. 1985 'Children of battered women: the relation of child behavior to family violence and maternal stress', *Journal of Consulting and Clinical Psychology*, 53(5), 657–65.

Women and Equality Unit 2003 *Cost of domestic violence: interim findings*, researched by Sylvia Walby, University of Leeds. www.womenandequalityunit.gov.uk

Women's National Commission 2004 Myths and facts: domestic violence and child contact, London: Women's National Commission, http://www.thewnc.org.uk/pubs/factsapr04.doc accessed 3 September 2004.

Women and Work Commission 2005 *A Fair Deal for women in the Workplace*, http://www.womenandequalityunit.gov.uk/women_work_commission/ accessed 25 June 2005.

Women's Aid 2004 *Celebrating 30 years of Women's Aid 1974–2004*, Bristol: WAFE.

Yeandle, S., Escott, K., Grant, L. and Batty, E. 2003 *Women and men talking about poverty*, Manchester: Equal Opportunities Commission.

Yllo, K. and Bograd, M. (eds) 1988 Feminist perspectives on wife abuse, Newbury Park, CA: Sage.

Index